GW00788716

A PICNIC W

THE NAT̄IⱯ̄Ɛ̄S

A PICNIC WITH
THE NATIVES

ABORIGINAL–EUROPEAN RELATIONS IN
THE NORTHERN TERRITORY TO 1910

Gordon Reid

MELBOURNE UNIVERSITY PRESS
1990

First published 1990

Printed in Australia by
Brown Prior Anderson Pty Ltd, Burwood, Victoria, for
Melbourne University Press, Carlton, Victoria 3053
U.S.A. and Canada: International Specialized Book Services, Inc.,
5602 N.E. Hassalo Street, Portland, Oregon 97213-3640

This book is copyright. Apart from any fair dealing for the
purposes of private study, research, criticism or review, as
permitted under the Copyright Act, no part may be reproduced by
any process without written permission. Enquiries should be made
to the publisher.
© Gordon Stephen Reid   1990

National Library of Australia Cataloguing-in-Publication entry

Reid, Gordon, 1929 Apr. 7–
  A picnic with the natives.
  Bibliography.
  Includes index.
  ISBN 0 522 84419 7.

  [1]. Aborigines, Australian—Northern Territory—Treatment—
  History. 2. Northern Territory—Race relations. I. Title.
994.29

For Campbell Macknight

Contents

Illustrations

Preface

In June 1875 Aborigines attacked three white men on the Roper River, Northern Territory, killing one and wounding the others, who managed to fight them off. This was one of the first serious clashes between Aborigines and the small parties of Europeans, who had come to establish the overland telegraph line from Port Darwin to Adelaide. When he heard of the incident, the head of the Territory's small police force, Inspector Paul Foelsche, wrote to a friend, saying that he had arranged for a police party to go to the Roper River to bring back the body and to 'have a Picnic with the Natives'. The parties of police and civilians operating separately along the Roper over the next six weeks several times attacked Aborigines suspected of having been involved. Some Aborigines were killed, camps were raided and burnt, and weapons destroyed. No attempt was made to arrest the culprits. The exact number killed is not known, reports simply stating that congregating blacks were quickly 'dispersed' a term commonly used by the Queensland Native Police Force when killing blacks who resisted white invasion of their lands. And so began the pattern of Aboriginal resistance to colonization and European counter-response already familiar in other parts of Australia.

This history concentrates on Aboriginal–European relations in the Northern Territory in the South Australian period of administration, 1863-1910; but it also briefly outlines contact between the two races before colonization began and quickly looks at the direction of official policy after the Commonwealth of Australia assumed control of the Territory in 1911. My chief concern throughout is with the application and failure of Aboriginal policy in frontier conditions. Because of the importance of the police in the relationship, they feature strongly in this history, particular attention being given to Paul Foelsche, head of the police at Palmerston (now Darwin) until 1904, when he retired. Reputed by some to know more about the Territory Aborigines than any other person of his period, he is important because of the information he gathered about several tribes, and because of his attitudes, which mirrored those of his associates on the frontier.

I have not attempted a complete survey but have examined certain events and situations in order to indicate comparisons with some other Australian colonies. In particular, I have summarized South Australian Aboriginal policy in the period in order to show why that policy failed when applied to the Territory. While Dr Mervyn Hartwig has studied the effect of white settlement in the Alice Springs district on the Aborigines, and other scholars, especially anthropologists and archaeologists, have closely studied contact in specific areas, no general history of Aboriginal–European relations in the Territory has previously been published.

This history is written from the top—that is, largely based on official, European records. The Aboriginal side of the story is not presented, simply because reliable Aboriginal records of events in this period apparently do not exist. No pretence at original research has been made in some areas. Rather, much use has been made of the pioneering work of Kathleen Hassell and R. M. Gibbs on South Australian policy before 1863, Hartwig on Central Australian relations, H. J. Schmiechen on the Hermannsburg Mission Society, Fr G. J. O'Kelly on the Jesuit missions in the Territory, and Peter Elder on C. J. Dashwood. The general histories of Alan Powell and P. F. Donovan have been used as guides to understanding the social and economic activities in the Territory during the South Australian period. The recent history of the South Australian Police Force by Robert Clyne has provided additional insights into police actions and policies, particularly in Central Australia.

I wish to thank several people for their help. Dr C. C. Macknight of the Australian National University and Dr Brian Dickey of Flinders University both commented on drafts. Richard Kimber of Alice Springs commented on two chapters dealing with that region. Helen Wilson, Colleen Pyne, Elizabeth Estbergs, Ian Sutherland and Bill McLaren facilitated research in Darwin. The staff of the South Australian Archives and the South Australian Museum, Milton Gooley of the Telecommunications Museum in Adelaide, the staff of the Australian Archives in Darwin and Canberra and the Australian Institute of Aboriginal Studies in Canberra all helped to locate sources.

A Northern Territory History Award for 1984 enabled me to research and write this book.

Gordon Reid,
Canberra

Introduction: *The South Australian Background*

The instructions issued to Boyle Travers Finniss before he left Adelaide late in April 1864 with a party of settlers required him to seek and maintain friendly relations with the Aborigines of the Northern Territory. On arrival, Finniss made no effort to do so and relations with the local people at Escape Cliffs, near present-day Darwin, quickly became hostile, particularly when they began stealing European property. Finniss sent out a punitive party which killed one Aborigine; the tribe responded by attacking a party of whites rounding up cattle, wounding one of them. So the pattern of distrust and over-reaction, so common in Australian colonial contact history, had quickly destroyed hopes for an amicable relationship with the Territory's indigenous people. In order to understand the official policy which the first administrators of the Territory were expected to follow, and how it readily failed, it is necessary to study briefly the development of Aboriginal policy in South Australia from its foundation.[1]

The powerful pressures for emigration to the colonies, felt in Britain after the victory at Waterloo in 1815, accompanied the emergence of humanitarian ideals stimulated by eighteenth century enlightenment and evangelical religious zeal. This humanitarianism had resulted in the abolition of slavery in England in 1772, the abolition of the British slave trade in 1807 and the emancipation of slaves in the British colonies in 1833. As historian R. M. Gibbs has written, 'The legacy of this campaign against slavery was profound, for it infected the British people with a responsibility for backward people at a time when plans for colonising South Australia were being developed'.[2] Also, Colonial Office policy became almost identical with missionary policy because of the powerful links between the office and missionaries. James Stephen, a member of the general committee of the Church Missionary Society for nine years, became Assistant Under-Secretary at the Office in 1834 and permanent Under-Secretary in 1836; Charles Grant (later

Lord Glenelg), a leading member of the Society, was appointed Secretary of State for the Colonies in 1835; and Sir George Grey, Parliamentary Under-Secretary, was also a leading member. Policy towards Aboriginal peoples in British colonies in South Africa and Australia, including Tasmania, New South Wales and Western Australia, had failed to protect the rights of indigenes on frontiers remote from official control.

South Australia was to be different: it was to be founded upon the principles of systematic colonization of Edward Gibbon Wakefield, who had argued that settlement would be centralized and controlled by means of the regulated sale of land as opposed to the almost indiscriminate granting and occupation of land which had occurred in other colonies. The Bill enabling South Australia to become a colony, passed by the British parliament in August 1834, declared the new lands to be 'waste and unoccupied' and omitted to mention the native people. Wakefield, however, had believed their interests could be protected, saying that the alternatives were 'between a Colonization, desultory, without Law, and fatal to the Natives, and a Colonization organized and salutary'. Grant (Glenelg) accepted this argument and, soon after assuming office in April 1835, requested that the Board of Colonization Commissioners give the treatment of the native race early attention as it was 'of the first importance in the formation of the new settlement of South Australia'. He advised conciliation of the Aborigines and acquainting them with the advantages of British civilization, morality and religion in order to avoid the evils seen elsewhere. The Board, which was not motivated by humanitarian ideals but rather was responsible for land sales and immigration on the Wakefield model, tried to ignore this policy direction. When Glenelg demanded a plan for securing the rights of the Aborigines, including the appointment of a protector and arrangements for purchasing land from them as distinct from the appropriation which had occurred elsewhere, the Board's chairman, Robert Torrens, realized that the protector would have a power of veto over the sale of land. 'To protect themselves from any interference from the Protector, the Board passed and sealed an order " . . . declaring *all* lands of the Colony open to Public Sale" '.[3] This action later helped to facilitate the defeat of Glenelg's objectives.

Nonetheless the Board pretended to have the interests of the Aborigines at heart. In October 1836 it issued instructions to the Resident Commissioner, James Hurtle Fisher, while the first settlers were still at Kangaroo Island awaiting the arrival of the first governor, Captain John Hindmarsh. These instructions provided for safeguarding Aboriginal proprietary rights and supplying Aborigines who ceded their land with food, shelter and moral and religious instruction. It was also suggested they be given free medical assistance. The Surveyor-General, Colonel William Light, was informed that any wild animals needed for food while searching the mainland coast for a suitable site for a permanent settlement must be purchased from the Aborigines. When the colonists arrived at Holdfast Bay in December 1836, more than half the proclamation read by Hindmarsh concerned the Aborigines — which was not surprising as the proclamation had to be approved first by Glenelg:

It is also, at this time especially, my duty to apprise the Colonists of my resolution to take every lawful means for extending the same protection to the NATIVE POPULATION as to the rest of His Majesty's Subjects, and of my firm determination to punish with exemplary severity all acts of violence or injustice which may in any manner be practised or attempted against the NATIVES, who are to be considered as much under the Safeguard of the law as the Colonists themselves, and equally entitled to the privileges of British Subjects. I trust, therefore, with confidence to the exercise of moderation and forebearance by all Classes in their intercourse with the NATIVE INHABITANTS, and that they will omit no opportunity of assisting me to fulfil His Majesty's most gracious and benevolent intentions towards them by promoting their advancement in civilisation, and ultimately, under the blessing of Divine Providence, their conversion to the Christian Faith.[4]

This was the strongest profession of good intentions towards the Aboriginal people since colonization had begun in Australia in 1788, and yet this policy began to fail immediately. It could not be enforced without the presence of a protector holding true powers. Early in 1836 Glenelg sought the services of George Augustus Robinson, who had impressed Governor Arthur of Tasmania and the Colonial Office with his work as conciliator on that island since 1829. While waiting for Robinson's decision, Hindmarsh appointed his private secretary, George Stevenson, as interim protector. But Stevenson did nothing positive after arrival with Hindmarsh, and by May 1837 he had fallen foul of Fisher. The interim post then went to Captain William Bromley who, while superintendent of educational institutions at Halifax, Nova Scotia, had produced a grammar of the local Indian language. He was expected to teach the Aborigines to regard the settlers as friends and lead them gradually to Christianity, but they soon took advantage of him, rejecting the official rations of oatmeal and rice and demanding biscuits instead. They frequently robbed Bromley and other settlers, who complained that the law was not being enforced against the Aborigines. This led to complaints about Bromley's inefficiency, and Hindmarsh dismissed him for 'physical and mental imbecility'. Robinson had finally rejected the post and Bromley was replaced as interim protector by Dr William Wyatt, to whom, as Kathleen Hassell explains, more explicit instructions were issued:

He was to ascertain the strength and disposition of the tribes, especially near the settled districts; he was to protect their property rights in land, encourage friendship with the settlers and induce them to work for themselves or the settlers. Wyatt was not to provide gifts but he was to see that the very old and very young, the very hungry and the very ill were given food and clothing. He was to supervise employment contracts and prohibit the supply of intoxicating liquors. A plot of land was to be enclosed where the Aborigines would be encouraged to work. It was hoped that Wyatt would bring them by degrees to civilization and Christianity. He was told to learn their language and to teach them English so that he could explain British law to the tribes, prevent aggressions and bring offenders to justice.[5]

When a white man was stabbed to death on a bank of the Torrens River in March 1838 and an Aborigine arrested, Wyatt pointed out the difficulty in applying British justice. Aboriginal evidence was not admitted in court because Aborigines could not give an oath based on Christian concepts foreign to them. This defeated the purpose of treating them as British subjects. Another example of the failure of the policy of bringing Aborigines under British law was the response of Governor George Gawler, who arrived in October 1838, to the massacre by Milmenrura people of the survivors of the *Maria* shipwreck on the south-east coast in mid-1840. Gawler was advised by Judge Charles Cooper that the Milmenrura, who were out of contact with the colonists and British authorities, could not be dealt with by the normal processes of law. It seemed that any attempt to try the murderers would fail, because of the inadmissability of their evidence. Gawler sent a detachment of police under the Commissioner, Major Thomas O'Halloran, to the area to administer summary justice. His party found the bodies of fifteen persons, who had been on the *Maria*. He hanged two Aborigines on the spot as an example to the Milmenrura and two others were shot while escaping. Hanging accused murderers at the scene of their crimes now became a tradition in South Australian justice, which continued well into Northern Territory history. Some colonists accused O'Halloran of being a murderer and Gawler of being an accessory. The Colonial Office and the law officers of the Crown absolved them of moral culpability but agreed that they were technically guilty. Gawler later attributed his recall in 1841 to this incident.

The inadmissability of Aboriginal evidence remained a problem until 1843, when the British parliament passed legislation authorizing colonial governors to take steps, if they wished, for the admission of native evidence. In the following year the new governor, Captain George Grey, who had preached Aboriginal policy close to that of the Colonial Office and the missionaries while a resident magistrate at Albany, Western Australia, forced legislation through the Legislative Council despite the opposition of the colonists' newspaper, *The Register*. The Aboriginal Evidence Ordinance provided for Aborigines to give evidence on affirmation to tell the truth. The degree of credibility of such evidence was to be left to the discretion of the court, except that no person should be convicted on the sole testimony of Aborigines. In 1846 this was amended to make Aboriginal evidence sufficient in itself to convict a person of any offences except those involving sentences of death and transportation; and in 1849 even this last proviso was removed.

Although it appeared that one of Glenelg's objectives—treating Aborigines and Europeans equally under British law—had been achieved, the balance still hung heavily in favour of the latter. Credibility of evidence still lay with the court, which needed to give little credence to the evidence of Aborigines who were, in the words of the Act, 'uncivilized'; also, the courts were composed of whites, and 'The Aborigine was completely subjected to the court procedures and criminal codes of the Europeans, both of which were entirely foreign to his experience and understanding'.[6] Recognition of the 'uncivilized' nature of the Aborigines did not lead to the creation of Aboriginal courts or a provisional code of law applicable to their situation. Even though some Aboriginal offenders were pardoned in court or before their sentences were completed, the legal bias against them was heavy. Thus in one case in 1849 four Aborigines were found guilty of murder after Aboriginal evidence was allowed against them; but a few days previously the same evidence had been rejected when given against Europeans; two of the four Aborigines were hanged at the scene of their crimes in the Port Lincoln district.

Despite the good intentions of the British government and its first governors, contact between the two races soon became violent. The first killing of a white man after foundation of the colony was at Encounter Bay in June 1837, when a man in a whaling party was murdered in a fight over one of the wives of an Aborigine. Similar acts had occurred in the whaling and sealing industry along the South Australian coast before foundation, leaving a legacy of hatred which may have contributed to the massacre of the *Maria* survivors. The first shepherd to die at the hands of Aborigines in South Australia lost his life in April 1839 seven miles north-east of Adelaide, apparently because his murderers wanted sheep meat. The government counselled settlers to show caution and forebearance and sought to solve the case in a dispassionate way, withholding rations until the offenders were caught. A party of three whites and fifteen Aborigines from Adelaide then went to the area, heard of the murder of another shepherd, and arrested those responsible for both. Provision of rations was restored. At two trials next month, two Aborigines were condemned to death and four acquitted, the murderers being hung before an Aboriginal crowd, most of whom, according to Hassell, 'seemed to agree with the punishment'. The whites, however, were not happy with the situation. They called a meeting which claimed a right of protection for settlers and natives alike, demanded a disciplined and effective police force and protested against the Aborigines' practice of carrying their weapons into Adelaide. The protector, Wyatt, was called inefficient. Soon after this Dr Matthew Moorhouse, who had just arrived in the colony, was appointed permanent protector and given amplified instructions which did not mention protection of Aborigines' proprietary rights.

Large-scale violence between the races erupted in April 1841, when Aborigines attacked a party of whites overlanding sheep at Rufus River (between Lake Victoria and the Murray River). Governor Grey was reluctant to use force against Aborigines, despite strong demands from the colonists. They, however, on 7 May sent out a private party, which clashed with an estimated five hundred Aborigines at Rufus River. One white man was wounded and five Aborigines were believed to have been killed. The whites returned to Adelaide defeated and demanding stronger action. In a state of crisis, Grey at last agreed, and on 31 May a force of sixty-eight police and volunteers, led by O'Halloran and accompanied by the new protector, Moorhouse, acting as a magistrate for the occasion, left Adelaide. They failed to make contact as the Murray tribes fled before them, but they did meet another overlanding party, which had lost four dead in an attack. Grey refused to sanction any further expedition, which might be motivated by revenge and likely to punish guilty and innocent alike. But in July, on hearing that yet another party was proceeding down the Murray, he sent a party of volunteers led by Moorhouse and assisted by Sub-Inspector Shaw to Lake Victoria, where they met the latest overlanders late in August. Their combined forces were now fifty-five men, confronted by some one hundred and fifty Aborigines in hostile mood, despite Moorhouse's peaceful overtures. Fearing that they were about to be attacked, the whites opened fire; twenty minutes later thirty Aborigines were dead and one European wounded. This was the largest clash between Aborigines and Europeans based in South Australia and marked the end of serious black attacks on whites along the Murray. To prevent further violence in the area, Grey established a police station on the Murray at Moorundee, near present-day Blanchetown. He appointed Edward John Eyre, the explorer, officer in charge and sub-protector of Aborigines.

The demoralization of the Aborigines as a result of contact with Europeans was by now quite apparent, and followed the process which had occurred in the first few years of other Australian settlements. Efforts to get blacks to work were frustrated by whites who were anxious to propitiate them by giving food and clothing without services being rendered in return. Aborigines soon became beggars and demanded money. Petty theft was now frequent. Despite the prohibition on supplying intoxicating liquor to them, drunkenness among Aborigines was increasing. Prostitution of Aboriginal women was common, and Moorhouse estimated that venereal disease affected half those Aborigines in contact with Europeans, together with inflamatory, rheumatic and dyspeptic attacks. Moorhouse treated them with some success and even vaccinated them against smallpox at the Native Location of twelve huts established in 1838 beside the Torrens. An interpreter had been installed, and all Aborigines who applied received food twice daily. Some Aborigines lived there, carrying water for the settlers and digging in the Location's garden, but the enterprise was undermined by lack of firm application of official policy. The Location was moved to a fourteen acre site on the north bank of the Torrens; land was given to every Aborigine who would cultivate it, and rations only for work performed — but it was easy to obtain food from the colonists, and work was neglected.

Although not a missionary, Moorhouse thought like one. He believed the Aboriginal children might be completely civilized if they could be removed from their parents. He established a school at the Location and attracted children from the town with biscuits, sugar and rice in order to teach them reading and spelling. Attendance was irregular, the average being thirteen daily. The first missionaries, C. W. Schurmann and C. G. Teichelmann, sent by the Lutheran Missionary Society of Dresden, arrived with Governor Gawler in October 1838 and spent a year in Adelaide building huts for the Aborigines and learning the local language. In contrast with Lutherans from a contemporary missionary society at Moreton Bay, Queensland, who believed that civilization must precede Christianity, they advocated Christian training as a precursor of change. In any event, both policies failed. The settlers in Adelaide, however, believed that training in industrious habits was preferable to any religious or intellectual teaching, a view with little chance of success in the urban environment, because of the ease with which the Aborigines could obtain food without working or learning.

Schurmann went to Port Lincoln at Gawler's request because of the deteriorating relations with the Aborigines there, but his efforts at conciliation had no effect. By December 1841 Aboriginal aggressions were so serious that they threatened the success of local settlement. In March 1842 they killed a station-owner and his hutkeeper and a few weeks later killed three whites in a shepherd's hut. Now in a state of panic, the settlers neglected their stock, which the blacks killed at will. This situation continued until April 1843, when the incidence of plunder and bloodshed declined in the settled districts of South Australia, although occasional killings of isolated whites did occur for some years later in the unsettled districts. The first two stages in Aboriginal contact in the first settled districts in South Australia — tentative approach followed by hostile reaction — had taken just seven years. Now these people entered the third and prolonged stage: accommodation with the invading whites and the consequent surrender of almost all traditional rights.

One of Glenelg's policy mainstays had been the assurance of

Aboriginal proprietary rights including rights to land. As we have seen, this was torpedoed by the Colonization Commissioners with their secret order that all land in the colony was to be open for sale. Nonetheless, successive governors did attempt to reserve land for exclusive Aboriginal use, even though the 1834 Act establishing the colony did not permit this. When some Aborigines applied in mid-1840 for land to cultivate, sixteen sections comprising 1151 acres were reserved, despite objections from some settlers. Announcing the reservation the *Government Gazette* of 22 July 1840 read:

The invasion of those ancient rights [of the Aborigines' title to land] by surveys and land appropriations of any kind is justifiable only on the ground that we should at the same time reserve an ample sufficiency for their present and future use and comfort under the new state of things into which they are thrown — a state in which we hope they will be led to live in greater comfort on a smaller space than they enjoyed ... on their extensive original possessions.

In 1842 the Waste Lands Act corrected the omission in the 1834 Act — land could now legally be reserved for public uses including the benefit of Aborigines. Since the first reservation in 1840 more land was set aside for Aboriginal use; some of it was then leased to pastoralists, the revenue going to the Aborigines Department. Further, expenditure of 15 per cent of gross proceeds from land sales for the benefit, civilization and protection of the Aborigines was now authorized. But in 1842 and 1843, of one thousand pounds spent by the Aborigines Department, more than half went on officials' salaries, the balance going on clothing and provisions for its charges. After a white man was killed by blacks at Streaky Bay on the west coast in 1850 the Governor, Sir Henry Young, stated that Aborigines had an undoubted right to traverse runs so long as the claims of European property were respected, and that no leases for runs should be issued without due provision for them.

   The background to the legal question was the question of land, although interference with Aboriginal women was also an important source of racial conflict. The establishment of reserves, sincerely intended by governors Gawler, Grey, Robe and Young, was seen by most colonists as a sop to the Colonial Office. The reserves were a valueless concession because, having no concept of individual ownership, Aborigines could not accept the allocation of a few acres as compensation for the vast tribal lands confiscated by settlers; and having no tradition as cultivators they rarely accepted the life of a 'tiny capitalist' and then never for long. More importantly, confinement to farms or small reserves was contrary to the nomadic life of the Aborigine and the practice of periodic acquaintance with significant features of tribal land. Thus the cultural and religious links between Aborigines and their land were severely weakened. To quote Gibbs again: 'The general result, then, of the contest for land between black and white was always the same — the colonists held all territory within their reach by the simple exercise of their superior might, and laid legal claim to the lands farther out'.[7] Glenelg's objective — of accepting the Aborigines' proprietary right in the land which must be purchased by settlers — failed from the outset. Quick to prevail was the standpoint of the founding Act of 1834, held from the outset by the colonists, that South Australia was 'waste and unoccupied'.

Aborigines in South Australia were thus dispossessed of their lands as easily as in the other colonies. But the dispossession resulted from failure of humanitarian policy and subtle manipulation of this failure by land-hungry settlers, rather than from any policy of appropriation and subjugation, by force if necessary, as sometimes occurred elsewhere. Official humanitarianism was evident in many gestures in the first years of South Australian colonization — in the ready offer of sustenance, encouragement of cultivation, creation of reserves, setting up of schools and genuine attempts to bring to the Aborigines the supposed gifts of European civilization and Christianity. British policy failed because of a want of firm application and understanding of colonial conditions.

In January 1836 Glenelg had announced that 'an amending act must at length be made to incorporate measures aimed at protecting native rights'.[8] This suggests that even at this stage Glenelg was dilatory, not fully realizing the need to act immediately to protect such rights. No such legislation was enacted. Glenelg had allowed himself to believe that the appointment of a suitable protector would be sufficient for the time being, but it was two years before Moorhouse was appointed and, although he proved to be genuinely concerned for his charges and aware of the adverse effects colonization was having upon them, without legal authority he could do little to assist them. Further, Glenelg and his immediate successors at the Colonial Office did not appreciate that systematic Aboriginal policy would be no more successful than systematic colonization. The Wakefield scheme had failed by 1842, because of factors which could not be properly controlled from London — faulty administration, speculation in land and stores, and a lack of unity of purpose among the colonists. Similarly, Aboriginal policy could not prevail in the face of the attitudes which land-hungry settlers brought to the colony. The Wakefield model was attempted in New Zealand after 1840 despite the lessons of South Australia, although there were some differences in situation. In New Zealand, under the terms of the treaty of Waitangi, land was to be purchased from the Maoris, some of whom were just as disgruntled as the European settlers because of the tight government control over land sales.

By 1849 Moorhouse had lost faith in past plans for civilizing Aborigines by directly assimilating them into the European community through secular and religious instruction. Even educating the children in special schools was considered not to have succeeded, because they were still in contact with their parents. Governor Young had little faith in civilizing Aborigines and was not impressed with the educational value of the Native School in Adelaide, which he said had an 'ephemeral usefulness'. For this reason, the proposal of Anglican Archdeacon Matthew Hale to establish a mission station at Poonindie near Port Lincoln was attractive. Henceforth young Aborigines were to be taken away from the influences of their tribes and undesirable whites, taught the white man's ways, trained in arts useful to the colonists, then returned to European society. Things went well at Poonindie for the first few years, but in 1856 Hale had to report that twenty-nine inmates had died since it was established and, although new recruits were constantly going to the station, there was no natural increase. After seven years, only seven children had been born there. A year later Hale's successor, the Reverend Octavius Hammond, reported that another twenty had died. Pulmonary diseases were believed to be the chief causes of death. By 1857 Poonindie had failed, although it struggled on for many more years. It was partly successful in that some of its graduates were among those Aborigines who became successful pastoral workers in the 1850s, their labour being readily accepted when white workers left South Australia for the Victorian goldfields.

Even the Colonial Office had by 1850 accepted that its Aboriginal policy had failed, the then Secretary for the Colonies, Lord Grey, stating that:

... under my own instructions and those of my predecessors too much has been at once attempted, and that the necessity has not been sufficiently recognized of resting content with a slow and gradual improvement in the condition of these people.[9]

Of course, the real fault had been 'resting content' from the outset. Policy had been taken out of the hands of the Colonial Office by the colonists, whose attitudes towards the Aborigines were dictated by the frontier experience, in which whites seized tribal land as a right and any objection by blacks or concerned whites were brushed aside in the name of economic necessity. Along with this lack of will at the Colonial Office, the humanitarian movement in Britain was waning—although it would from time to time, chiefly through the London-based Aborigines' Protection Society, and with little effect, cause the Colonial Office to question Aboriginal affairs in the Australian colonies. The granting of self-government in 1856 meant that Aboriginal policy was finally and effectively taken out of the hands of the British authorities. By this time the Aborigines of the settled districts were conquered people. Some tribes, including the Adelaide tribe, had almost disappeared. Those tribes which did manage to survive were dislocated by the demands of whites for labour and sexual services, and their numbers were seriously reduced by the effects of alcohol, disease and malnutrition. L. R. Smith has estimated that total numbers had declined from about 15 000 before the coming of the Europeans to about 9000 in 1861.[10]

The South Australians, even at this stage, had had a slight experience of native police, although a force formed in the 1850s was apparently small and did not contribute to the decimation of tribes as did the native police forces in the Port Phillip District, 1842–52, New South Wales, 1848–58, and Queensland, 1849–97. As early as 1838 Aborigines 'were appointed Native Constables and used as trackers, interpreters and for explaining European law and justice to their people',[11] with limited success. Ronald and Catherine Berndt have mentioned that an Aborigine, arrested and tried in 1842 for killing a calf, was formerly a native constable.[12] In 1850 Governor Young suggested the establishment of a corps of native police auxiliaries but after consulting Moorhouse, the police commissioner and others he took no action. When Aborigines murdered a shepherd on the north-west coast of Eyre Peninsula in September 1852, Young immediately ordered the establishment of a native police unit there. The following January fourteen constables, including twelve natives recruited from Murray River and Lake Alexandrina tribes, took charge of the 'feeding station' at Venus Bay and the troubles there ceased. Other such detachments were placed at Wellington and Moorundee. But those at Venus Bay became 'quite usless' and the whole native police force was disbanded in 1856.[13] By this action, South Australia had now adopted the practice of the eastern colonies of using Aborigines from remote districts as policemen to control local trouble-makers, a method of racial suppression which was to be used in the Northern Territory with mixed results after 1884.

Conquest having been completed by 1860, the South Australians were willing to consider the effects of colonization upon the indigenous people, possibly prompted by the Aborigines' Friends' Association. This association was formed at a public meeting in August 1858 attended by the Governor and the Commissioner for Crown Lands—a cabinet minister now responsible for Aborigines following the abolition of the protectorate in 1857. In March 1859 the association appointed George Taplin, a Congregational minister and teacher at Port Elliot, as its missionary agent. Later that year Taplin established a mission on crown land granted at Point McLeay on the southern side of Lake Alexandrina. The selection of the site antagonized several white settlers in the area, particularly John Baker, a member of the Legislative Council, who in September 1860 proposed that the council set up a select committee to inquire into the whole state of Aboriginal welfare and administration in the province. The committee was established with George Hall as chairman and Baker as a member. It heard evidence from seventeen Europeans, including Moorhouse and Taplin, and 'certain Aboriginal

Natives'.[14] It was told that eight thousand acres had been allotted as Aboriginal reserves. The intention that the natives should settle on them and cultivate the soil had been frustrated by their nomadic habits. Most of this land was now leased for about one thousand pounds a year, which went into general revenue. Originally one-tenth of the proceeds of all 'waste lands' had been set aside for the benefit of the Aborigines but as sales had increased this was found to be more than sufficient. The committee recommended a special fund for the relief of the Aborigines into which the revenue from the lease of reserves should go. Additional reserves should be created until the revenue so derived was equal to the necessary expenditure of the Aborigines Department.

Evidence given to the committee had proved that the strict application of British criminal law to the Aborigines was not in accordance with principles of equity and justice. Some people, not charged with any offence but required as witnesses, had been handcuffed, bound in chains, imprisoned and 'otherwise treated as the meanest of felons'. To prevent this, the committee recommended the appointment of a chief protector to watch over the general interests of the Aborigines and be the means of communicating with the government. He would itinerate and inspect 'sub-protectors' and ration and clothing depots, ascertain the numerical strengths of each tribe annually, and be armed with judicial powers to dispense summary justice to Aborigines and commit Europeans for trial — except in capital cases, which he would report. He would adjudicate in the presence of the tribe concerned, 'whose recognition of the justice of the punishment to be inflicted should be sought to be obtained'. Sub-protectors would be appointed in districts where the Aborigines were numerous. Their primary duty would be to attend to physical necessities, especially of the aged, sick and infirm, to train them in 'steady industrial habits and manners of civilized life' and later, as the committee said, to attempt to eradicate their 'vile superstitions and barbarous rites, leaving the mind open for the reception of the simple truths of Christianity'. Settlers in the outlying districts would be authorized to supply government clothes and provisions to them.

The committee was impressed with past attempts to educate Aboriginal children in Adelaide, where at one time 107 boys and girls had made satisfactory progress. It expressed dissatisfaction with Poonindie, which had suffered commercial mismanagement recently, but did not mention the many deaths there. It was strongly convinced that permanent benefit from attempts to 'Christianize' the natives could only be expected by separating children from their parents and the 'evil influences of the tribe to which they belong'. This would be a 'work of mercy to the rising generation of aborigines'. It recommended that a central elementary school be provided from which, after preliminary training, children would be transferred to an establishment where complete isolation would be secured. In other words, the committee advocated segregation as an end in itself, contrasting with Hale's 1850 objective of segregation, training and return to society as useful servants of the Europeans. This proposal was already practised at Point McLeay by Taplin and was to become the standard practice in South Australia.

The select committee acknowledged that the Aborigines had an equitable title to the lands they had occupied but of which they had been virtually dispossessed. 'All the evidence goes to prove that they have lost much, and gained little or nothing, by their contact with the Europeans; and hence it becomes a question of . . . compensating them for the injuries they have sustained, or of mitigating the evils to which . . . our occupation of the country has led'. While the committee acknowledged an obligation, the only compensation it recommended was some protection from abuses and more clothes and rations. Its view was pessimistic. Although it recognized the great social problem resulting from colonization, it did not see the problem as a long-term one. The Aborigines themselves would solve it by dying out. It was universally admitted, the committee said, that their numbers were fast decreasing because of lack of clothing, pulmonary complaints, syphilis, infanticide and sexual relationships with the whites. It was a melancholy fact that 'the race is doomed to extinction' and it would only be a question of time before the reserves set aside to raise revenue to support the Aborigines would revert to the crown — a view held later by settlers in the Northern Territory.

This view of the Aborigines was to become conventional wisdom in Australia. C. D. Rowley has written: 'It was easy for the gentlemen who considered the results of over two decades of settlement to assume that reasonable effort had been made and that all positive steps had failed: that Aborigines defeated welfare policies by dying out'.[15] Blaming the victims of conquest for what befell them characterized the racist attitudes towards Aborigines, which were to develop and become a fundamental rationale of white Australian society towards the end of the nineteenth century. As a result of the select committee's recommendations, the protectorate was revived and two officers appointed, one in Adelaide and another in the far north. But their responsibilities were generally limited to administration of ration depots, channelling of aid to missions and investigation of suspected ill-treatment of Aborigines. The protectorate lapsed again in 1868 and was not again revived until 1881.

All official attempts to civilize Aborigines and assimilate them into the European community by means of education had been abandoned. According to Fay Gale, the Adelaide Native School had been closed in 1852 because, after eighteen pupils were removed to Poonindie mission, the remaining children feared the same fate and ran away.[16] Under the 1844 Aborigines Act, the Protector had become the legal guardian of all part-Aboriginal children. By 1860 thirty-five of the forty-two reserves set aside for Aborigines had been leased to white settlers and of the others only Poonindie was being used for the benefit of the Aborigines. The only official help Aborigines were now receiving was a meagre distribution of rations. The responsibility for helping the Aborigines was now left largely to private benevolence, shored up by government assistance. Following the formation of Poonindie mission in 1850 and Point McLeay in 1859, Moravians and Lutherans established Kopperamanna and Killalpaninna missions respectively in 1866, some ten miles apart on Cooper's Creek. Two years later, local residents in the Wallaroo, Moonta and Kadina mining towns were granted land for a mission at Point Pearce on Yorke Peninsula. No other mission was established in South Australia until the Evangelical Lutheran Church leased land at Koonibba on Eyre Peninsula and a pastor was appointed there in 1901. Particularly in the outlying areas, the only other whites responsible for Aborigines were police officers, simply because they were the only white officials available. As the Berndts have put it:

In these places local police officials were automatically appointed (honorary) Protectors of Aborigines, but seem to have been regarded with some antagonism and fear. Their stations, however, were often used as ration depots. This helped to modify the hostility of the aborigines, who came to rely on them for economic support and, instead of actively opposing the new system, began to accept as a matter of course, what benefits they could.[17]

This statement may be true of South Australia proper, but it gives the impression that it applies also to the Northern Territory. Rowley says in some remarks on the Territory that 'The South Australian system of appointing sub-Protectors, who might be police officers or officers in charge of the telegraph stations, began in 1877 to be used for the management of a limited number of ration stations, mainly to feed the old and ill'.[18] This also suggests that policemen were used as protectors or sub-protectors of Aborigines in the Northern Territory during the South Australian period, whereas, as will be shown, no policemen served as protectors in the Territory before 1908. Policemen did, however, distribute rations after drought began in the Centre in the late 1880s.

It is thus clear that the original British policy towards the Aborigines of South Australia could not be implemented in the light of prevailing colonial conditions. Competition from white settlers for land and other resources led to a steady weakening of any official resolve to carry out the intentions expressed in Hindmarsh's proclamation of 1836. When South Australia achieved self-government twenty years later, official protection was not being extended equally to the Aboriginal population and the settlers. Acts of violence or injustice against Aborigines were no longer being punished, and they were no longer considered to be 'as much under the Safeguard of the law as the Colonists themselves, and equally entitled to the privileges of British subjects'. Instead, much of their land had been appropriated and many had been confined to missions and reserves. The objective of promoting their advancement in civilization, and ultimately their conversion to the Christian faith, had lost force over two decades and by 1860 whites thought it just a matter of waiting until the Aborigines themselves solved the social problems resulting from colonization by conveniently dying out. In 1864, when South Australia began to colonize the Northern Territory, the Europeans had no better idea of how to deal with indigenous people than they had in 1836. The first party of colonists to sail from Adelaide to the Territory were instructed to apply the same benevolent principles as proclaimed by Hindmarsh — but they carried with them the same pernicious colonial attitudes, which had quickly undermined those principles.

Chapter 1

Early Overtures

South Australians, like most other Europeans, knew little about the vast lands to the north, which some of them coveted. Until the overland explorers set foot on it, the only information had come from seafarers. The reports of the Dutch seaborne explorers and the British hydrographers did not inspire a rush of settlement. Van Colster in 1623, Pieter Pieterszoon in 1636 and Abel Tasman in 1644 saw nothing of value on the Arnhem Land coast, and the local people were to them 'wretched naked beachcombers ... and wicked men'. Martin van Delft and his men, visiting Melville Island in 1705, tried to fraternize with the Aborigines they met until two sailors were wounded during an attack by the local people, causing the Dutch to dismiss them as 'foul and treacherous'.

The chief interest in the northern coast of Australia before 1863 came from the British Admiralty, which was more concerned with imperial defence than settlement. In 1803 Matthew Flinders had completed surveying only the eastern half of the Territory's coast when he had to cut his voyage short because his ship's condition was deteriorating. In 1818 Phillip Parker King called at and named Port Essington on Cobourg Peninsula while completing Flinders's work, warding off an attack on his small ship without loss to either side. King also discovered and named Apsley Strait between Melville and Bathurst Islands, and encountered the antagonism of the local Tiwi people who harried his men and stole his theodolite. In 1824 the British government, suspicious that the French, Dutch and Americans might have designs on unclaimed parts of the continent, decided to establish military and trading settlements at Port Essington and Apsley Strait; a lack of water at the former led to the latter only, named Fort Dundas, being founded. This outpost, and the two others which followed at Raffles Bay and Port Essington over the period 1824 to 1849, did provide the first sustained contact between Aborigines and Europeans in the Territory.

The Tiwi people of Melville Island greeted the British in 1824 with the same hostility they had shown van Delft and King. Captain Gordon Bremer arrived on 23 September with fifty marines and soldiers, and several wives and children, but without official instructions as to how he should handle the local people. He had merely been told they were 'understood to be of a ferocious disposition'. Within a month the Tiwi had attacked, and one was shot in reprisal. Thereafter the Aborigines were seldom seen but they tore down huts, speared the livestock, stole the tools of working parties and, in October 1826, killed a white man. In November 1827 the surgeon, John Gold, and storekeeper, John Green, walking near Fort Dundas, were attacked and killed. By this time it was apparent that Apsley Strait was unsuitable as a trading settlement, being well south of the route taken annually by the Macassan trepangers visiting the Arnhem Land coast, and that it was unhealthy, several of the garrison having died of malaria. In 1828 Fort Dundas was abandoned in favour of Fort Wellington, which had been set up at Raffles Bay in July 1827, but where relations with the Aborigines were no better. The commandant, Captain Henry Smyth, possibly mindful of the experience on Melville Island, sent out armed patrols with his working parties. In February 1828 one of these patrols had killed an Aboriginal man, woman and child and wounded several others. When Smyth reported this to Sydney, Governor Ralph Darling condemned the action as an 'unofficered expedition of private soldiers and convicts undertaken against the natives upon the promise of pecuniary reward'. He regretted that atrocities had been committed upon women and children but believed that the natives had brought the trouble upon themselves.[1] No action was taken against Smyth but he was replaced by Captain Collett Barker.

Barker was an exceptional man in the history of black–white relations in Australia. He treated the Aborigines with tact and respect, demonstrating his trust by walking with them unarmed and unescorted through the bush, even sleeping in their camps overnight. Soon his fame as a white man to be trusted spread to other tribes. The last year at Raffles Bay was one of peace, but the continued unfavourable reports on the second settlement caused the British to terminate it. On his way back to Sydney via South Australia, Barker called at the Murray estuary in April 1831 and, although warned of the hostility of the local people, swam alone across a channel to take soundings; he was attacked and killed. No doubt he was another casualty of the hostility of the Murray men to the white whalers and sealers who had abused them and their women for years.

Despite these failures at northern settlement, the British were still concerned about French and possibly American interest in northern Australia, and decided that an outpost should be established again on Cobourg Peninsula to ensure British sovereignty. Although there were advocates of another Singapore on the north coast of Australia, this had little influence on the decision to return to Cobourg Peninsula; strategic considerations were paramount. The British meant to have all of Australia. In October 1838 Bremer arrived with a force of marines, civilians and families, this time finding water at Port Essington where he set about building a town he called Victoria. The Macassan traders called, but the Arafura Sea and Torres Strait were not major trade routes. Free settlers were welcomed, but 'successive British governments could never bring themselves to sell land cheaply or offer any real inducement for either European or Asian merchants to come to north Australia'[2] — although traders did bring supplies and buffalo, ponies and cattle for the use of the settlement. There was nothing to offer in return, the soil being poor and the climate harsh. Eventually shipping lines declined to use Port Essington as a port of call. After a serious malaria epidemic in 1843, health and morale steadily declined. By the time Victoria was abandoned in February 1849, more than forty whites had died there. By September 1841 the Aborigines were suffering catarrh, inflamation of the chest, ophthalmia, and a bronchial disease killed many, including sixty in one area, as malaria and a bronchial disease again struck in 1846. The British were not responsible for introducing all the illness suffered by the Aborigines of the peninsula. 'Malaria, leprosy, smallpox and venereal diseases were endemic in the Indonesian islands and could easily have been passed from the Macassans to the Cobourg tribes.'[3]

Race relations at Port Essington were amicable throughout the eleven years of British settlement, possibly because of the failure to attract pastoralists and their flocks and herds. Disruption of Aboriginal society was minimal; the tribes of the Cobourg Peninsula were used to foreigners such as the Macassans calling and staying for long periods; and no doubt Collett Barker's exceptional behaviour at Raffles Bay, only a few miles away, had allayed any antagonism towards the whites. Guards had been set as soon as Bremer arrived but it was soon realized that they were not needed. The local people set up camp on the shore near Victoria, occasionally pilfering articles which took their fancy, but this was soon discouraged in favour of exchanging fish, crabs and oysters for biscuits and clothing. Before long they were entertaining the whites with corroborees. Occasional thefts still occurred but, when two Aborigines escaped after one incident, they returned in two days, acknowledged their guilt and submitted to punishment. By 1841 Aborigines were availing themselves of the surgeon's services and even asked the commandant, Captain John McArthur, to arbitrate in their personal disputes. Soon the Cobourg tribes were working as servants, guides and seamen on British ships. Father Angelo Confalonieri, a Roman Catholic priest who survived the sinking of the *Heroine* west of Torres Strait in 1846, attempted a mission to the Aborigines, setting up a camp with them at Black Point on the outer harbour of Port Essington. He quickly

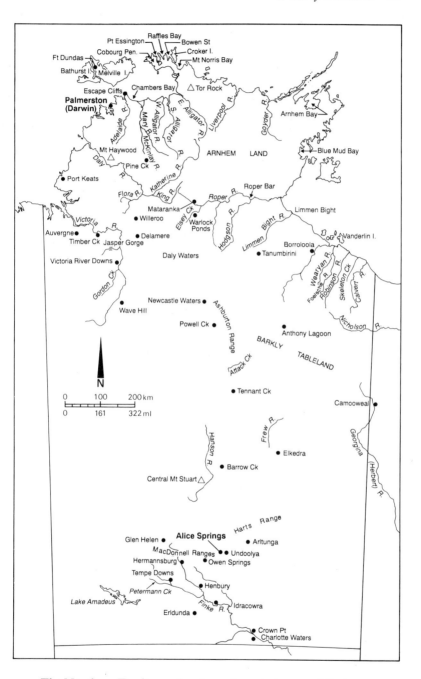

The Northern Territory, showing relevant places and features

learned the language of the people there and was soon accepted because of his attempts to reconcile tribal differences, sharing his provisions and adopting their nomadic life. Confalonieri compiled vocabularies of the seven tribal languages used on the peninsula, drew a map of the tribal areas and familiarized himself with their customs. But some of the elders were antagonistic towards him and robbed his hut. He despaired of converting them to Christianity, telling McArthur that he was not making any impression on them. He may in fact have made an impression on them as had Barker at Raffles Bay, but he was not to see the results of his work. He died of malaria at Port Essington in 1848 a disappointed man, his anthropological work incomplete.

The French explorer, Dumont D'Urville, and his party visited Raffles Bay and Port Essington in 1839 and on landing he was approached by Aborigines who presented him with weapons and showed him how to use them. He gave 'knives and other trifles' in return. One acted as pilot when the French visited Croker Island. D'Urville made few comments on the Aborigines he observed in that area, merely saying that two men who asked for food and ate it gluttonously had 'brutish natures'. George Windsor Earl, one of the early promoters of northern settlement, who arrived with Bremer in 1838, also studied the people of Cobourg Peninsula, separating them into four tribes. Earl attributed the good race relations at Port Essington to every white being employed by the government; that is, there were no settlers. In eleven years there, the British were responsible for the death of only one Aborigine. Sergeant William Marland, taking Aborigines accused of theft under arrest across the harbour to Victoria by boat in 1846, shot one when they dived overboard. McArthur was 'greatly distressed' by the killing, having prided himself that until then there had been no deaths by violence. Marland was arrested, charged and placed on bail and the case referred to Sydney. He was found to have acted justifiably to prevent a prisoner escaping. The Aborigine killed was a member of the Monoba tribe, which sought revenge, but instead of attacking a European the Monoba murdered Neinmil, a member of another tribe who was a favourite of the whites.

Although Port Essington and its two preceding outposts on the northern coast were failures in the European colonization of Australia, generally they were not failures in Aboriginal–European relations. Instead they showed for the first time since 1788 that the whites could intrude into black society and remain without stimulating violent reaction. Both sides appear to have gained from the experience because of remarkable tolerance and adaption to each other. When the first whites reached Cobourg Peninsula with cattle in 1874, they found that the goodwill towards whites created thirty years before still remained. Certainly, the circumstances were exceptional because of the absence of pastoralism, mining, timbergetting and the other European

B. T. Finniss, who failed to establish a settlement at Escape Cliffs

G. W. Goyder, South Australian
Surveyor-General, who established a
settlement at Port Darwin

Mitchell Street, Palmerston (later Darwin), June 1879, looking north-
westward

Inspector Paul Foelsche, first police chief in the Northern Territory

Foelsche's residence in Palmerston, n.d., one of many photographs he took himself

industries which had undermined tribal economies and traditional societies elsewhere — although the destructive elements of attraction, concentration and disease on Aboriginal culture, clearly seen later, were apparent by 1849. The northern experience had shown that the first European assessment of these people as being 'wicked men' and 'foul and treacherous' was not justified. Yet, there is no evidence that the British authorities in Australia learned from this successful exercise in relations with indigenous people, which contrasts strongly with the hostile response to European settlement in South Australia at the same time.

The first overland contact with the native peoples of the Northern Territory had been made by Ludwig Leichhardt's expedition of 1844–45. Leichhardt was a careful observer, noting the way in which European and Macassan influences had intruded inland from the coast. Moving from the Gulf of Carpentaria towards Port Essington he saw a cut post, which suggested the use of an iron tomahawk, on the Roper River and he spotted iron axes and English cloth on the South Alligator plain. He recorded that Aborigines on the Alligator plains were aware of gemstones and also of buffaloes, which had strayed from Cobourg Peninsula. A week before the end of his trip, Aboriginal women and children consented to enter his camp whereas previously only men would approach his party in groups of two or four or one man backed up by others standing in the trees. The closer the white explorers got to Port Essington, the more friendly became the local people who acted as guides, gift-givers, mendicants and even procurers. As the whites descended the tableland to the South Alligator River on 21 November 1845, four Aborigines offered them presents of red ochre, a spear and a spearhead of baked sandstone. Finally, near the mouth of the East Alligator River, on the last stretch of the journey, an Aborigine named Bob White greeted Leichhardt with the words: 'Commandant! Come here! Very good! What's your name?' He was then led to Port Essington.

The next land expedition might have been expected to contribute more to European understanding of the indigenous people, but it did not. Augustus Gregory led the North Australian expedition which explored the Victoria River district and southwards along Sturt's Creek (now named Stuart Creek) into Western Australia in 1855 before returning to the Victoria and then striking eastwards on the way to the Gulf of Carpentaria. Gregory was accompanied by the eminent botanist, Ferdinand von Mueller, who concentrated his attention upon the flora they encountered. Gregory, who became Queensland's first surveyor-general in 1860, was considered later in that colony to be an expert upon the Aborigines, a reputation which was never justified. The references in his journal of that expedition to the native people he encountered are perfunctory.

Although the journal does not indicate Gregory's thoughts about the Aborigines, his notes occasionally indicate how the Aborigines reacted to him and his party. Returning to his main camp on the Victoria River in March 1856, he found that the men left there had been

... somewhat annoyed by the blacks, who had made frequent attempts to burn the camp, and also the horses, by setting fire to the grass, and on some occasions had come to actual hostilities, though by judicious management none of the party had been injured; nor was it certain that any of the blacks had been injured although it had been necessary to resort to the use of firearms in self-defence and for the protection of the horses.[4]

Previously Gregory mentions only seeing and hearing Aborigines, but this large expedition had been in the Victoria River district since September 1855 and by March it would have seemed to the local tribes that the whites had come to stay, thus the attempt while Gregory was absent to drive them out. The Victoria River people had had no history of contact with foreigners as had the Arnhem Land tribes, and the explorers made no effort to fraternize with them, keeping guard at all times. Although Aborigines occasionally visited the Victoria River camp and bartered 'trifles' the situation was always tense, as the following incident shows. In June 1856 the expedition's artist and storekeeper, T. Baines, landed from the schooner *Tom Tough* in company with the master, Captain Gourlay, and two others to barter with about twenty Aborigines on shore. Some of them stole a tomahawk and one of the seamen seized an Aborigine, intending to hold him until the tomahawk was returned. An Aborigine then seized the seaman's rifle and attempted to wrest it from him, but when Gourlay approached the man ran into the bush, the others retired and the whites returned to the schooner. The geologist, J. S. Wilson, whom Gregory had left in charge of the main camp, asked Gregory to investigate this incident, which he said might have 'terminated the hitherto undisturbed harmony which had been maintained by the parties in his charge in my absence in their intercourse with the aborigines'. But Gregory decided to drop the matter.[5]

At last, moving eastwards in July, Gregory and the surgeon and naturalist, Dr J. R. Elsey, were reconnoitring the way ahead on a creek — which Gregory named after his companion — when they met the first Aborigines they had seen since leaving the Victoria. The meeting was a nervous encounter, the Aborigines following them at a distance down the creek. When Gregory and Elsey stopped, the blacks ran away and hid until the whites unsaddled and commenced a meal, conscious of being watched from a hiding place. Gregory wrote:

... after some time spent in making signs, they were induced to approach, the oldest of the party feigning to weep bitterly till they got close to us; when we commenced an attempt at conversation, and they appeared to recognize some words of the language of the Victoria River. Their spears were formed of reeds with large heads of white sandstone, and also with three wooden points for fishing. They were circumcised and had their front teeth remaining . . . [6]

Proceeding farther down the Elsey, the party found the remains of a hut made by whites seven to eight years beforehand. Gregory thought the whites had camped for several weeks, judging by the ashes which still remained. Several trees had been cut down by iron axes. This may have been one of Leichhardt's camps of 1845, although eleven years old and apparently too far west of his route. If Gregory's estimate of seven to eight years is correct, then the only explanation appears to be that it was made by Leichhardt's last party in 1848 or 1849 when he was attempting to cross Australia from the Darling Downs to the Swan River Colony, as the settled districts of Western Australia were sometimes then known, only to disappear without certain trace. There is no record of any other whites being in that area between the time of Leichhardt's first expedition and Gregory's expedition.

Gregory's last recorded contact with Aborigines in the Northern Territory occurred on 19 July on the Roper River, when he was forced for the first time to resort to firearms. Aborigines were seen stealing into camp at 8 p.m.; they did not retreat, so Gregory ordered a shot to be fired in the air, thus causing them to scatter. In all his explorations Gregory had never provoked Aborigines but was always cautious, never allowing them into camp. He commented in his journal:

What their object was in thus approaching the camp at night, unless for hostile purposes, we had no means of ascertaining; but the Aboriginal Australian considers it an act of positive hostility to approach a camp in silence at night. [7]

The above quotations comprise the sum of Augustus Gregory's comments on his dealings with the Aborigines of the Northern Territory. Totally lacking in observation, except for the generalization in the last remark which was probably based on his Western Australian experience, his journal entries suggest that the Aborigines he met were merely figures in a landscape and, apart from their potential danger, of no lasting interest to him. However, the Aborigines of the Elsey and Roper districts apparently did not forget him. Many years ago old Goggle Eye told Baludja, known as Bunny, a member of the Mungari people whose territory includes Elsey cattle station, that he had seen six white men come from the west and ride down Elsey Creek. Goggle Eye was at Elsey during the time of Aeneas Gunn and Baludja was born in 1899. In 1948 H. E. Thonemann, managing partner of Elsey station, retold the story. According to Thonemann, Goggle Eye told Baludja that the white men were members of Gregory's party: 'They seemed very tall and confident, these white men, as they walked, although they must have been tired and dusty'. The Mungari laughed at von Mueller and followed him about to watch him cut leaves and seeds off trees and grasses and put them in little hollow sticks made of glass. Gregory was recognized as the chief of the whites and it was noted that he wore a fish-hook in his hat. Years previously Goggle Eye had seen fish-hooks on the north side of the Roper River, apparently obtained from Leichhardt's party. With four other Aborigines he went to Gregory and asked for them by making signs. They were given only one, so hoping to get more they followed the whites all the way to Stuart's Rocky Hole in the Strangways River. Nothing came of this because they were frightened of the 'fire-sticks which had already wounded one member of the tribe'.[8] If this last statement is correct, Gregory either did not know that his warning shot on the Roper had been aimed too low or he did not wish to admit in print that he had spoiled his otherwise impeccable record of non-violence.

A similar story appears in McDouall Stuart's journal of his last journey. On 30 June 1862 he and his party crossed the Roper River on their way northwards and met a group of Aborigines, including a tall old man.

Mr Kekwick having a fishhook stuck in his hat, which immediately caught the old fellow's eye, he made signs for its use, and that he would like to possess it. I told Mr Kekwick to give it to him, which seemed to please him much. After examining it, he handed it over to a young man, seemingly his son, who was a fat stout fellow, and who was laughing all the time.

Next day before sunrise Aborigines again appeared and Stuart sent Kekwick to see what they wanted.

On his coming up to them they put two fingers in their mouths, signifying that they wanted more fish-hooks, but we had no more to spare ... After starting they followed us for some miles, when Mr Waterhouse observing a pigeon shot it. They did not like the report of the gun, went off, and we saw no more of them.[9]

The fish-hook incident is not mentioned by Gregory and so it is more likely that the meeting related by Baludja was with Stuart's party. While they had traversed the Strangways River and stopped at a place they called the Rock Camp, there is no evidence that Gregory went there. Also, Waterhouse's shooting of a pigeon corresponds with Gregory's warning shot on the Roper, and the laughing son corresponds with the amusement which von Mueller gave the Mungari. Quite possibly elements of both encounters are contained in Baludja's story, which is important for its contribution to Aboriginal folklore of the coming of the white man.

The last of the overland expeditions before 1863 were led by John McDouall Stuart in 1860–62. Stuart was ambitious to emulate the work of Charles Sturt, his illustrious leader in the 1844–45 expedition which pressed outwards from Adelaide to ascertain whether there was an inland sea. Stuart was financed by graziers William Finke and James Chambers, two of those land-hungry South Australian graziers who had become frustrated when the limits of South Australian grasslands were reached late in the 1850s. In March 1860, with two men and thirteen horses, Stuart set off on his fourth expedition into the interior, heading westwards of Lake Eyre, then northwards through the ranges of Central Australia which he named after the expansionist Governor MacDonnell. On 22 April he reached a mountain he calculated to be at the heart of the continent, naming it Central Mount Sturt (later renamed Stuart). When he and one of his companions, William Kekwick, climbed its peak and raised the Union Jack they, to quote Stuart's words, 'gave three cheers for the flag, the emblem of civil and religious liberty, and may it be a sign to the natives that the union of liberty, civilization, and Christianity is about to break upon them'. In view of the subsequent events, this must be the most ironically futile announcement in Australian history.

Stuart has a justified reputation for having been courteous towards the Aborigines he met, always showing reasonable restraint in the face of hostility. His first serious confrontation in Central Australia occurred during this expedition at Bishop Creek, just north of Tennant Creek, to which he had returned after failing to reach the Victoria River, one of the possible sites which the South Australian government was to select for settlement. On the second day after their return, several Aborigines approached the white men's camp and by their gestures showed they wanted them to go away. Stuart tried appealing to a young man who advanced towards them, spear raised.

He came fully prepared for war. I then broke a branch of green leaves and held it up before him, inviting him to come across [the creek] to me. That he did not fancy, so I crossed to him, and got within two yards of him. He thought I was near enough and would not have me any nearer, for he kept moving back as I approached him, till at last we both stood still. I tried to make him understand, by signs, that all we wanted was water for two or three days. At last he seemed to understand, nodded his head, pointed to the water, and held up his five fingers.

Stuart's party stayed there five more days during which they were not again threatened. Farther north, at Kekwick Ponds, on 23 June, two young men presented the whites with four opossums and a number of small parrots, even though they were 'much frightened at first'. The well-wishers overcame their fear enough to attempt to steal 'everything they could lay their fingers on', possibly because they expected something in exchange for the food. Later these young men returned with their father who was very talkative and, after making a sign which Stuart took to be Masonic, the old man patted Stuart on the shoulder, stroked his head, and departed, 'making friendly signs until out of sight'. The whites 'enjoyed a good supper from the opossums, which we had not had for many a day'. Three days later, at

Attack Creek, occurred the incident which gave the place its name. While they were looking for a spot to camp for the night, about thirty Aborigines approached, fully armed, shouting defiantly. Rejecting Stuart's attempts at friendship, they attacked with a shower of boomerangs, one striking Stuart's horse, and began setting fire to the grass. Stuart ordered his men to hold their fire, but after another volley of boomerangs and some spears, one of which struck his horse, he 'gave orders to fire, which stayed their mad career a little'. It was now dark and, fearing that they would be surrounded and destroyed, Stuart and his two companions retreated to the previous night's camp, followed by the Warramanga. Now exhausted, with supplies running out and the country fast drying up, Stuart decided to return to Adelaide.

On his next expedition, which left Adelaide at the end of 1860 and reached Attack Creek in April and Newcastle Waters on 20 May, one of the party, J. Woodforde, was attacked by Aborigines while duck-shooting alone, and found himself trapped in water. While a black was in the act of throwing a spear, Woodforde 'gave him the contents of his gun in his face, and made for the camp'. Arthur Ashwin wrote in 1927 that Woodforde told him a few years after this incident that he 'shot one of the natives dead', but Ashwin was apparently writing from memory. There is no reliable evidence that any member of Stuart's parties killed an Aborigine. On the contrary, their behaviour in Warramanga territory seems to have built up credit for Stuart. On their way homewards after Stuart's last expedition had successfully reached the north coast at the Adelaide River mouth in July 1862, two of his men were washing clothes at Attack Creek when a tall Aborigine befriended them. One of the men, Stephen King, later related:

He came up to us, and after talking and making signs he untied the lace of my boot. Then I made signs to him to take it off, which he did, and then gave a whistle. Next he took off the stocking, gave another whistle, and tried to peel off more. I made signs to him to replace them, which he did, doing up the lace and tying it in a bow the same as it was before. He seemed very much astonished at the whole process. We packed up our clothes, bade him a most polite good-day, and returned to the camp.

Next day at Hayward Creek the party was preparing to make camp when a group of Aborigines 'danced and yelled and looked as if they intended an attack':

Making signal-fires, they became more frantic until our tall friend made his appearance. He had feathers on his head and arms. He walked up to us boldly, and made a sign to the others. They immediately sat down and became quiet. It appeared that we had taken possession of their water. We made signs to them to come and help themselves. We filled two leather buckets and carried them some distance from the camp for them. Our friend was the chief, and a splendid man he was — over six feet high and as upright as a soldier. We christened him 'Major O'Halloran'.

It was an inappropriate nickname in view of the summary justice which O'Halloran had dealt out to the Aborigines who had killed the *Maria* survivors in 1840.

Stuart's good record is further supported by T. G. H. Strehlow in his *Comments on the Journals of John McDouall Stuart* in which, after speaking to tribesmen who were alive at the time, he says firearms were used on Stuart's journeys only as a means of self-defence and then only as a last resort to warn off attackers. As an indication of the Aborigines' reaction to these strange humans and animals who passed through their country, men — who were boys at the time but had not seen them — told Strehlow about their tracks:

We were terrified by those footprints. The boot-tracks looked as though they had been made by human beings; but what kind of creatures could men be who had broad, flat, toeless feet, and a heel that was a hard lump, sharply edged from the main part of the foot? As for the horse-tracks, we could tell that they must have been made by huge four-footed creatures, larger than any we had seen before. These creatures, too, had no toes, and their heavy feet had cut their way even into hard clay ground, and left their scars on the rock plates. Surely, we thought, both these kinds of creatures must be evil, man-eating monsters! Perhaps they were some of those man-eating monsters who prowled about at night and normally attacked men without leaving any tracks behind.

Apart from the early misfortunes at Melville Island and Raffles Bay, contact between the British and the Aborigines before 1863 had generally resulted in nervous but cordial relations which white strangers in Aboriginal territory had experienced in other parts of Australia. Aborigines were motivated by curiosity and fear; the few hostile acts had not been designed to destroy the European parties but to persuade them to move on — anywhere out of local territory. Sometimes, as we have seen at Attack Creek, relations improved with acquaintance. This was not to be the case, however, when the South Australians began to settle the Territory.

Chapter 2

Escape Cliffs

The creation of the colony of Queensland in 1859 had caused New South Wales to be split into two parts, the home colony and the Northern Territory. To the latter was attached a strip of land between 129 and 132 degrees east longitude, separating South Australia and Western Australia. Although this tract was worthless, the Colonial Office agreed in 1861 to a South Australian request for it. The colony also suggested that the Northern Territory be transferred to it but this was rejected. The Secretary for the Colonies at the time, the Duke of Newcastle, was not convinced that any settlement on the northern coast should be governed from the other side of the continent — a judgement justified by subsequent events.

Because their colony had little productive pastoral and agricultural land compared with the eastern colonies, South Australians seemed to believe that more land was the answer to their economic problems; further, they were led by two expansionist governors, Sir Richard MacDonnell, 1855–62, and Sir Dominic Daly, 1862–68. McDouall Stuart's expeditions into the interior were motivated by this search for more usable land, and his return to Adelaide in 1862 after finally crossing the continent led the colony to ask for the Territory as well. In 1861 Queensland had successfully requested that its border with the Territory be moved westwards from 142 to 138 degrees east longitude to include the Plains of Promise at the head of the Gulf of Carpentaria, into which its pastoralists were then moving. This stimulated South Australia to request what was left of the Territory, especially as it was possible that the submarine telegraph cable from India would come ashore on the northern coast. If granted, this would ensure that an overland link could be constructed entirely within South Australian boundaries. In May 1863, Newcastle informed Daly that the request would be granted, and letters patent effecting the transfer were issued on 6 July.[1]

South Australia's claims were based chiefly on the explorations of

Stuart (who had proven that the Top End of the Territory could be reached by a direct land route), on the professed intentions of some of its pastoralists to apply for land in the Victoria River district, and on its willingness to finance the construction of the overland telegraph. Newcastle had considered dividing the Territory, granting the southern part to South Australia and the northern part to Queensland, but Queensland declined the gift. As it happened later, South Australian pastoralists generally confined themselves to the Centre while Queenslanders developed the industry in the Top End. In the first flush of excitement of this doubling of South Australian land, the rush was for grazing land on or near the north coast; on 1 March 1864 land sales were opened in Adelaide and London and the first 250 000 acres were sold off the map.

To prepare the way for expected development, a survey party of forty officers and men under Boyle Travers Finniss was hastily assembled in Adelaide and despatched in April with orders to select a site for a settlement near the mouth of the Adelaide River. One possible site was the Victoria River district, which was favoured by pastoralists on the basis of Gregory's reports. The other was the Adelaide River mouth on Adam Bay, which had been surveyed by Captain John Wickham and Lieutenant John Lort Stokes in the *Beagle* in 1839, and reached by Stuart a few miles to the east of the river. The government believed tropical agriculture, which would attract small settlers, should be attempted on the flood plains of the Adelaide. This view was supported by Finniss, who on arrival chose Escape Cliffs on the eastern side of Adam Bay for the site of the first settlement.

The place was so named because of an incident involving men of the *Beagle* in 1839. A mate, L. R. Fitzmaurice, and the ship's clerk, Charles Keys, had gone ashore to check their compasses. Lort Stokes wrote in his journal:

From the quantity of iron contained in the rocks it was necessary to select a spot free of its influence. A sandy beach at the foot of red cliffs was chosen. The observations had begun when 20 feet above their heads a large party of natives appeared with poised and quivering spears, as if about to immediately deliver them. It was not a little surprising to behold their paroxysm of rage evaporate before the happy presence of mind of Fitzmaurice, who began to dance and shout, though in momentary expectation of being pierced by a dozen spears. In this he was imitated by Keys. They succeeded in diverting the natives from their evil designs. Fitzmaurice and Keys had firearms within reach but the moment they ceased dancing and attempted to touch them a dozen spears were pointed at their breasts. Their lives hung upon a thread and their escape must be regarded as truly wonderful.[2]

By this time one of the *Beagle*'s boats had pulled into shore and, with the Aborigines in pursuit, Fitzmaurice and Keys made a successful dash for it. In December of that year Stokes was speared in a shoulder when he went ashore at the mouth of the Victoria River, but after a night close to death he slowly recovered.

Finniss was appointed government resident and magistrate. His credentials appeared to be good: a Sandhurst graduate, he had served in Mauritius as an Army engineer and had arrived in South Australia with the first colonists in 1836, being appointed deputy to the surveyor-general, Colonel William Light. Later he became a resourceful farmer, businessman, politician, acting governor and South Australia's first premier after self-government was granted in 1856. Escape Cliffs proved to be unsuitable largely because much of the hinterland was under water during the wet season and therefore impassable. The survey teams could not move about in the boggy soil but, although instructed to do so, Finniss refused to seek another site. He was recalled in September 1865, leaving his deputy, J. T. Manton, in charge, to face a royal commission which 'condemned him for poor judgement and for spending some 40,000 pounds of public funds on a hopeless venture'. Finniss, despite his unsuitability as a planner and leader, became a scapegoat for the government's failure of judgement in deciding to settle a region, of which it knew almost nothing, and at a time of economic recession, during which South Australia had few resources to develop its new province. The rapid succession of thirteen governments over six years from July 1863 only contributed to the muddled thinking in Adelaide, while those intending settlers and speculators who had bought land in the early rush of enthusiasm for the North were demanding return of their money by 1866.

In his instructions Finniss had been informed that the Aborigines in the Adelaide River area were represented by some as friendly and inoffensive and by others as treacherous and quite ready to attack anyone who might visit their shores:

Your duty will be to exercise the greatest caution and forebearance in communicating with them, to warn your party to studiously avoid giving them the slightest offence, and should you find them sufficiently trustworthy to have intercourse with them, or to enter into any dealings with them, you must insist upon every transaction being carried out on your part with the most scrupulous exactness; and while it may be well to encourage communication with them, by showing them that you are prepared to trust them, you will take every precaution against their taking you by surprise, by always being prepared to act on the defensive, by keeping regular watch in your camp, and by ordering our party not to move about the country in small parties or unarmed. Above all, you must warn your party to abstain from anything like hostility towards them; and avoid the extremities of a conflict, which must only be had recourse to in self-defence, and only then from absolute necessity. You will show them that, while you are anxious to gain their goodwill and confidence by kindness and judicious liberality, you are able to repel and, if necessary, punish aggression.[3]

In addition, Finniss was referred to the special instructions issued to the surgeon, Dr F. E. Goldsmith, who was also to be protector of Aborigines. Goldsmith was told to 'win the confidence and respect of the Aborigines and make them aware of their legal rights as British subjects, as well as to prevent sexual intercourse with them or the sale of liquor to them; and to use the law against settlers who ill treated them'.[4] These two sets of instructions, carefully enjoining caution and restraint in dealing with the Aborigines but omitting any acknowledgement of Aboriginal right to their land, were like those given to all colonizing leaders since Governor Arthur Phillip. Perhaps there was even more attention to the need for avoiding conflict, which may have stemmed from a desire on the part of the South Australian parliament to avoid criticism. The evangelical George Fife Angas had told the Legislative Council select committee in 1860 that he knew of 'no subject in the whole course of the history of the colony that has been so shamefully shirked as the welfare of the aborigines'.[5] Also, the Aborigines Protection Society in London, which had a South Australian branch, could be expected to watch carefully events in the north.

The Aborigines at Escape Cliffs soon proved to be as aggressive as Fitzmaurice and Keys had found in 1839. Finniss and some of his party arrived on the *Henry Ellis* on 20 June 1864. On 2 July two blacks appeared at the camp and went away at sundown without hostile incident; the following day, twelve visited the camp; and sixty days later the number of visitors had grown to forty as Aboriginal curiosity and desire for European goods increased. The *Yatala* arrived on 29 June, having run aground on the journey north; she was unloaded but her cargo was left on the beach for some time, guarded by Finniss's force of volunteer police, who had no legal authority and were wont to leave the cargo unattended during meal periods. Thieving became common and tension between the two races soon developed. When called before the commission established in 1866 to inquire into his management of the expedition, Finniss claimed that in the early contact with the natives he had 'by scrupulous forebearance, and by kindness and liberality, tried to win their confidence'.[6] But it was obvious, he said, that they resented the whites' occupation of the country and nothing would restrain them from stealing; 'and their numbers and strength, and the nature of their weapons, and the nature of the country, made them formidable enemies'. Fear soon caused official caution to be replaced by a siege mentality, as Finniss explained. Early in August, while stores from the *Yatala* were being moved about two hundred yards to the depot, a party of blacks plundered the stores in sight of sentries whom they threatened with spears. They were driven away only by other guards firing at them. Next morning a well-armed party of four under a man named Pearson rode out to recover the stolen goods but was attacked. Pearson was unhorsed and wounded; another man, F. H. Litchfield, was struck and disabled; and two horses were speared. A second party of whites went to their aid and one of them, Alaric Ward, shot a black. The Aborigines then retreated. According to Finniss, this affray had caused Manton and his men, who had been moving the stores, to be terrified of the Aborigines.

Later that day Dr Goldsmith, who, as well as being protector of Aborigines, was a stipendiary magistrate, held an inquest with an appointed jury. The jury found the death was due to justifiable homicide but stated that the 'disasters' which had occurred were solely attributable to the camp having been pitched on a site surrounded by dense mangrove in which the Aborigines might lie in ambush, as they had done that morning. There the matter ended, but Finniss took this to be a personal criticism, which only helped to estrange him more from his officers. On 4 September Aborigines appeared at the Europeans' camp. Some were painted white, which, Finniss said, was the mark of mourning and indicated that they were out to avenge a death; some were painted red, 'their war paint'. They were recognized as belonging to the tribe which had attacked Pearson's party, and the Europeans were convinced that 'their intentions were hostile'. On 7 September one of the horses came into camp with a spear sticking into its hock, and men sent to bring in the cattle found that another horse had been speared three times.

Finniss decided that strong measures must be taken. 'Neither property nor life was secure so long as the natives were lurking in the neighbourhood of the camp and neither the work of the camp, nor the task of the exploring party could be carried on', he said. To have remained on the defensive, as had been been done until this time, would have encouraged the Aborigines to choose the time of attack and plunder. He organized a party of seven mounted men and nine on foot to go out and recover the stolen goods, and placed them under the command of his twenty-year-old son, Frederick, because, as he said, he had to 'select a person he could trust and whom his followers would willingly obey'. Manton, his second-in-command, was out of the question because of his handling of the affray at the river camp. Other officers were ill and he would not send Goldsmith, the protector, 'because of his avowed hostility towards myself and his expressed determination to thwart all my proceedings'. Finniss had antagonized most of his officers on the voyage from Adelaide because of his militaristic attitude, and at Escape Cliffs Goldsmith was one of his leading critics. Finniss said he had not 'fettered' his son with written instructions but had told him he was, 'at all hazards, to get in contact with the natives whom he must treat as armed bushrangers and felons, and pursue and capture, or kill if he could not capture'.

As they set out on 8 September eastwards towards Chambers Bay, William McMinn, who had charge of the foot party, asked Frederick Finniss what was to be done. Young Finniss replied:

'Shoot every bloody native you see'. When asked later by the royal commission whether he understood that the orders implied an indiscriminate massacre of the natives, McMinn replied: 'Everyone could interpret the orders in his own way'. He could see 'from the feeling coming from them' that his men would slaughter the Aborigines. Three of them trapped an Aborigine behind some scrub and, instead of taking him prisoner, one of them shot him dead. The whites then went to the native camp, recovered stolen property and destroyed the camp. They then encountered the surveyor, J. W. O. Bennett, who 'ordered them not to kill a native within fifty yards of his camp', apparently because he feared the Aborigines would associate him with this action. It was too late; they had already done so. When the party returned to Escape Cliffs, Finniss complimented his son by saying, 'Well done, Freddy, I thought you would let them see'. Some time later Alaric Ward was out of the whites' camp and was killed by the natives. The government's charges against Finniss were presented by F. Rymill, who claimed that the death of the prisoner was murder. He also believed that, if it had not been for the previous gross provocation, Ward would still be alive. Finniss had approved of the actions taken on 8 September, as was shown by his letter written nearly a month later to the Chief Secretary. Rymill said that Finniss had an extraordinary idea of the manner in which his instructions were to be carried out, his conduct towards the Aborigines being 'most inhuman'. The matter had brought disgrace not only on him but on the whole colony. The commissioners agreed, stating in their report that his proceedings in retaliation against the Aborigines were not in the spirit of his instructions, and that sending an armed aggressive party against them in the charge of an inexperienced youth without precise written instructions was highly indiscreet and reprehensible.[7]

Nothing was done about the alleged murder of the prisoner and, although Finniss suffered some ignomy as a result of the commission's damning report on his management, he was unfazed by the experience and was back in the Territory in 1870 as representative of the British Australian Telegraph Company, formed to bring the undersea cable to Port Darwin. The government could do little to chastize him, because he raised questions before the royal commission to which the government had no answers. It had not fully considered, before it sent him to Escape Cliffs, what he was to do if the Aborigines resisted the whites' intrusion or even persisted in stealing. In his defence Finniss said he could have gone through the normal legal procedures, issuing warrants for the searching of Aboriginal 'huts' and if the stolen goods were found warrants for the arrest of the owners of these 'huts'. But, he asked, what was to be the result of such a course? Who was to identify the owner of a 'hut'? What was to be done with a prisoner? Where was he to be kept? On what evidence was he to be committed? How was he to be transported to Adelaide for trial? Finniss added that to have attempted to deal with the Aborigines as through they were British subjects was 'not only absurd in principle, but even certain to result in complete failure'. He said that his only course was to treat them as outlaws. They were to be made to feel that the whites possessed the power to defend themselves and to attack and punish those by whom they were assailed and injured. He had revealed the moral dilemma which any colonial power created for itself when it annexed other people's land contrary to their wishes and yet wished to establish friendly relations with them:

The government had sent the party to occupy their territory without regard to their wishes, and if we were to remain there we were to overcome their hostility; and this, as we had proved, could not be done by means of conciliation and forebearance.[8]

The actions taken by him were effectual, he said; the tribe not showing itself again in the neighbourhood of Escape Cliffs. Most colonists would have agreed with his attitude and actions.

While the Aboriginal people near Port Darwin later were to prove friendly, those to the east in the Alligator Rivers district were by this time distinctly hostile. The latter appear to be those responsible for the hostilities at Escape Cliffs, since the punitive parties sent out moved eastwards to Chambers Bay. The repressive actions taken during Finniss's period at Adam Bay probably led to the aggressive reaction to the presence of John McKinlay who, following the recall of Finniss, arrived in November 1865 with instructions to find another site. As Carmel Schrire writes, relations between blacks and whites at Port Essington had given the impression that Aboriginal reaction to European invasion was benign: 'This had changed some 20 years later when McKinlay journeyed from the settlement at Escape Cliffs in 1866 and encountered open hostility, spears and threats on the Cannon Hill plains'.[9]

McKinlay delayed his search until January when the wet season had set in. Ignoring the merits of Port Darwin a few miles to the west, he set off eastwards with a party of fourteen men, forty-five horses, a number of sheep and rations for ten weeks. The country was so boggy that nearly five months later they had reached only the mouth of the West Alligator River, 160 kilometres from Adam Bay. Short of rations and unable to return overland, McKinlay and his men killed their horses, jerked the meat, made a raft of logs and greenhide and returned by sea to Escape Cliffs. While they were building the raft, McKinlay's party was threatened by Aborigines:

It was fortunate that the natives did not show their evil disposition until we had got all the timber from the jungle. Then, on the 27th, they pounced upon us under cover of smoke. They tried to attack the camp and those at the punt simultaneously but we dispersed them without any damage being sustained by us. A few rifle shots settled the question.[10]

Following McKinlay's failure to find a better site the Murray River navigator, Francis Cadell, was sent in 1866 to sail along the Arnhem Land coast. Although he reported enthusiastically about the Liverpool River area, the government was not impressed. In 1867 the settlement at Escape Cliffs was abandoned. Finally, late in 1868 it was decided to send the surveyor-general, George Goyder, to the north coast. He selected Port Darwin on the basis of Stokes's report of 1839 and the recommendations of both Manton and McKinlay, who had now changed his mind about Port Darwin. Goyder arrived with a party of 120 men in March 1869, and surveyed the site for a provincial capital and three other towns to the south. The name 'Palmerston' had been given to the settlement at Escape Cliffs but rarely used; now it was transferred to the new one at Port Darwin.

Relations with the local people, the Larakia and the Woolna (now identified as the Djerimanga), were relatively peaceful during Goyder's time. The Aborigines accepted the coming of the whites to the extent of assisting them to build stores, stables and smithies by bringing bark to the settlement. The whites were surprised one day when the Larakia spontaneously sang 'My Old Kentucky Home', which they had picked up from the whites at Escape Cliffs. This did not make them immune from retaliation from the Alligator Rivers tribes for the misdeeds of Finniss's party. One of Goyder's party was J. W. O. Bennett, who had tried to stop the white aggression of September 1864. Bennett, who had originally been antipathetic toward the Aborigines, had gradually come to count them as his friends and had begun to compile vocabularies of local languages. In May 1869 he was murdered, the only casualty among Goyder's party. Goyder refused to retaliate for Bennett's death, and showed that he had some understanding of the Aboriginal attitude when he wrote:

We were in what to them appeared unauthorised and unwarranted occupation of their country ... Territorial rights are strictly observed by natives ... it is scarcely to be wondered at if, when opportunity is allowed them, they should resent such acts by violence upon its perpetrators.[11]

Although he understood the Aborigines' position, Goyder had no respect for Aboriginal rights and looked forward to the time when those who would follow him would civilize 'these miserable specimens of humanity', teach them Christianity and the benefits of working for the Europeans destined to take and use their lands.

Goyder's task was completed in August, when he and most of his party returned to Adelaide. He left a small group at Palmerston in the charge of the medical officer, Dr Robert Peel, to continue the surveying and to erect better accommodation. In mid-December a relief party led by a new medical officer, Dr J. S. Millner, and including Sub-Inspector Paul Foelsche and six police troopers, sailed from Adelaide, arriving next month. Millner took charge of the settlement until the first permanent government resident, Captain William Bloomfield Douglas, arrived in July 1870.

In addition to his other duties, Millner was protector of Aborigines, a responsibility which he took seriously to the extent of going out of his way to provide food for those in need and to dress their wounds. Yet, in his official reports over the next few years, Millner showed no awareness of the broad ethical, social and political issues which the initiation of European settlement on the north coast of Australia would entail. Nor did the governments which had sent him and other Europeans to this place over the past five years.

Chapter 3

Colonization Begins

In its campaign for acquisition of the Territory, South Australia had claimed that it could colonize the northern lands by the overland route pioneered by Stuart. Having acquired the Territory, it changed plans and sent the first settlers there by sea. There was good reason for this: a sea voyage might take only a month and a ship could carry the heavy stores, materials and equipment required for a permanent settlement, whereas an overland expedition would have taken several months in extreme discomfort and without carrying heavy equipment, such as prefabricated houses. By contrast with Stuart's ordeal in reaching Chambers Bay in 1862, the voyage of the first permanent party led by Millner was a comfortable excursion in the *Koh-i-Noor*, which arrived in Port Darwin on 21 January 1870. After relieving the men left behind by Goyder to prepare for them, Millner's party of six officers and thirty-eight men set about its primary task — to prepare for the selection of land near Darwin. As P. F. Donovan has said, 'It was little more than an extension of the Adelaide Lands Office'.[1]

The Aborigines of the Port Darwin region were well used to the presence of Europeans when Millner's party arrived, but they showed no interest in the newcomers until 6 February, and did not go into the camp. Six days later a few camped at the 'Gully well' and approached the fence which had been constructed across the 'tableland' but were not allowed into the camp. Relations, nonetheless, were good. On 22 February a man brought an oar, which he had found on the beach near Point Emery, into the camp and over the next three days two other oars, all supposed to have come from the *Koh-i-Noor*, were brought in. The Aborigines were rewarded on each occasion with biscuits. But despite this friendly situation, Millner maintained Goyder's wary attitude and instructed that firearms be carried at all times when out of the camp. On 6 March Foelsche reported five white men for being with their wives and children at the native camp, two of the men being unarmed. Millner fined each one day's pay. He was also concerned about the practice of bartering with the local people and forbade it, except with his permission, because articles had been taken from them without anything being given in return. When Foelsche and the gardener and naturalist, Alfred Schultze, and another man went by boat to Shoal Bay in search of natural-science specimens, Aborigines in canoes approached them with turtles and shells, exchanging them for damaged flour. Three days later the party returned from Shoal Bay with a large collection of shells, a few birds and crustacea.

Millner, who was a lay preacher, soon showed that he took his responsibilities towards the Aborigines seriously, both as a protector and doctor. On 21 March, when an Aborigine became ill after eating too much flour, he 'prescribed for him and he was well in a couple of hours'. In April relations with Aborigines began to change. The Larakia of Port Darwin were never any trouble to the Europeans but the Woolna to the east were becoming hostile. On 6 April a Larakia woman warned that the Woolna intended to spear the white shepherds by crawling through the grass and taking them by surprise. The shepherds were warned and none was speared. Two days later, however, the Larakia left the camp outside the boundary fence and crossed to the other side of the bay to West Point. A further two days later, numerous tracks, supposed to be those of Woolna, were seen at Fanny Bay. Millner, Foelsche and the surveyor, George MacLachlan, Goyder's nephew, rode to Fanny Bay and examined the neighbourhood; although they saw several tracks, there were not enough to cause concern. Early in May the Larakia returned to the camp outside the boundary fence, their number varying from 30 to 150 men, women and children. They were peaceful but several times warned that the Woolna were coming to attack the whites' camp. At 5 p.m. on 9 May more than 100 Woolna, well armed and many in 'war paint', were detected outside the boundary fence. Millner ordered the usual armed guard to be increased by four overnight. Next day the European camp was on the alert all day as the Woolna insolently demanded food and 'white lubras'. That night they moved away, but the Larakia stated that the Woolna intended to attack the whites after dark by creeping through the mangroves. Additional guards were posted and two drays placed across the road to the tableland and another two at the camp as a cover for the defenders. All men in camp were organized into three parties and issued with arms and ammunition.

Early next morning, about dawn, the Larakia called out that the Woolna had attacked them and were about to attack the whites' camp. They requested assistance to drive off the Woolna. Millner and other whites went to the Larakia camp and found that two men and a woman had been speared. He took the most seriously wounded, a man named Orunga, to the whites' camp, laid him in a spare tent and extracted a spearhead from his chest. But it had gone into his lungs, and Orunga died half an hour later of internal haemorrhage. His father and brother, who were present during the operation, wrapped his body in grass and paperbark and carried it to their camp. At 9 a.m. that day Millner sent out a mounted party of five troopers and eight civilians, with MacLachlan in charge and accompanied by some Larakia, to disperse the Woolna and send them back to their district. In the meantime, Millner sent some damaged flour to the Larakia women and children. In the evening the mounted party returned. With the assistance of the Larakia they had been able to track the Woolna to Knuckey's Lagoon but MacLachlan had considered it useless to follow them farther as his party was then out of provisions. Also, the Larakia had told him at Knuckey's Lagoon that they were satisfied the Woolna had gone back to their own country.

On 12 May Millner sent some damaged biscuit to the Larakia camp and then visited it himself with his medical assistant, E. C. Rix, and dressed their wounds. He continued to do this regularly, feeding them and dressing their wounds, until 24 May. On 16 May Millner instructed MacLachlan to employ a few Larakia in cutting timber and brushwood outside the boundary fence; over at least the next five days, eight cleared bamboo and brushwood, for which they each received two rations of damaged flour each day.[2]

In March the South Australian government chose Captain William Bloomfield Douglas, a former mariner and now public servant, as permanent government resident. Douglas arrived at Port Darwin with his wife and many children in the government schooner *Gulnare* on 24 June after a leisurely voyage via Brisbane. In January the British Australian Telegraph Company had announced it would bring the undersea cable from Java ashore at Port Darwin. On 27 May the government — fearing the company's original plan to continue the line overland to Burketown, where it would connect with the Queensland telegraph system, would draw the benefits to be gained from the Territory towards Queensland — announced that it would build a line from Palmerston to connect with the South Australian system at Port Augusta. On learning of this decision, Douglas, a man of action but little wisdom, immediately despatched MacLachlan to survey a route for the line from Palmerston to the Roper River.[3]

Related by marriage to Sir James Brooke, first rajah of Sarawak, Douglas had served briefly in the Royal Navy as a steward in 1842, resigning in Hong Kong; for the next two years he fought pirates with Brooke in Sarawak before joining the Indian Navy. He was in command of a coastal mail vessel in 1854 when he was appointed naval officer and harbourmaster at Adelaide, and in 1858 also became collector of customs; in 1860 Douglas became first president of the South Australian Marine Board and was responsible for surveying parts of the South Australian coast; in addition he served occasionally on the Immigration Board, as an inspector of distilleries and as a stipendiary magistrate before he was appointed government resident at Palmerston. P. L. Burns has said of him that, perhaps inspired by Brooke's example, he tried to govern the northern province like a 'white rajah' but lacked the competence to introduce a suitable administration.[4]

Douglas found the settlement at Palmerston in a 'very satisfactory condition, the party under good discipline' and relations with the Aborigines of the district 'encouraging'. The police force was under 'excellent discipline' and performed its duties 'most satisfactorily'. Foelsche was 'eminently qualified for the Post he fills' and his 'cordial co-operation' with Millner and bearing towards Douglas himself deserved special mention. He thought the police barracks and quarters should not have been placed in the middle of the camp and proposed moving them to the tableland near the proposed site for the official residence. Reporting a fight between the Larakia and the Woolna of Escape Cliffs, he said he would visit the Woolna and 'impress upon them the necessity of peaceable conduct towards the Larakia in the vicinity of the settlement as well as to ourselves'.[5]

In April 1871 Douglas was reporting to Adelaide that, although he had not yet had an opportunity to form an opinion of the individual characters of the police force, it was very evident there was not any 'zealous desire' to undertake the 'active and arduous duties devolving upon a police force in a new settlement'. Foelsche's health was poor and he would get Millner to make a final report on it which he would forward for the consideration of the government. Foelsche had been unable to travel 'up country' to search for a party of whites whose tracks had been seen at Yam Creek, 114 miles from Palmerston, and similar tracks on the banks of the Katherine River. They were believed to be those of a party of whites pushing through from the east coast. Douglas said that the duties of the police since he had arrived were nominal, and that he intended to reduce the number of European police and replace them with native police obtained from Queensland or New South Wales. If a goldfield started, he could use the government boat's crew as occasional police and, should coolies be introduced in a sugar industry, the native police would be 'quite competent to keep them in order'. The police were quite lazy, he believed. They had given themselves a 'healthful occupation' in putting up the wall poles of their quarters, but had absolutely refused to assist in putting on the roof or in preparing the rough windows and doors. He thought it a great farce to have a body of men sitting down in a new settlement 'literally doing nothing'. It was a sore point with him that one of the senior troopers was paid more than a lieutenant in the Royal Navy. Although a merchant navy captain, Douglas was a lieutenant in the Royal Navy Reserve. He had no cause to complain about his own salary — £700 a year. By contrast Millner received £500, MacLachlan £350, Hood, the storekeeper, £300, and Gardner, the draughtsman, £280 — all higher than Foelsche on £230 a year. The number of officers and men who had signed on for twelve months service in the Territory was thirty-one. Two others had refused to sign but would stay on, and three had refused to sign and had requested a passage to Adelaide. In the order of things Foelsche did not rank very highly, a matter which was to rankle with him for the rest of his career.[6]

Paul Heinrich Matthias Foelsche was the antithesis of Douglas. He was born at Moorburg in Hamburg, Germany, on 30 March 1831, the son of Matthias Foelsche — about whom nothing is known, the Hamburg records having been destroyed by Allied bombing during 1939–45. Apparently of 'lower middle-class' background, he joined a Hussar regiment at the age of eighteen and sailed for South Australia in 1854, arriving in the brig *Reihersteig* on 26 October. In November 1856 he joined the South Australian Police Force as a trooper third-class, stationed at Strathalbyn, rising steadily through the ranks until promoted in December 1869 to the Port Darwin post as sub-inspector. Foelsche had spent the whole period of his service at Strathalbyn. He had married Charlotte Smith, daughter of a local man, in 1860 and they had two daughters. Foelsche became a naturalized British subject on 9 December 1869.

At Strathalbyn Foelsche had established himself as a capable officer. An obituary in the *South Australian Register* of 2 February 1914 recorded that he took infinite pains with his tasks and was often selected for special duty which required 'exceptional tact and discretion'. Regarded as a well-educated man, he was versed in the law and was said to be 'the best lawyer outside the South Australian Bar'. He was an expert on firearms and his hobby was making rifle sights and gun stocks and colouring the barrels of weapons used by local volunteers. At Strathalbyn also he 'acquired a considerable reputation as a dentist', possessing many instruments frequently used to 'relieve his neighbours of painful molars'. Universally liked, he had participated in local affairs and had been a member of the Angas lodge of the International Order of Oddfellows for more than ten years. On 13 December, on the eve of his departure, Foelsche was given a farewell dinner hosted by the mayor of Strathalbyn who praised him for his 'courtesy, tact, kindness and ability'.

What Foelsche thought of Douglas is not known, but one of the troopers was unrestrained in private comments. Edward Catchlove arrived with Douglas on 24 June 1870. After dinner on the second day he strolled to the top of Fort Hill and the Aboriginal camp of about eighty men, women and children, who were all anxious to know his name and tell him theirs. This tribe, he recorded in his diary that evening, were far more civilized than the others. Catchlove said Douglas was always 'sporting about on horseback, making himself more disliked' and he particularly objected to Douglas's demand that at all times, when on horseback, he be accompanied by a trooper dressed in full uniform under the tropical sun. Douglas and his 'great lumps of daughters' practised target shooting with Foelsche and Captain Sweet, using carbines and revolvers, and Catchlove had to concede that the daughters were 'tolerable shots'. Foelsche, however, was the best of them all. One of the troopers, Todd, showed some initiative by building his own house, assisted by the Larakia; this man, however, soon had an argument with Douglas. Two labourers out felling trees one day left their axes while eating and the axes were stolen by Aborigines. They informed Douglas who instructed Todd to find them. Todd refused until Foelsche instructed him to do so. Douglas threatened to send Todd back to Adelaide but did not. Catchlove said that on arrival Douglas had allowed the Larakia to walk about the settlement, a privilege not previously granted. But, because of the theft of the axes, Douglas ordered them to leave the place, which had antagonized them. Consequently a double guard had to be kept by the police at night. After banning the Larakia, Douglas permitted them to camp about a mile from the whites and they again became friendly, but while at Escape Cliffs he had invited 'some of the most murderous natives in the Territory to come to the camp, knowing they had murdered poor young Bennett and two other whites'. Having done that, he had not permitted the guard at night to have a dog loose; as Catchlove observed, 'while on guard we could be speared at any minute from behind any of the trees'. Late in August 1870 Catchlove was saying that Douglas was more disliked every day by all in the camp.[7]

For all his urbanity and genial demeanour, Foelsche was very sensitive of official dignity. When one of the troopers, William Stretton, gave an old pair of his uniform trousers to an Aborigine in November 1870, Foelsche threatened to make all the troopers suffer. Catchlove thought this threat 'shows a meanness on the Inspector's part which will not be forgotten'. Nevertheless Catchlove had had reason to be thankful for Foelsche's presence: after suffering toothache all one night he went next morning to Foelsche, 'who kindly extracted it with much difficulty, it being so firm a piece of the gum bone came with it'.[8] Stretton did not bear Foelsche any ill-will. He said many years later that Foelsche was highly respected by all who knew him. He ruled the police force with a great sense of discipline and, in Stretton's opinion, any penalty he inflicted upon his subordinates was just but merciful.

Douglas showed his 'white rajah' attitude towards his job in April 1871. One of the most valuable horses in the settlement was speared in the hock and died four days later. Douglas instructed Captain Samuel Sweet of the *Gulnare* and the coxswain of the government small-boat to seize some Aborigines from their canoes as hostages until the man who had speared the horse was apprehended. This was done, but some of the hostages jumped from the *Gulnare* and escaped. Douglas then 'turned out the police' and, accompanied by them and Millner and two of his own staff, proceeded to the Larakia's camp intending to seize two men if the culprit was not given up. They were met by a large body of armed Larakia who were persuaded to allow two men to accompany the whites back to the settlement and to retire beyond East Point, some four miles from the settlement. Douglas then learned that the horse had been speared by a young man named Binmook who had been employed at the telegraph station in Palmerston. A white man had shot Binmook's dog because it had been destroying his fowls. Binmook had speared the horse as an act of revenge. Instead of attempting to remove the causes of such disputes between individual whites and blacks, Douglas decided to punish Binmook. He had the two hostages imprisoned on the *Gulnare* until Binmook was produced so that he could be flogged. In his report to Adelaide, Douglas declared: 'This may be deemed to be illegal but I cannot carry out legal measures and to avoid bloodshed which must have occurred . . . I attempted to take Binmook by force from the assembled tribe'.[9] Binmook was subsequently brought in and flogged — a dozen strokes with an ordinary riding whip. Millner approved of the punishment, but then he was not a disinterested party. The speared horse had belonged to him.

A day or two later the Larakia returned to the camp near Palmerston, friendly relations were re-established, and the men and women returned to working in the gardens at Doctor's Gully, where there had been trouble before the spearing of the horse. A Woolna man and his wife, who were friendly with the Larakia, had destroyed sugarcane plants by biting and sucking them, and the Larakia had been blamed. Two months previously Aborigines had destroyed some fifty coconut plants at Fanny Bay, and Douglas had warned them that they would be punished if they harmed plantations or other European property. In reporting this, he said:

I am and have been most anxious to avoid any collision with the natives but before settlers arrive who will not probably be so lenient as myself . . . it is essential that I should let the natives fully understand the risk they run in committing depredations in plantations or among the cattle. If they do not learn this lesson the settlers here will not be likely to be more lenient than they have been in Carpentaria Queensland [*sic*] where the blacks have been driven back in all directions and on too many occasions with loss of life.[10]

The Woolna were still hostile late in 1871, rumours continuing to reach the whites through the Larakia that their eastern neighbours intended to attack. Douglas claimed to pay little attention to these reports but kept the settlement on alert. On 30 October the Woolna attempted to steal women from the Larakia camp, a fight ensued and one of the raiders was speared. The alarm was given in Palmerston but the Woolna immediately retreated. Douglas told the Larakia that if they feared another attack they could send their old men, women and children close to the settlement, but he expected the fighting men to 'take care of themselves'. He did not intend to interfere with their intertribal quarrels unless after 'absolute defeat' the Larakia, being in their own district, claimed his protection.[11] Douglas had told the Woolna, when at Escape Cliffs soon after arriving, that they were welcome at Palmerston, provided they conducted themselves well and did not interfere with the Larakia.

Official attitudes were generally conciliatory and condescending, every effort being made to show the Aborigines that the arrival of the Europeans was beneficial to them. Three Larakia had travelled to Adelaide by ship and, on their return, Millner said in June 1871 that this had a good effect, 'giving them a better opinion of what the white people are, and a better reliance on our good faith'.[12] What the three Aborigines thought of Adelaide is not known but while there they may have noticed the cash payments made by the whites and wondered why Aborigines at Port Darwin never received money for their labour. A year later, on 10 July, Douglas reported that no payment had been made to Aborigines during the previous year but just over £600 had been spent on Chinese, Malay and other coolie labour. Aborigines were still being employed at clearing land and cutting firewood. Where their labour could be made useful and was economical, Douglas said, they were remunerated with supplies of damaged flour, peas, oatmeal etc. unfit as staff rations. Six blankets and five sets of clothes had also been issued to them in the previous twelve months. Remunerating Aborigines with food and clothing continued the practice now established in outlying parts of South Australia and led to the same practice in the Territory's pastoral industry, one which effectively bound workers to their employers.

Construction of the northern section of the telegraph line began at Palmerston on 15 September 1870, when Douglas's eldest daughter, Harriet, turned the first sod, and at first it proceeded southwards quickly. Curious Aborigines were soon taught not to interfere with it. One operator gave several an electric shock to discourage touching the wires and poles. When he heard of this, Edward Cathlove remarked: 'I think it will have the desired effect as they appear to be very timid of it now'.[13] By 22 October the line had reached Mitchell's Creek and by the end of the year 121 miles were constructed; but, as the wet season set in, work slowed until, against great odds, the northern gang reached King River, 225 miles south of Palmerston, early the following year. The government was not satisfied with progress, dismissing the contractors on 3 May and taking control of the northern section, but little was achieved during the ensuing dry season because many of the workers had gone south and because of Douglas's interference. In November 1871 a government party under Robert Patterson, a railway engineer, resumed the task with fresh supplies and materials. The southern and central sections had already been completed and on 22 August 1872 Patterson joined the two lines at Frew's Ironstone Ponds, near Tennant Creek.

Despite the deep intrusion into other Aboriginal homelands which construction of the telegraph line entailed, reaction was not immediately hostile. To April 1871, small parties travelling southwards had no difficulties with the local peoples, no attacks having been made. From this Douglas inferred that 'no danger need be feared in settling the country districts so long as ordinary precautions are taken against the natives who will if they can pilfer any articles left exposed, and might attack a single unarmed man if they could secure a supply of food by such an act'.[14]

One of the few full expressions of Europeans attitudes towards the Aborigines in those early days at Port Darwin comes from Harriet Daly, one of Douglas's daughters and wife of D. D. Daly, a young surveyor in the Territory during Goyder's time and nephew of a previous Governor of South Australia. Writing in 1887, she gave her impressions of the Aborigines she and her family had encountered on arrival. They differed slightly, if at all, from the ordinary Australian Aboriginal, she said: 'Just the same low type of physique, the same nomadic habits, the same vices, and the same customs that prevail everywhere else. Darwin's theory of the law of selection seemed to hold good amongst them'. Some of the men were fine, well-made fellows but others were 'lean and ill-shapen, and the least interesting specimens of at best an uninteresting race'. Some of the women were plump and good-looking but the older women were 'literally "old hags" lean and shrivelled, and excessively ugly'. The women were 'a most wretched, down-trodden set' who were 'cruelly treated by their lords and masters, who make them do all the hard work of everyday life'. The women searched for wood, carrying the heaviest loads when they shifted camp and were not fed until their husbands were satisfied. The Aborigines, she said, were a lazy race and not alive to making the most of their opportunities; 'Had they been, they might have made money by supplying the wants of the community with fish, game and turtle'. Waddies were used in everyday life and the Aboriginal women 'feel the effect of them, if the husbands are in an angry mood; the children suffer also, and perhaps deserve it!' Harriet Daly's memory was not perfect. She wrote in 1887 that the horse speared in 1870 was lame for several months after Millner extracted the spear, whereas her father wrote at the time that the horse died four days later. Also, she stated that the two hostages taken at this time were induced to go aboard the *Gulnare* by the promise of 'tum tum' and that one of the hostages was Binmook. Daly's recollections are not reliable, but her sentiments probably reflect those of many Europeans then in the Territory, particularly the officials. After stating that every man in the Territory was armed and habitually wore a revolver in his belt, she expressed the racist attitude of fearful colonizers surrounded by natives they did not understand when she wrote:

Much has been written and much has been said about the proper treatment of natives. My experience teaches me that there is only one rule that holds good — firmness accompanied by kindness, fair play, and honest payment for work done. And, above all, to keep the aboriginal in his proper place—stand no insolence, or disobedience; for when a native shows signs of sulkiness and defiance, it is perfectly certain that trouble is brewing. And with natives, above all others — to be forewarned is to be forearmed.[15]

By 1873 Harriet Daly had given up anticipating any troubles with the natives. The Larakia had become 'very much more useful, and had gained some idea of working in a systematic manner'. They had also become more self-reliant, less afraid of attack by the Woolna. Even so, the settlers always carried arms when they left the settlement. Riding one afternoon with her father on one of his many inspections, accompanied by a trooper, they struck off along an unbeaten track until stopped by a party of unknown Aborigines 'armed to the teeth' and decorated with streaks of white and yellow clay. Drawing their weapons the whites proceeded past them until they were out of sight. Then on the way home they met a black named Scotchman, 'who was not unknown to the police' and who spent some time with the Woolna but called himself a Larakia. This confirmed their suspicions that some trouble was brewing. When Scotchman barred their way, Douglas ordered him to lower his spears, but the black threw two spears which missed. Two shots were fired. Then a third spear grazed one of Douglas's arms, drawing blood. At the same time the trooper dismounted and seized Scotchman. Harriet rode alone to Foelsche who ordered some police out and brought in the assailant who, she says, was tried the following day. He was sentenced to a long term of imprisonment with hard labour and served his time 'very close to our doors, for he cut wood and carried water for the use of the Residency; and the clank of his chains were [*sic*] a familiar sound at all hours of the day'.[16]

A little gold had already been found by Litchfield in the Finniss River in 1865, by Goyder's men in 1869 and by a land-speculation party in 1870. It was found at Yam Creek in December 1870 by telegraph construction workers, and then more finds were made as the line pushed southwards. In February 1872 an Adelaide gold-prospecting company sent a party north; by August 1872, 40 men were on the fields along the line between Yam Creek and Pine Creek; in September 1872, 150 miners arrived at Port Darwin followed by 200 more within a month. Many stayed in Palmerston, deterred by the wet, the cost of getting to the fields and fear of the Aborigines. The penniless miners stranded in Palmerston were in a desperate position. Foelsche had to use all his tact to persuade 300 of them, who wanted relief-work and rations, not to rob the store and take possession of the town, as they threatened. Those who did go to the diggings found little payable gold and, as Alan Powell says, 'By the end of January 1873 nearly all had gone and the "rush" of independent men, the mainstay of the Victorian fields in their early days, was over in the Northern Territory when it had hardly begun'.[17] Gold-mining, the hope of early wealth to justify South

Australia's investment in the Territory, was left to a few mining companies and the Chinese.

By early 1873 the South Australian government was seriously concerned at the administration of the Territory. Douglas had hoped to find fame and fortune on this new frontier but he had squandered money, ignored instructions and, as we have seen, quarrelled with his subordinates. P. L. Burns has said that he failed to control the gold rush he encouraged and 'probably delayed the introduction of the 1872 mining regulations in order to protect his own investment'.[18] Early in 1873 his ambitions were 'shattered' and he had to be warned about his drinking. His administrative control was lax, having permitted some of his officials to take leave to go looking for gold. He tried to put his administration in order, but in June 1873 the Commissioner of Crown Lands, Thomas Reynolds, visited Palmerston and witnessed the confusion caused by the gold rush. Back in Adelaide he reported favourably on the mineral resources of the north but unfavourably on Douglas, who was forced to resign, returning to Adelaide financially ruined.

Foelsche, a portly and unflappable man, adapted well to the tropics and his new life. A two-roomed tin hut had been his first home and he had spent a good deal of time grooming his chief companion, a dog called Rough. When he and the rest of the camp moved to the tableland late in 1870, Foelsche was allotted a new home where he set about establishing a garden on his small plot of land to help meet the serious lack of vegetables experienced by the early settlers at Palmerston. He did all he could to 'beautify' the place, and then sent for his wife and daughters. The house was small, two or three rooms, probably like the police station, which was composed of poles and plaster and measured twenty feet by twelve. While others complained of the hardships and sacrifices of residence in the Territory, Foelsche 'never lost his cheerfulness and he invariably made the best of the most trying conditions'.[19] He was considered the best man who could have been selected for the position because of his qualifications and his capacity for adapting to new conditions. His wife and family helped to make their house 'one of the most cheerful and comfortable homes in the settlement'. There was also a small stone building with two or three cells. When Reynolds arrived in 1873, he noted that Scotchman was held in a building a few feet square and chained by the legs; 'Very improper and illegal', he noted.[20] It may have been improper and illegal but, given the primitive conditions at Palmerston then, it is not surprising; without chains Scotchman had been able to escape with ease. The police buildings, in present-day Mitchell Street, were so insecure that by the end of the first decade termites had demolished the roof of Foelsche's quarters.

The discovery of gold and the building of the telegraph line gave little economic benefit to the Territory. On 10 July 1872 the number of white residents, excluding the construction workers, totalled only 351, comprising 302 men, 16 women, 17 boys and 16 girls. In addition, there were a few Asians, mainly Chinese, who were eagerly sought as servants. Foelsche and Millner both had a Chinese 'boy'. As gold production declined and white miners left the country, the South Australian government urged the mining companies to use Chinese labour. In April 1874 it appointed Douglas to recruit Chinese and he obtained 186 in Singapore on two-year contracts, but when they arrived in Port Darwin the companies, now on hard times, would take only 123. Early in 1876 the total non-Aboriginal population including Chinese and Malays was only 756, and later in that year the new government resident, Edward Price, reported that there were now 140 coolies in the Territory, all usefully employed. More Chinese arrived late in 1877, and in March 1878 the non-Aboriginal population was about 1160 including about 540 Chinese. Until this time relations between the Aborigines and Chinese had been peaceful, but in August 1878 an Aborigine was arrested and committed for trial for spearing two Chinese. The Chinese population was now soaring as more poured into the country to work the fields abandoned by the European diggers. The total number of Chinese in the Territory was 1568, about 200 working in Palmerston and the remainder on the alluvial fields. Chinese numbers peaked in December 1880 when some had already begun to leave the Territory. There were then 4358 Chinese as well as 713 Europeans and 40 Malays. Such a large number of foreigners crowded into a small district was certain to lead to violence by the local people: in October 1881 Aborigines attacked Chinese at Saunders' Rush, spearing three and killing one. Hundreds of Chinese had been present but, although they had firearms, they did not attempt to defend themselves. The police had gone there and Price ordered that a police camp be established at Saunders' Rush. This appears to have been the most serious conflict between Aborigines and Chinese in the Northern Territory.[21]

The Aboriginal population was always large relative to the European and Asian figures. There were an estimated 50 000 Aborigines before the coming of the Europeans, but numbers decreased steadily until there were only 22 000 in 1911. The Chinese population dropped from a peak of 6122 in 1888 to 1387 in 1910 whereas Europeans increased very slowly, the total being only 1182 in 1910. Although the Aboriginal numbers dropped to about half those before the arrival of the Europeans, they always greatly exceeded the non-Aboriginal population in the South Australian period, not being surpassed until about 1955, except during the Pacific War.[22] This balance of numbers in favour of the Aborigines was to be one of the most significant differences between the Northern Territory experience and Aboriginal–European contact history elsewhere in Australia. It was to be the chief reason why the original people of the Northern Territory were to endure in the face of European ingression, which almost everywhere else in Australia had led to devastation and subjugation.

Chapter 4

The Overlanders

When work on the northern section of the telegraph line stopped at King River early in 1871, the men were nearly starving and threatening mutiny. Getting supplies to the workers on the northern section remained a constant problem until the following year. To provide food for them, Ralph Millner, owner of Killalpaninna station on Cooper's Creek, had decided in September 1870 to drove sheep and cattle along Stuart's track to the Top End of the Territory. Millner was under the misapprehension that the South Australian government had offered a reward for the first one thousand sheep or one hundred cattle overlanded from South Australia to Port Darwin. The Aborigines had previously seen no more than forty horses on Stuart's expeditions and these had always been reduced by death and wandering at night. Millner's historic expedition was the first to drove stock across the middle of the continent and was to be an important test of the reactions of cattlemen and Aborigines to each other. The exact date on which Millner set out is not known but it was probably about Christmas 1870. By the time he left the Peake station, just west of Lake Eyre, he had assembled a party of nine whites, three Aboriginal men and an Aboriginal woman (who ran away a day or two later) to take charge of seven thousand sheep and three hundred horses. Second in command was his brother, John, and the group included Arthur Ashwin, who told the story of the expedition in 1927.[1] They lost about two thousand sheep, which ate poisonous plants near the Devil's Marbles, south of Tennant Creek; then at Attack Creek came their first trouble with the Aborigines.

The Warramanga had been making tentative contact for some days, but one big man had behaved so suspiciously that he had been sent out of the European camp. The next day Ashwin saw native tracks and then the big man of the previous day. Ashwin raised his rifle to show him that he had been seen and the man dropped out of sight in the grass. Ashwin then accompanied John Millner and an Aboriginal woman, Fanny, to the creek about a mile from the camp and saw the same man about half a mile ahead. Ashwin drew his revolver and signalled him to clear off, which he did. After about an hour attending to the sheep, Ashwin returned to Millner and Fanny and found the big Warramanga sitting with them on the ground. On seeing Ashwin the man stood up, holding a club in his hand. All his weapons were with him. Ashwin remonstrated with Millner for allowing the Aborigine to come up to him but Millner ordered him to leave the man alone, saying that he was 'a fine specimen of a native' and there was no harm in him. Ashwin was not convinced. After he tied up his horse he kept an eye on the man, leaving his rifle and revolver on the horse but retaining a double-barrelled duelling pistol on his belt and a large butcher's knife in a sheath.

Ashwin, who had given the impression that there were no Aboriginal women with the party after one ran away soon after leaving Peake station, does not explain the presence of Fanny. Possibly she had accompanied the expedition or had been acquired along the way by one of the three Aborigines in the party. It is more likely that she was a Warramanga, offered by her people to the whites in return for goods. If so, the big man probably was her husband and his subsequent action may have resulted from Millner's failure to fulfil obligations under Aboriginal law.

Continuing the story, Ashwin says that Fanny at this stage commented: 'Wild fellow no good. Piccaniny time him growl'. Ashwin took out the pistol and checked it and then slipped it onto his belt. For some minutes the big Warramanga and Ashwin watched each other carefully. Millner lay on the ground between them, ignoring Ashwin's warnings of danger, saying there was no harm in the black man, now only five feet behind him. Ashwin later recalled:

After a short while I said to John we had better get around the sheep, they are getting a long way. He said, all right and rose onto his elbow and was going to get up when I took my eyes off the native and turned towards my horse. At that moment the native clubbed Milner [*sic*] and smashed his skull. 'Fanny' shouted to me, and I had my bridle rein in my hand. I turned around and saw the native coming at me, and Milner's favourite dog 'Dick' flew at the blackfellow and got hold of him under the arm and the native turned. I dashed round the thick bush my horse had been tied to, and in a second had the pistol out and cocked both hammers and fired into his stomach or low in his chest as he faced me with the dog on him. He had a boomerang in the air in the act of throwing it when I fired and it flew out of his hand and he fell, but got on his feet again, and I fired at his back as he was running away and he fell again but got up again. My horse bolted when I fired the first shot. I ran over to Milner's horse and took his revolver out of its holster and got his rifle from where it was hanging from a limb of a tree where his horse was tied to. I put up the 200 yards sight and aimed low at the native as he was running, the old dog 'Dick' having just left him. The rifle would not go off, although I snapped it three times. I then tried at 300 yards, but it would still not go off.

Ashwin sent Fanny to the camp on Millner's horse to tell the men there to bring the spring-cart and towels and water. Then he attended to Millner. It had been a heavy blow, smashing his skull 'from the ear to the eye. Both his eyes were out on his cheeks'. Men soon arrived with the cart and John Millner died as they lifted him onto it. Ralph Millner had been absent with two of the whites and one of the Aborigines in the party, but returned next day. He took the loss of his brother to heart and 'it was a miserable camp for a week or two'. The men buried John Millner under a large tree, fenced in his grave with heavy timber and nailed a metal sheet, pricked with his name, date, age and cause of death, to the tree. Later Ralph Millner paid a carpenter in the telegraph construction gang to carve a large ironwood slab and place it at the head of the grave which, Ashwin says, by then was riddled with spears: 'The natives had been corroboreeing round the grave and throwing spears into it, and were too superstitious to remove them again. They were demonstrating their hatred of the white man'.

North of Powell Creek, fearing an attack one night, Ashwin released six staghounds; when they returned to camp about ten minutes later they were covered in blood. In the morning he found an Aborigine lying dead about four hundred yards from the camp, his throat torn out. Blood was on the tracks of others for two to three hundred yards farther afield. Ashwin estimated that about two hundred Aborigines had been near the camp, judging by their tracks 'a quarter of a mile wide, and all making for the Ashburton Range about one mile distant'. As they moved northwards Millner's party found 'the natives were very numerous all along the range, but they did not come near us. I think that the stag hound episode was known to them'.

Later about two hundred Aborigines approached while they were camped, yelling and shaking their spears. Millner ordered his men to make sure their firearms were ready and not to fire until he did: 'Let them come up close about 100 yards and then make sure of a nigger every shot'. They did not attack but withdrew, and after dinner Ashwin and two others followed their tracks and, coming upon them 'corroboreeing', surprised them and they dispersed. While camped at Newcastle Waters, Ashwin went exploring by himself a mile or two eastwards in the hills at the northern end of the Ashburton Range, and chanced to come upon a native encampment.

I tied my horse up and took the rifle and revolver I always carried on my belt since poor John Milner's death to examine the place. There was one large mia-mia about 7 feet high in the middle and about 16 feet diameter. It was round and arched off the ground. There were large bundles of spears stored there and large wooden dishes four and five feet long filled with grass seed as large as rice with the husks or skin on the seed. I think it was a specie of rice which grows in the flooded country 40 or 50 miles in extent and North of Newcastle Waters. There must have been about a ton of seed stored there in 17 large dishes full and all covered with paperbark. The dishes were nearly all five feet long and a foot deep, scooped out of solid wood. There were more weapons and shields. I made a fire and carried all the weapons out and burnt them alongside the large Mia-Mia. All around this storeroom there were about 50 small Mia-Mias or Miahs or Gunyahs as some tribes call them. The fence enclosing the lot was about 200 yards across, and appeared to be kept in good order. There were also numbers of netted bags containing red ochre, plumbago, and white chalk, and numbers of flint stones, from which they chip their knives from. I would have examined the smaller Mia-Mias, but I heard a weeya (child). I think there were some old men and gins camped there looking after things whilst the tribe were away. My horse was getting restless, so I decided to start back to the sheep.

As Millner's party approached the Roper River they encountered a small party led by H. D. Packard from the telegraph construction gang, which had managed to proceed only as far south as Elsey Creek during the 1871 dry season; the workers were all on half-rations. Packard had been to the Roper Landing at Leichhardt's Bar for supplies brought in by ship, and was making his way back when the two parties met on 11 December. Packard had been attacked three times in November while making a previous attempt to get through to the Roper Landing. Two of his horses were speared and he was forced to bury some of his stores and beat a retreat to the Katherine River camp. The number of attackers was estimated at between one hundred and two hundred on each occasion. J. A. G. Little, who was telegraph stationmaster at Palmerston at the time, thought this collision with the Aborigines had been brought about by Packard's own carelessness in allowing them to come too freely into his camp — and that burying the stores had been unnecessary as the Aborigines merely dug them up and destroyed them.[2] Packard's men were all Queenslanders and, according to Ashwin, there were some 'hard cases among them, good men in bad nigger country'. At this spot on his way to the Landing, Packard had given handkerchiefs, looking-glasses, combs, knives and a tomahawk to the local people. Next night they had attacked his party on the Strangways River, spearing a horse but not injuring any of his men. A day after the two parties met 'a big mob of niggers' showed up a quarter of a mile away on a range of hills. Three of the Queenslanders rode away to get behind them 'to give them a lesson', asking Packard not to allow any of the others to fire until he heard their first shot. But one of the main party fired a shot and the Aborigines fled. Clearly, the Queensland tradition of violent action against apparently treacherous and ungrateful Aborigines was now established on the Roper.

The wet season was beginning, but Millner's party managed to get through to Red Lily Lagoon, on Elsey Creek, on Christmas Day. They were preparing a dinner of grilled mutton — all they had because they had run out of flour, tea, sugar and salt five days previously — when Patterson arrived from the construction camp on the Roper. Millner had only three thousand sheep left and immediately sold one thousand to Patterson at twenty-five shillings a head. In January 1872 Charles Todd, head of the South Australian Telegraph Department, sailed up the Roper

John Lewis, 1870, prominent
South Australian pastoralist
and confidant of Paul Foelsche

Aborigines on the cattle station established by Lewis at Port Essington on
Cobourg Peninsula, November 1877

F. J. Gillen, telegraph station-master, ethnologist and, from 1892, Protector of Aborigines at Alice Springs

Alfred Giles, who drove stock fro[m] South Australia to found Springva[le] station, near Katherine, in 1879

Attack on the Barrow Creek telegraph station—the first serious clash between Territory blacks and whites after settlement

with two steamships and a barque laden with supplies, and the northern workers' food shortages were ended.

If Ashwin's account is reliable, Millner's expedition is significant because of the lack of retaliation by the whites following Aboriginal aggression, particularly after the death of John Millner. When Ashwin and two others came upon the corroboree after the confrontation at Powell Creek, they did not 'disperse' the Aborigines. Although Ashwin destroyed weapons in the Aboriginal village near Newcastle Waters, he did not return with other whites to destroy the buildings and food stored there. There appears to be no vindictive attitude towards the Warramanga in Ashwin's account which, given European attitudes in 1927 when he wrote it, need not have hidden any violence.

Millner's expedition was soon followed by another overlanding party led by John Lewis of the Burra copper-mining and pastoral district north of Adelaide. In 1871 George MacLachlan had applied on behalf of Lewis for a pastoral run on the Cobourg Peninsula. Francis Cadell had sought leases covering the entire peninsula in May 1868, but he never took them up. In January 1872 Lewis, his brother James and two others set out overland for Port Darwin. They were travellers, not drovers, and made good time. Like Millner in the previous year, they found green feed and water without difficulty throughout the trip and, although they occasionally met Aborigines, they had no trouble. Even so, tension in Warramanga territory was high. Lewis's party reached Tennant Creek on 23 May, and on the second night blacks were reported to be sneaking into the camp under cover.

All hands were turned out with their revolvers and rifles. Every now and then we could see a little flicker in the distance. We discharged our firearms in that direction, but it turned out that the flicker was from a stump fired by one of the whites a few days before, which was still burning.[3]

At this time a gap of nearly three hundred miles remained in the telegraph line between Tennant Creek and Daly Waters; and the South Australian government, anxious to establish some sort of connection in order to fulfil its obligation to the British Australian Telegraph Company, engaged John Lewis to run a pony express between the two points. With three men and twenty-five horses, he commenced on 1 June. On 22 June the undersea cable failed, taking the pressure off Patterson and his men up north; when it was repaired the gap had been closed. Lewis made only two or three trips before the closure and then continued northwards, reaching Palmerston on 2 October. There he engaged men to go prospecting on behalf of the Telegraph Prospecting and Goldmining Company, in which he had an interest, and in 1873 set up the first ore-crushing battery in the Territory at Pine Creek. In October 1874 a miner, August Henning, was killed by Aborigines on the road from the goldfields to

Darwin, four miles south of the Adelaide River. At the same time fears were being held for two men, Permain and Borradaile, who had set off four months earlier to select land near Port Essington but had not arrived. Lewis was asked by G. B. Scott, who had succeeded Douglas as government resident in October 1873, and a committee of local citizens to search for them. Lewis provided ten horses and Scott seven for the expedition, which Lewis used as an excuse to pay the first visit to his Cobourg Peninsula selection. Two police troopers, a Doctor Guy, who had arrived in Darwin from Singapore with the first consignment of Chinese labourers, a European cook, and Neddy Lewis, an Aborigine whom Lewis had apparently engaged at Powell Creek, started with him from the Union mining camp just north of Pine Creek. In Scott's opinion John Lewis was a 'most competent person'.[4]

The first Aborigines they met were numerous and threatening, but after they had crossed the South Alligator River the people were friendly and walked or ran with them for twelve or fourteen miles, clearing sticks and stones in their path. They seemed anxious to assist but often indicated that the travellers should go back. When these people would go no farther, John Lewis and his party gave them a few presents — red handkerchiefs, butchers' knives and two pounds of raisins — 'and they went away rejoicing'. Having crossed the East Alligator, the whites headed northwards through the land of apparently hostile people but without incident to Port Essington, the first party to complete the journey by land. There they met Flash Poll, an Aboriginal woman who spoke exceptionally good English, having been a servant to one of the officers at Victoria. She looked about fifty years of age, was very active and stood 'as straight as a die'. She addressed Lewis as Commandant and told him that her people were hungry for tobacco. From them Lewis learned that Permain and Borradaile had been killed by Aborigines near Tor Rock, about twenty miles from Mount Norris Bay.

John Lewis took out a second lease on Cobourg Peninsula, thus extending his claim there, and with Philip Levi, who owned the Peake station, and a man named Campbell, formed the Cobourg Cattle Company. In the dry season of 1875 he set out with another party including Charles Levi, brother of Philip, a Chinese cook, some stockmen and 'blackboys' to form a buffalo-shooting station there. After crossing the East Alligator River they encountered the hostile resistance which had developed in that area since the generally friendly times of the Port Essington settlement. When the intruders separated into two parties, a horse was attacked, then a shower of spears was hurled at one of the parties but fell short. The attackers came nearer and attacked again, but all the spears missed. Lewis and his men then opened fire, discharging twenty-one rounds, hitting many. With only revolvers left to use, they charged the Aborigines, who fled. A few miles farther, the combined party was attacked, but this time the whites had prepared a good supply of 'nicely greased' bullets. The Aborigines got close enough to hurl more spears, many sticking in the baggage behind which the intruders sheltered. Then the party opened fire and kept it up for nearly half an hour. Many Aborigines were injured and taken away by women before the attackers retreated. Later, when passing through a narrow gorge, they were showered with spears and, when they reached Port Essington, the local people told them they knew about the fight with the East Alligator people, who had warned them by means of smoke signals.

Lewis and his men set about forming the station, building a two-roomed log hut with paperbark roof and verandah front and back, flooring it with bricks from some of the old Victoria buildings, adding a kitchen and men's quarters with a fence around them all. Then they erected a boatshed and built two stockyards. They fenced off the peninsula with the help of the local people, who felled the timber and carried the logs, about six feet long, putting up a mile in fourteen days. When all this work was done they began herding buffalo from outside the peninsula through the fence, sometimes including a few Sourabaya cattle, English shorthorns and Timor ponies left from the early settlements. Lewis trained some of the local men to ride by putting them on Timor ponies, then he turned them out on other ponies and horses. If a man could stay on a pony for a mile-and-a-half around the paddock he was considered competent, but only one in ten qualified. Flash Poll was anxious to ride and 'waltzed onto a pony like a girl of fifteen' but as soon as the pony moved off she sprang to the ground. Lewis found the Cobourg Peninsula people friendly and useful. He gave the men doing the clearing and fencing half a stick of tobacco and a pannican of rice daily with a little tea and sugar. He employed an old man and his two wives to gather yams and other parties to gather honey, to fish, capture turtle and wild fowl. 'With a Chinese cook, we lived remarkably well', he wrote. After three months at Port Essington, Lewis returned to Palmerston, leaving Charles Levi in charge. Soon afterwards Lewis left the Territory and returned to the Burra district of South Australia.[5]

This was the first pastoral station established in the Top End of the Northern Territory, although it was not a true cattle station but rather a buffalo-shooting lodge formed to provide meat to the gold-fields. The first true stations were established on the Herbert River (also called the Georgina) by Queensland pastoralists moving westward in the early 1860s and probably not aware that they had crossed the unsurveyed border. This was temporary settlement and by 1866 all these leases had been abandoned. The first permanent pastoral stations in the Territory were Undoolya and Owen Springs, both in the Centre and both stocked at first with sheep. They were never abandoned and are the oldest continuously stocked runs in the Territory.

The original application for two Undoolya leases was made by E. M. ('Ned') Bagot in 1872; they were instead issued to Andrew Tennant and John Love in 1876, when the leases for Owen Springs were also issued. The first permanent stations to be stocked in the Top End were Springvale and Glencoe, both in 1879. Even so, Lewis had founded a special kind of pastoral enterprise built upon the goodwill created by Collett Barker at Raffles Bay and John McArthur at Port Essington many years before. So powerful was the effect of that early contact with the local people that, after a break of twenty-four years since Victoria was abandoned, Lewis found they still spoke English clearly:

What English they spoke, they spoke properly. There was no pidgin English among the old hands who had been there at the time of the military camp. If you sang out to one of them, he would immediately jump to his feet and answer by saying, 'Sir!' and would always raise his hand to his forehead when addressing you. I never saw more honest or trustworthy men.[6]

The Queensland 'hard cases' among Packard's party on the Roper, mentioned by Ashwin, apparently were workers brought in by sea for the overland telegraph project. There is no record of any European travelling by land from Queensland after Leichhardt, although Gregory and his party made the journey in the opposite direction. The first man to make the trip after settlement began in the Territory came with cattle, and he was one of the hardest cases of all. D'Arcy Wentworth Uhr (incorrectly spelt Ure by some contemporaries, including Lewis) was working for Matthew Dillon Cox, who had taken his cue from Millner and decided to try to sell stock to the telegraph workers. Uhr drove four hundred head of cattle from Charters Towers by following Leichhardt's route through the Gulf Country to the Roper River, arriving at Leichhardt's Bar on 18 September 1872. Cox had overtaken him on the way with a mob of horses, and both cattle and horses sold readily in the Territory. Uhr and Cox thus blazed the way for the rush of cattle from Queensland into the Top End which was to follow from 1878. Uhr, a former Queensland Native Police officer, was well used to meeting Aboriginal resistance with force. He and his black troopers are reputed to have killed thirteen Aborigines on the Belyando River in 1864 in retaliation for the killing of two white shepherds. On the other hand, Uhr was a tough and relentless horseman with an almost manic determination to fulfil a task. He left Rockhampton on 22 December 1865 with five troopers to establish a Native Police post at Burketown in the Gulf Country. He arrived on 11 April 1866 to find that the town was stricken by fever and many inhabitants were dying. Obtaining a boat, he took some of the sick to Sweer's Island in the gulf and then, returning to Burketown, found his best trooper was dead and the others were helpless with the fever. The epidemic had hardly passed when, on 29 July, he started out from Burketown in pursuit of two horse thieves. He soon caught one and, taking him in tow, continued to track the other as far as the New South Wales border. Still with his prisoner, he pushed south as far as the Castlereagh River and was within one day's ride of his quarry when his horse collapsed. He then handed over his prisoner to the New South Wales police and returned to Burketown on 19 November, having ridden some two thousand miles in three months. Such a man as Uhr was not likely to be deterred by the difficulties of getting a mob of cattle to the Territory! According to Ernestine Hill, 'Some say he shot his way through the blacks'.[7] Hill is not always reliable — but this could partly explain the later hostility of the people of the McArthur River district to whites travelling though their country.

Alfred Giles was the second man to drove stock from South Australia. He made two trips, in 1873 and 1875, and on both occasions was working under contract to the South Australian Telegraph Department to supply mutton to its staff along the line. On the first trip he lost six hundred head at the Devonport Range near Wauchope Creek, when he unwittingly camped in the field of *Gastrolobuis grandifolia* which had killed Millner's sheep two years before. Giles had only one serious incident with Aborigines, after he drove through a Warramanga camp at Central Newcastle Waters and stopped after about a mile. When an old man 'dressed in the royal robe of scarlet cockatoo feathers stuck on all over his body, and legs and hair' approached the whites and menaced them, Giles and seven others rode off, leaving only the cook in the camp. The Warramanga then began attacking it, but the whites wheeled back, charging them and firing over their heads. Giles said later that they used stockwhips, scattering the blacks into the creek and up trees. He commented: 'There is no doubt that we gave them a salutary dispersal and one that they remembered, indeed, I believe they never gave any trouble after that lesson'.[8]

By the early 1870s some Europeans were, with a little luck, able to wander at will across the vast, dry expanses of inland Australia. On the Roper River, Millner's party had encountered Andrew Hume, who in 1862 left Cullin-la-Ringo station in Central Queensland, riding westwards to find traces of the Leichhardt expedition. Three years later he showed up at Hornet Bank station, south of Cullin-la-Ringo; then, while riding south to Maitland to see his father, he was wrongly arrested at Coonamble as a bushranger and sent to prison for ten years. In Parramatta gaol he claimed that he had found Adolf Classen, Leichhardt's second in command, living with a tribe of Aborigines in the Northern Territory. He was so convincing that the New South Wales government released him and sent him to Darwin by steamer to contact Classen again. Hume was with the telegraph workers on the Roper when Millner and Ashwin encountered him on 11 December 1871. He claimed that he had orders to get two good hacks from Millner, which were to be charged to the government. Hume said Classen was living with a tribe in the Newcastle Waters area, and Ashwin thought at first this might explain the large storehouse of grain in the settlement he had seen there; but serious discrepancies in his story persuaded Ashwin and Milner that Hume was an impostor. John Lewis encountered Hume later, and also dismissed his story. In November 1873 Hume returned to the Roper River telegraph station claiming to have seen Classen again and carrying a leather satchel containing, he claimed, Leichhardt's journal, watch and telescope. Back in Sydney he alleged that these effects had been stolen *en route*, and the government washed its hands of Hume; but some citizens still believed him and financed another expedition to contact Classen, accompanied this time by two reliable companions. They left Nockatunga station in western Queensland on 1 November 1874, heading for Cooper's Creek in a time of drought; ten days later one of the companions staggered back to Nockatunga exhausted. A search party found Hume and the other companion both dead.

Most likely Hume was an impostor. According to Ashwin he told them Classen was living with a tribe in the Newcastle Waters area. If this is so, his attempt to reach Newcastle Waters overland from western Queensland during drought — when he could have returned to the Roper by ship and then had a comparatively short ride to complete the journey — suggests irrationality and unreliability. The significant thing about Hume is that for years he was able to wander the arid wastes of inland Australia alone and with comparative ease, living off the land. By contrast, well-equipped exploration parties, such as those of Leichhardt and Burke and Wills, only a few years before him had perished. Men like Stuart, Millner, Giles, Lewis, Uhr and Hume could now go where they liked in Australia with reasonable chance of success. Their long, sweeping penetrations into and through Aboriginal homelands were now commonplace, and the effects of such men on Aboriginal society in the Territory was potentially devastating.

Not only the men droving cattle overland, but also those building the telegraph line had affected the tribes through whose lands they cut their way. Patterson recorded several incidents which, as Francesca Merlan writes, 'illustrate the Aborigines' and Europeans' mutual lack of understanding of behaviour and motives'.[9] Patterson had seized as hostages two Aboriginal men who had come into the Roper camp, in an attempt to 'smoke out' those who had stolen some European clothes. Neither the Aborigines nor the Europeans spoke the others' language, and the hostages had difficulty understanding why they were being held. They called to some women across the river, who swam across. 'It became evident that our captives wanted to propitiate the camp by sending for their women, but before they could land we drove them back', Patterson said. When it became clear the clothes would not be returned, he ordered the captives' release and sent them back to their camp after giving them a meal and some biscuits for their families.

Aborigines quickly appropriated anything of use which the construction workers left behind or unattended. Tools left on the line overnight were stolen, bullock drays bogged and abandoned at Red Lily Lagoon were cut up and carried away, buckles were cut out of a harness left near Bitter Springs (near Mataranka), even empty *boulli* tins were taken. In some areas Aborigines attempted to institutionalize trading and protective relationships with telegraph workers. One worker, S. W. Herbert, noted that a Larakia would change names with a white man to whom he took a fancy, 'an act which implies protection, assistance with obtaining food, and warning against danger'. Herbert also claimed that Aborigines assaulted No. 2 Depot, ninety-seven miles south of Palmerston. Aborigines had at first been given bully-beef and damper by the workers there but when supplies ran low they were refused. They attacked the camp but did not succeed in storming the workers' hut. As a result, two mounted troopers were despatched to protect workers on the northern section of the line, one being stationed at No. 2 Depot and the other at the Elsey camp. 'This seems to have been the first police presence in the Elsey area', Merlan writes.

Workers on the southern and central sections of the line had similar experiences, although not so violent. Christopher Giles, brother of the explorer Ernest Giles, was a member of the first party of whites working its way northwards from South Australia in 1871.

At first we saw but little of the natives though we had good reason to know that they saw a good deal of us. Axes began to disappear in a mysterious way, and the men's clothing hung out on bushes to dry near the camps, would be missing in the morning. A large and heavy tarpaulin vanished also and was never again seen. Though I never saw the missing axes I saw traces of them. While piloting a cutting party to the Finke River for poles I frequently found the natives had been there before us cutting down saplings with our own axes, to make weapons with.[10]

Although the tribes may have resented the intrusion of the telegraph workers, they saw the line as another source of European goods. Reporting in 1884, Charles Todd said the Aborigines, principally about Newcastle Waters, 'where they are very numerous and treacherous', at one time frequently damaged the line, breaking the insulators and using the fragments for spearheads. Binding wire on the line was taken and converted into fish-hooks and the iron footplates of the poles were dug up, broken and made 'with much ingenuity, into tomahawks, of which I possess some very creditable specimens'. Todd said that the telegraph department now distributed fish-hooks and a few cheap tomahawks to friendly Aborigines for occasional services rendered and wilful damage to the line was now rare. Within the last few months to October 1884, cattle had been speared at some of the telegraph stations. 'From the first, every effort has been made to maintain friendly relations with the natives and generally with fair success; there have, however, been occasional outbreaks of hostilities from time to time of a more or less serious nature', Todd wrote.[11] Apart from the attack on No. 2 Depot and two incidents not yet outlined, there appears to have been little violence involving the telegraph workers and Aborigines, chiefly because the former did little to disrupt the latter's life and in many cases were an easy source of European goods. As a measure of the success of Todd's policy of propitiation, in the period 1872–83 only nine of the interruptions to the telegraph line were caused by Aboriginal interference. In a tenth case a pole was accidentally destroyed when Aborigines burnt off grass. In the period 1884–95 no interruptions were caused by Aborigines.

The overland telegraph line construction gangs, like the overlanding parties of cattlemen, provoked only minor Aboriginal resistance. These groups of strangers were seen to be passing through on their way somewhere else. While some settled at waterholes and rivers, their competition for resources was not great. The strangers who brought antagonistic attitudes, such as the Queensland 'hard cases', invited conflict but they were still few in number. Most Europeans were under some form of sanction to keep the peace and to seek good relations with the people they encountered. This applied particularly to all government employees, who were dominant during this early period. The occasional parties of settlers and drovers may have brought frontier attitudes from Queensland and other parts, but they seem to have been aware that they were in a province at least nominally controlled by a southern government much removed in spirit and antecedants from the eastern Australian experience of colonization. This was the normal early-contact period of Aboriginal–European relations, a period in which the former viewed the strangers with suspicion, some hostility and much interest, while the Europeans generally did their best to insinuate themselves peacefully into a world which a beneficent government in London had handed them on a plate. The first period of tentative contact would soon be replaced by one of misunderstanding, hostility and bloodshed.

Chapter 5

Frontier Practice

The Territory's administration was always small: in July 1870 it numbered thirty-one people, reaching forty-four in January 1872, when it was reduced by the government to twenty-six as a cost-cutting measure. In the reorganization following the 1873 visit to Darwin of Thomas Reynolds, Commissioner of Crown Lands, only three of the early public officials remained — Millner, Foelsche and the sub-collector of customs, J. A. G. Little, who had been appointed in August 1872. In December 1873 steps were again taken to strengthen the administration with the appointment of Edward Price as stipendiary magistrate, together with a small staff to manage the court, and of J. G. Knight as secretary-accountant to the new government resident, G. B. Scott. Both Price and Knight later became government residents. With the increasing weight of Territory affairs, the government in July 1874 transferred responsibility from the Commissioner of Crown Lands to the Minister of Justice and Education.

Foelsche had arrived in January 1870 with six troopers, and at first had very little to do. The telegraph-construction workers, stretched across hundreds of miles of Aboriginal territory, were left largely to defend themselves; but as the gold rush got under way, the government was forced to accept the need for more police. In 1873 the number of troopers was increased to fifteen and three water police were stationed in Port Darwin. Police posts were established on the goldfields, the first at Pine Creek in 1873 and another at Adelaide River in 1875. Generally, police posts were established at the principal telegraph stations.

The first troopers employed in Central Australia were sent to the telegraph stations at Charlotte Waters — the most southerly such station, just north of the South Australian border — and at Barrow Creek in 1873. These men were members of the newly created far-northern division of the South Australian Police Force with head-quarters first at Melrose and later at Port Augusta — an arrangement maintained until the end of the South Australian administration of the Territory. The authorities in Adelaide could now exercise more direct control over the police in the Centre than would have been possible through Palmerston. Because of this arrangement, Foelsche was not responsible for the whole Territory. Initially he had had some sort of independence, being responsible directly to the Commissioner of Police in Adelaide, but Scott objected to this and was given control of the Top End police. There was one consolation for Foelsche: with the increase in police numbers, he was promoted to inspector.

The division of the Territory's police strength into northern and southern sections, and the direct control of the latter from Adelaide, was clearly demonstrated in the aftermath of the attack on the Barrow Creek telegraph station in February 1874. The Kaititja, who occupied country between the Aranda of the MacDonnell Ranges and Warramanga of the Tennant Creek area, had not strongly resisted European intrusions including the building of the central section of the telegraph line. They had not attacked Stuart or the overlanding parties of Millner and Lewis. When Alfred Giles followed northwards in 1872 and 1873 with stock for the telegraph stations, he was not attacked until he also reached Warramanga country between Gibson and Hayward Creeks, when at least two Aborigines were shot. Unlike the Warramanga, the Kaititja appeared to be willing to allow strangers to pass through and even remain in their country. The telegraph station at Barrow Creek occupied only a tiny space and apparently its presence did not disrupt tribal life, culture or resources. F. J. Gillen, later stationmaster at Alice Springs and an important early student of the Central Australian people, visited Barrow Creek in 1901 in company with Walter Baldwin Spencer, professor of biology at the University of Melbourne. Gillen remarked then that 'in the annals of Native treachery there is no crueller or more unprovoked attack'. He added that the stationmaster, John Stapleton, had been 'kind to the point of weakness to the natives giving them almost everything they asked for until their demands became wholly unreasonable and he was unable to comply with them'.[1] It seems that Stapleton had taken Todd's instructions to establish and maintain friendly relations too much to heart, especially a request that the telegraph stations provide rations to the old and infirm Aborigines and those who worked. If so, the motive for the attack appears to have been greed for European goods. But it may have resulted, as in so many other cases, from the Europeans not fully compensating the Kaititja for living in their country and, possibly, for services rendered. The motive for the Barrow Creek attack has never been satisfactorily explained.[2]

The station's staff were sitting outside the north-west corner of the building after their evening meal on 23 February, when a group of armed Kaititja descended a hill at the rear of the station. They made for the building, which was in the form of a stockade, having an internal courtyard and only one entrance — on the eastern side facing the hill. Seeing some of them approaching along the northern side, the Europeans, all unarmed, ran around the southern side but found the gateway barred by another party. The whites then rushed the gateway, braving the spear-thrusts. A linesman, John Frank, reached the kitchen door but was pierced through the heart; Stapleton was speared in the groin; the assistant stationmaster, E. E. C. Flint, was severely wounded in a thigh, while the others managed to get into the building with only a few scratches. They seized their weapons; the attackers withdrew. Gillen was the operator in Adelaide who received the first news of the attack, and later relayed medical advice from a doctor and messages to Stapleton's anxious wife. Frank had died immediately in the attack and Stapleton did so a few hours later, while Flint recovered. The Kaititja returned next day, but this time they were repulsed with bullets, one being killed.

The police officer at Barrow Creek, Mounted Constable Samuel Gason, who does not appear to have been present during the first attack, sent the first official report. On receiving Gason's telegram, the Commissioner of Police, George Hamilton, recommended to the government that action be taken against the Aborigines, but Barrow Creek was so far from the settled districts that it was difficult to organize a punitive party quickly. Hamilton wanted to send six or more troopers south from the Territory goldfields. He was concerned that there was no police station nearer than Charlotte Waters, about 430 miles to the south, where the one trooper was required to protect the two-man telegraph staff from unfriendly natives in that district. The next was at the Peake, 170 miles south of Charlotte Waters. When the matter was discussed by the government, the Commissioner of Crown Lands, W. Everard, said police could not be spared from the goldfields; the Commissioner of Police was therefore compelled to send up reinforcements from the south. Trooper Born at the Peake was instructed to obtain volunteers, horses and arms and to set out for Barrow Creek as soon as possible. In the meantime, the force at Barrow Creek could be strengthened by calling in a party working on the line north of the station. Two days after the attack, warrants were issued for eight Kaititja believed to have taken part — Harry Boy, The General, Spritely, Sunkeyes, Coonarie, Apongita, Tongala and Umpiganna. Two men at Strangways Springs, Edwin Warne and William Handby, rode northwards to join Born at the Peake. With an Aborigine, Sergeant, they set out on 1 March and reached Barrow Creek on 31 March without incident, except that on the Hanson River, just south of Barrow Creek, Sergeant was attacked by an Aborigine while looking for lost horses. Defending himself, he shot the assailant through an arm.

Meanwhile, on 25 February the Kaititja had again tried to surround the station, but the defenders had dispersed them with three shots and another was killed. Next day, a small party led by a man named Cowan left Barrow Creek to warn a party of about five teamsters nearing the station from the south. On 27 February the party of linesmen working to the north under a man named Tucker arrived, having had a 'brush' with the Aborigines about twenty miles out. To this reinforcement was added the party of teamsters who arrived safely, escorted by Cowan and his men, about 1 March. On 2 March Gason and ten men left Barrow Creek in search of the attackers, leaving ten at the station. At the spot where Tucker's party had been attacked, Gason and his volunteers encountered the Kaititja and a number were killed. He reported by telegram that:

At dusk, while following the course of the Taylor in search of water for camping four natives were sighted on opposite side of the creek. They immediately took to the scrub. On galloping up to where the natives were seen a large body of natives rushed out. They were evidently lying in ambush, all fully armed with spears. Some of our horses took fright, and in consequence of scrub being so thick, it was with the greatest difficulty that the party kept clear of spears. Shots were fired on them, killing several. The density of the scrub and lateness of the hour prevented us from more effectively punishing them . . . [3]

Gason and his party returned to Barrow Creek on 4 March, and three days later began searching along Taylor and Stirling Creeks. Failing to find any traces of the blacks there, he went to Hanson River, where he followed fresh tracks. His party pursued some Aborigines who fled into a scrub so dense that 'a horseman could not be seen at a distance of 20 yards'. On 10 March, while still on the Hanson, the whites saw a large body of blacks, all of whom escaped into the scrub. After searching for three hours, during which they located only a few women and children, they abandoned the search. Gason now lost the services of some of his men, who had to return to their work on the line, and so he awaited the arrival of Trooper Born and his three assistants. With this party he searched Taylor Creek again for fifty miles without result. On 8 April he paid off Warne and Handby, but two days later made a final search along the Hanson. On 3 April he reported by telegram:

Fourteen miles south of Central Mt Stuart a large camp of natives sighted on approaching camp. They made for the scrub, when three of them were overtaken and shot in an attempt to capture them, they resisting by using their weapons. These natives were recognised by the assistant operator and a native boy as having been at the station previous to attack. One of the party had a narrow escape in attempting to capture one of the natives and would have been speared but for the prompt assistance of one of his companions. [4]

According to the official records, the above details describe what happened in the aftermath of the Barrow Creek attack, which to some extent has become the subject of legend. Two Aborigines died in the second and third attacks on the station. It is not clear how many Gason claimed to have accounted for — his reports merely referring to 'several' and 'three'. One historian has made a total of eleven from the official reports, but says the number appears to have been much higher, one story being that ninety died at Skull Creek.[5] The Kaititja side of the story is difficult to find, only a few scraps being available to Europeans. In 1901 Gillen met an old man, Arabinya-urungwina, who helped him and Spencer with their research on the Kaititja and who was 'undoubtedly one of those concerned in the attack on this station'. This man told Gillen of his escape from the avenging whites who passed within a few feet of where he had hidden himself in a cleft rock, using tussocks of grass to conceal his retreat. When Herbert Basedow visited the district early this century, he found several old Kaititja who well remembered the affair and told him they had been 'more or less mixed up in it'. Basedow said: 'The tribe had, of course, since paid dearly for the outrage at the hands of a punitive expedition which included several expert sharpshooters'.[6]

First reaction to the news in Adelaide was similar to that in eastern Australia after such Aboriginal outrages as those at Hornet Bank in 1857 and Cullin-la-Ringo in 1861. South Australia had not experienced a massacre of a large number of whites since the *Maria* disaster in 1840. The Adelaide editorial writers, like those in Brisbane and Sydney before them, generally responded with anger based on preconceived ideas of how Aborigines should behave in the face of European occupation of their lands — rather than concede any grounds for grievance. Two days after the first attack the *South Australian Advertiser* called, in effect, for war. A day later it urged sharp, swift and severe retaliation, while the *Register* accused the government of procrastination. One person down south urged restraint: a Strathalbyn lawyer, J. H. Gordon, argued that 'defence of corporeal possessions could not justify the breaking of the laws of justice and humanity'.[7] He was ignored and, as we have seen, troopers Gason and Born were given a free hand to exact summary punishment. Robert Clyne has remarked: 'The tone of race relations in the north was determined by the police response to the native attack at Barrow Creek, when Hamilton argued that a strict adherence to the letter of the law was unnecessary'.[8]

The South Australian attitude towards Aborigines had reached a new stage. In 1840, after the massacre of as many as twenty-six survivors of the *Maria* about two hundred miles south of Adelaide, the police commissioner had executed two Milmenrura after a brief investigation; it was intended largely as an example to others of the tribe, and no other punitive action was taken. Thirty-four years later, and one thousand miles north of Adelaide, about ten and possibly many times that number of Kaititja were killed without any formal investigation and without any attempt at restraint. By 1874 Aborigines had become so removed from the sight of most South Australians that those of the Northern Territory could be treated as members of an alien race who had unjustifiably waged war against innocent and defenceless whites. There was no suggestion in the general reaction to the Barrow Creek attack that the Aborigines of the Territory were British subjects with the same rights under the law as Europeans. After the Hornet Bank massacre, warrants were issued for the arrest of Aborigines suspected of having been implicated, but by 1874 the Queensland Native Police did not bother with such formalities after Aboriginal 'outrages'. On the other hand, South Australian authorities in 1874 did issue warrants for arrest but, significantly, all those killed by Gason, Born and their associates were killed while supposedly resisting arrest. Of all the Aborigines encountered, the white parties did not take one male prisoner. The Barrow Creek 'outrage' probably heralded the end of the conciliation phase of official policy towards Aborigines in Central Australia and the beginning of pacification — that is, making the Aborigines submit to force if necessary. The proof that the Barrow Creek retaliation was not just a momentary overreaction to an incident arising out of special circumstances lies in the official reaction to the next major 'outrage'.

The telegraph master at Daly Waters, Charles Johnstone, two other employees, Charles Rickards and Abram Daer, and two Aborigines left Daly Waters towards the end of June 1875 with a waggon for the Roper Landing. They were to recover horses and cattle which had strayed from Daly Waters. At McMinn's Tableland they met more Aborigines who accompanied them to the landing, where they arrived on 29 June. The blacks were 'very quiet', some of them riding on the waggon. The whites had seven dogs and did not think they were in any danger. After the midday meal, Johnstone and one of the Aborigines from Daly Waters went to the river to swim, and Daer went there also for water. Without warning, a native speared Rickards, who was left in the camp. Daer heard Rickards shout and ran to Johnstone to warn him, but was too late. He had already been speared and was trying to wrest a second spear from his attacker, who bolted as Daer approached. Because the blacks had appeared to be friendly, Daer had left his revolver in the camp. He took Johnstone's revolver and twice tried unsuccessfully to fire at a man with spear raised. Daer ducked, but the spear struck him in the bridge of the nose, penetrating about three inches. Daer tried again, and this time fired but missed the assailant, who ran away. Rickards, although severely wounded in the chest, also came to Johnstone's aid, but his revolver was on the waggon. Daer continued to fire, forcing the attackers to flee. Johnstone died next morning. Because of their wounds, Rickards and Daer could not bury Johnstone, but left him rolled in canvas at the foot of a tree. Then they set out for Daly Waters, every jolt of the waggon giving intense pain to Daer, who managed to extract a piece of the spear through the roof of his mouth. They reached Daly Waters and medical assistance on 13 July. Reporting the incident, Daer said he believed that one of the Daly Waters Aborigines knew there was to be trouble but was afraid to warn them. He thought both had been forced to flee with the assailants. The whites' dogs, which had failed to discourage the attack, stayed with them on the way back and, in his opinion, were the main reason for the Aborigines' not trying again. No Roper River Aborigines were among the assailants who, Daer said, were chiefly from Mole's Hill. He could identify a 'great number of them'.[9]

Reaction to news of this event demonstrated the Adelaide authorities' lack of understanding of Territory conditions and lack of faith in their local representatives. Paul Foelsche had struck up a friendship with John Lewis, who was at this time at Port Essington. On 15 July he commented in a letter to Lewis that on receiving the 'sad news' he had arranged for his second-in-command, Corporal George Montagu, and a trooper to go to Daly Waters. They were to organize a party to go to the Roper, bring back Johnstone's body and 'have a Picnic with the Natives'. He had obtained warrants for the arrest of four Aborigines whose names were known and a warrant for those not known, adding that 'this is the loophole'. He said he had also communicated with Little — the former sub-collector of customs, now senior inspecting officer at the Palmerston telegraph office, and apparently Johnstone's brother-in-law — who was at Yam Creek at the time, to ask what men he had close to Daly Waters who could join Montagu. Little replied that he had just received a telegram from his chief, Charles Todd, in Adelaide stating that arrangements were being made to despatch a lawfully organized party to punish the culprits. The matter now having been taken out of his hands, Foelsche took no further steps. Then the Minister of Education, who controlled the Northern Territory, telegraphed the government resident, Scott, saying warrants had been issued in Adelaide and a party was to be organized at Yam Creek or the place nearest to the Roper River to arrest those who killed Johnstone. A small party of civilians led by Little left Yam Creek on the morning of 15 July to pick up a trooper at Pine Creek and to meet Montagu and the other trooper at Warlock Ponds on Elsey Creek. Next, the minister telegraphed Foelsche, telling him to locate Montagu at Daly Waters, which was much farther south, until further orders. Foelsche, annoyed by all this unhelpful interference, simply wired back that the party had already started. It seems he had no intention of trying to implement the minister's orders and he commented to Lewis that he expected that 'a regular mess will be made of the whole affair. The authorities in Adelaide will meddle with our affairs'. He added enigmatically:

I hope that the party that have gone out will not see any Natives, for I want to have a trip into the Roper country; I know I can identify all the niggers about there whether they have a name or not, but I don't care for a party of ten—no doubt you will say why don't you go this time, my reply is there are too many tale-tellers in the party; but my official excuse is that it would have delayed the party at least four days.[10]

Exactly what tales some of the party might have told is not made clear. Neither is the implication of what Foelsche would do which the others would not. One member of the party was A. Dewhurst Gore, who arrived as a settler in the Territory in 1872. Writing from the Roper Bar in 1899, he said, when objecting to the 'inhuman' treatment of the Aborigines on the north coast of Arnhem Land, that he had gone on the Roper expedition only as a guide. He referred to it as 'that unfortunate expedition' which had been sent to 'avenge' Johnstone's death, inferring that things had happened of which he did not approve. Reporting to Todd by telegram on 29 August, two months after the murder, Little did not give the composition of the party, but it can be assumed that it comprised three policemen and seven civilians. He said they had arrived at the Roper Bar on 2 August without seeing any Aborigines on the way. They had found notices left by a man named Batten, who was leading a party of nine *en route* to Queensland, saying he had found a notice left by Daer and Rickards reporting the death of Johnstone. Batten's party had then found the blacks 'mustered strongly' at Mount McMinn, 'whom they quickly dispersed and did their best to avenge poor Johnstone's death'. One of their party was almost speared. Ali Baba, the 'chief', Roger, Billy, Larry and several other blacks were recognized. Batten's party recovered a quantity of clothing, the camp was burnt and all spears and other weapons destroyed.[11]

After collecting and interring Johnstone's remains on 3 August, the group of police and civilians split into two parties to search both sides of the Roper. They found numerous camps, especially near Mole's Hill, including the one attacked by Batten's party; there one dead Aborigine was found with a bullet wound in the chest. One of the parties then started down the river towards Mount St George and on 18 August attacked a small camp at Harris's Lagoon, about eleven miles below the old depot at the Roper Bar. Two 'chiefs' named Abareeka and Harry Bing were killed in attempting to escape. Other blacks were seen but got away in the long grass. Some women and children were found that afternoon but, according to Little, were not molested. This party returned to the Bar on 20 August and the other started down the south side two days later. The second twice saw Aborigines, who also got away in the long grass. On 29 August, the day on which he reported, Little said another group of whites on foot had attacked a camp on the north side of the river near Calder's Range and dispersed more blacks but 'none were killed'. A lot of spears were obtained and the camp was burned. When Montagu set out from Daly Waters on 27 July he had warrants for the arrest of five Aborigines including Bungawar Lowrie, known as Ural. The government cutter *Flying Cloud* had been sent to the Roper to meet the police party. Ural was one of several Aborigines induced to board the vessel late in August and on 21 August a trooper named Farrell arrested him. Ural was taken back to Palmerston. Apparently the authorities realized that no charge against him could be made to stick, so Scott sent him to Daly Waters in the care of another trooper, to be held there until he could be returned to the Roper.[12]

On 1 June 1875 a gold-prospecting party led by Thomas Walker had left the Union Camp just north of Pine Creek with five saddle horses, fifteen pack horses and six months' provisions to look for gold in the Blue Mud Bay area of eastern Arnhem Land. The government had provided five of the horses and three months' provisions. Seventeen days later, Walker's party encountered Aborigines who appeared to be friendly although their faces were painted. They came into camp and were given some empty *boulli* tins, which they seemed to want, and then left. An hour later they returned with others, all heavily armed, and surrounded the camp. The whites tried to drive them off, spears were thrown and one of the whites, Charles Bridson, was struck on a hand which became severely infected. On 7 August the party reached Blue Mud Bay. Two days later about thirty Aborigines, whom they had thought to be friendly, entered their camp and speared two others, including Walker who died next day. The other man, David Marchall, was severely wounded but Bridson's wounded hand had improved. The Aborigines kept up their harassment, one night attacking the horses and one of the whites on horseback, who had to fight his way back to the camp, firing his revolver at them. Later, they attempted to burn the whites out.[13] It was subsequently said that forty Aborigines had been killed in these clashes. The government cargo vessel *Woolner* sailed from Port Darwin on 9 September 1875 for Blue Mud Bay with a party of prospectors. While in that area they heard there had been a 'great fight' between the blacks and whites and 'forty' blacks had been killed. The prospectors were unable to get the local people to help them locate either Walker's party or gold, and they returned to Port Darwin without any auriferous samples. The overlanding party returned to Union Camp on 21 October; Marchall recovered, but they had lost four of the government horses because of the hardships encountered. They found no gold. It seems that no punitive action was taken directly in response to this incident, which coincided with the Roper River episode.

Foelsche later became known as an expert on the Aborigines of the Territory, a claim which meant only that he appeared to know more about them than did other Europeans. His knowledge, however, seems limited and he lacked any sympathy for them. He seldom travelled and when he did he confined his movements to the Palmerston district, the goldfields and Cobourg Peninsula. He took many photographs of Aborigines, answered E. M. Curr's ethnological questionnaire and prepared a paper for the South Australian branch of the Royal Geographical Society. Some writers present Foelsche as being sympathetic towards the Aborigines: 'His constant quest was for every detail of their way of life and their outlook, and how it could be arranged that they could carry on despite the totally alien civilization that had been thrust upon them'.[14] His true attitude towards the Aborigines can be gauged from another letter to Lewis:

Of course you have seen all about our Nigger Hunt in the papers. There has been no end of telegraphing from the Minister about the affair and orders have been sent to the effect that in pursuing Natives for offences committed by them, no firearms are to be used except in extreme cases and in self-defence, but we'll be able to regulate all that; I should have gone out myself, but too much time would have been lost in overtaking them with the plunder in their possession, so I left it to Stretton, and I could not have done better than he did so I am satisfied and so is the public here.[15]

This was a reference to the action of police and volunteers who pursued Aborigines after a teamster, James Ellis, was killed on the road between Yam Creek and Pine Creek in January 1878. Mounted Constable W. G. Stretton, two other troopers, civilians and a South Australian Aboriginal tracker located a party of suspects near the Daly River. The blacks resisted arrest, seventeen were shot and the others dispersed. One volunteer was wounded but not seriously. No sooner had this action been completed than the police and volunteers were sent out again to apprehend Aborigines who had speared two Chinese near Pine Creek, both of whom had been badly wounded. When pursuing Ellis's murderers, the police had been instructed to arrest any Aborigines found with any goods from his waggon or any goods 'which they have the slightest suspicion of'. In reporting this matter to Adelaide, Edward Price, who had succeeded Scott as government resident in 1876, observed that 'Blacks lately have been getting more dangerous and a severe lesson will be required to check them'. He claimed that the blacks had always been treated kindly by the whites and had shown great ingratitude.[16] As Foelsche suggested in his private comment to Lewis, Price's report on this episode caused some consternation in Adelaide. The minister, Neville Blyth, a member of the Boucaut government, directed that, in pursuing Aborigines supposed to have committed crimes, severe measures were not to be taken except in 'the last extremity'. Firearms were not to be used unless on fair evidence that the Aborigines were part of the tribe criminally concerned in outrages; resistance was such as to make it impossible to capture them; or it was necessary in self-defence. Blyth sent a copy of these instructions to the Attorney-General, Charles Mann, who commented:

I think the instructions given of the Hon. Min. to the G.R. are the best that can be given. It is in my opinion utterly out of the question that he can deal with the natives of the Northern Territory in the same way as if they were civilized — I think however that the case is hardly one of 'law' but essentially of policy as I have before observed. I entirely agree with the Hon. Minister.[17]

In a general report in March that year, Price defended local practice when he wrote that the great difficulty in detecting actual offenders had encouraged the Aborigines to become bolder. He acknowledged great difficulty in handing out even-handed justice according to civilized laws, but he claimed that no injustice had been done. He believed criminals had escaped punishment because of insufficient reliable evidence to convict them under English law. It was almost impossible to obtain evidence from Europeans in cases of crimes committed by Aborigines, and their own evidence was utterly unreliable as they 'rather pride themselves in not telling the truth in a Court of Justice' and only a few could be trusted to bring a criminal to justice. Price said that whenever a crime had been committed near Palmerston he had threatened to order the whole tribe away unless the criminal was brought in. Even then, he said, great care had to be taken to ensure they did not bring in an innocent man, but in most cases they had given up the offender.[18]

Price could defend his actions on the basis of the difficulties of implementing government policy in view of Aboriginal untrustworthiness and hostility, but it is clear that the government realized, in part at least, the weakness of its own position. Official reaction to Price's reports of the latest 'Nigger Hunt' suggests that in 1878 the government would not sanction unrestrained punishment. On the other hand, the new instructions did allow considerable discretion, and the attorney-general's opinion that any action taken was a matter of policy rather than law suggests the South Australian government had now accepted that the bloodshed on the northern frontier arose from conflict between two races rather than from the criminal actions of subjects of the Queen. Foelsche's remark that 'we'll be able to regulate all that' suggests that he fully understood the government's position and that, in interpreting instructions based on policy, neither he nor any other Territory official would be breaking the law. The Queensland practice of wholesale killing as a means of pacifying hostile Aborigines had now become Territory practice. By 1878 the South Australian government had lost control of Aboriginal affairs in the Territory. It hardly mattered now what the government or South Australians generally thought of Constable Stretton's actions, because frontier attitudes now guided official practice.

Chapter 6

A Policeman's Lot

Although a man of placid nature, Foelsche had some ambition and was conscious of the professional disadvantages of accepting a post in the Territory. In September 1876 he wrote to Lewis in South Australia that he was aggrieved that after volunteering for the Territory, when the authorities could get no one else, with the distinct understanding that this would not interfere with his service in the South Australian force, he was being disadvantaged. He was certain no officer would volunteer to take his place now out of fear of similar treatment. Foelsche wanted an assurance that if his health failed he would be permitted to return to South Australia and remain in the force without loss of rank. Foelsche thanked Lewis for the trouble he had taken in furthering his interests in Adelaide and mentioned Ben Rounsevell, a member of parliament; but he urged Lewis not to press anything as the government might think he was using parliamentary influence, which was against civil service rules. As an indication of how slowly things moved in the Territory, he said that stones were being cut for a new house for him and his family but he believed it would not be completed for another twelve months. In the meantime, they were still living in an 'old shanty'. Contrary to Douglas's early doubts of his fitness to undertake arduous travel, Foelsche made occasional trips 'up country'; on 20 August 1876 he travelled from Palmerston through the goldfields to Pine Creek and return. He was met at Southport by his wife and they camped on the Elizabeth River on 1 September 'where the mosquitoes serenaded us and Mrs Foelsche kept watch all night for fear of the niggars [sic], but they did not come'. About 1873 Foelsche had taken over from Captain Sweet as the Territory's leading photographer, but his activities were intermittent. In January 1877 Foelsche said he had taken no photographs during the past four months and would take no more until his new house was finished.[1]

With the decline in gold fever, many people had left the Territory, among them Thomas Reynolds, the man who had reorganized the administration in 1873. Impressed with the mineral potential of the

Territory, he had resigned his parliamentary seat in August 1873 to return to the Territory to try his luck; but he had gone away disappointed and to his death on the steamship *Gothenburg*. This ship had sailed from Port Darwin early in 1875 with many prominent Northern Territory residents on board; on 25 February she had foundered in a storm off the Queensland coast near Bowen with the loss of 102 lives. Among the victims was the Aborigines' early friend and protector, Dr Millner. Other victims were the wife and five children of Edward Price, the magistrate. This loss was later said to have greatly affected Price and, although he followed Scott as government resident in 1876, he had a lonely and apparently miserable life in Palmerston. Foelsche at first liked Price, writing to Lewis in September 1876 that 'We are all getting on well with our new Resident, he is a jolly fellow and very fond of a lady, who engages all his spare time and I fancy his game leg is getting shorter from all the toddling he does between the residence and where Joshua Jones used to live'. When the lady, Mrs A. W. Sergison, moved to the official residence with her husband, 'the old man' was 'occasionally seen nursing the baby'. In May 1877 Foelsche was not so amused by Price who, he told Lewis, was a 'little two-faced man'. Price had telegraphed the minister that he could do without Foelsche's services. He would make Montagu a sergeant, as that was all that was required. He had heard that Price had told Donaldson, the deputy sheriff, that when they had 'done away' with Foelsche, Donaldson could have his quarters. Price had also deprived him of any assistance in his office. Despite his earlier caution about asking parliamentary favours, Foelsche again asked Lewis to 'have a word with Ben Rounsevell and any other of your friends in Parliament and induce them to interest themselves on my behalf'. He did not wish to leave the Territory without knowing that the government would give him a similar appointment in South Australia. He could not afford to be out of employment, he said. He had been in the police force twenty years and did not like to be 'kicked out in the gentle manner Mr Price intends to do it'.[2]

When he heard that Montagu had been appointed Inspector of Public Houses, Foelsche saw it as a step towards replacing himself. He telegraphed an influential friend in Adelaide who tried to assure him it would not mean any disadvantage to him. Nonetheless, Foelsche was anxious, telling Lewis that, if the government cut off the head of the force in the Northern Territory by adopting Price's recommendation, 'the whole will die a natural death'. He damned the government, saying it would save only £350 a year by doing as Price proposed. Foelsche attributed Price's change of attitude to his having forced A. W. Sergison to pay the rates on Jones's house after having used it for eight months rent-free. Price had then invited the Sergisons to stay at his residence; he had subsequently shown a coolness towards Foelsche and would not look him or any of his family in the eye 'even if we are on the verandah'. No one in Palmerston, Foelsche claimed, seemed to care for the company of the government resident and the Sergisons. Sergison had been a member of the party led by the senior surveyor, Gilbert McMinn, brother of William McMinn, to the lower reaches of the Katherine River in 1876 to examine it for mineral and pastoral prospects. McMinn reported unfavourably but Sergison disagreed and next year went to Sydney and interested several pastoralists in northern land. Foelsche was pleased when the Sergisons left for Sydney in May 1877. 'These people are all the cause of Price's ill-feelings towards us', he lamented. But Sergison and his wife were soon back and staying again at the official residence. Sergison led his own expedition to the country between the Daly and the Victoria, while Price nursed Mrs Sergison, who was expecting another baby — 'and since she is back he is more struck on her than ever'. Drink had already taken its toll on some of Palmerston's officials. While the Sergisons had been absent in Sydney, no one cared for Price's company, according to Foelsche, except Donaldson 'who is not satisfied being wheeled home in a wheelbarrow, but has lately taken to sleeping in a fowlhouse, where he was found after being missing for 6 hours'. Donaldson, Foelsche later commented, was 'a little sneak'. The drink had even got to one of the ladies. Foelsche had found Mrs Finniss, wife of B. T. Finniss's son Fred, lying in the street 'beastly drunk'. She and her husband had left the British Australian Telegraph Company's quarters and were going to live in A. D. Gore's cottage, but the Foelsches believed that the Finnisses were going to leave Palmerston soon. 'She seems to have lost all respect for herself or husband', Charlotte Foelsche remarked.[3]

By December 1877 Foelsche was despondent, feeling very unwell. He had been on a trip to Port Essington, taking photographs for Josiah Boothby to take to the Paris Exhibition. He had worked himself into the doctor's hands, he told Lewis, having worked in a tent when, he said, the temperature was 110 degrees Fahrenheit in the shade — too hot for any European to work ten hours a day. He had taken a few views of Lewis's settlement there. In May 1878 he was able to report that he had sent his first batch of photographs to Adelaide. Foelsche's new house was now constructed — to his own plan — and it was very comfortable, but in July of that year he was still worrying about his career after twenty-two years in the police force, having almost concluded that it would be his lot to live and die in the Territory. He often thought about how to improve his position which was about as high as he could get in that branch of the service. Foelsche asked Lewis to use his influence to have him appointed visiting justice to the prison; he thought he would have no difficulty in achieving this now that the Chief Justice, Sir Samuel Way — a fellow Freemason — was Acting Governor of South Australia.[4]

According to Foelsche, the 'whole gaol establishment, as at present carried out, is a rotten system', but he did not intend to complain about it, being sure that this situation would soon be discovered. He was disgusted with Donaldson, because of his failure to keep prisoners in gaol. An Aborigine, Addoolah, had escaped from the Palmerston gaol twice, each time taking another Aborginal prisoner with him. The companions were still at large, although Addoolah had been recaptured by Foelsche and Montagu who had had to risk their lives by descending the steep cliff at Lameroo beach in pitch dark between one and two o'clock one morning. Addoolah had been tried at the last court sitting, had pleaded guilty and been sentenced to twelve months' imprisonment in irons, of which Foelsche wrote:

He has more liberty than any prisoner in gaol. He is very seldom in gaol all day, always working about Donaldson's place and is sent on errands about the town. This is poor encouragement for me to bring offenders to justice . . . such things would not be tolerated in South Australia.[5]

Foelsche sailed to Port Essington in July 1878 to inquire into an allegation that Captain Francis Cadell had illegally shipped and detained Aborigines. This matter had come to the ears of the Adelaide authorities, who had asked him to investigate. Foelsche learned from the then manager of the Cobourg Cattle Company, David Morgan, as well as from two Aborigines, Jack Davis and his son Harry, that Cadell had obtained eleven 'Darkies' from Raffles Bay during the previous October and twelve with their wives from nearby Mount Norris Bay. His pretext was that he wanted them to get trepang and that he would bring them back in one month. Cadell was back in Bowen Strait, between the peninsula and Croker Island, at the end of March; he tried to induce more Aborigines to go with him but they refused. At about the same time, in Mount Norris Bay or the neighbouring bay, opposite Tor Rock, he enticed some Alligator Rivers people on board — but they jumped overboard and swam to shore. Since then he had not been back. Foelsche commented that the people at Port Essington seemed 'to be in a great way about those taken not coming back'.

Francis Cadell, born in Scotland in 1822, had joined the growing number of mariners operating in the northern and north-eastern waters of Australia, particularly in the trepang and pearling trades. The methods by which they obtained Aboriginal crews and the conditions aboard their vessels were to become an important issue in Queensland over the next twenty years. In 1884 the Griffith liberal government introduced the *Native Labourers Protection Act*, but the penalties provided were so weak that it was ineffectual. The kidnappings, beatings and deprivations suffered by the Aborigines along the Cape York Peninsula coasts continued. They became so serious that public and parliamentary concern were among the reasons for introducing the much more effective *Aboriginals Protection and Restriction of the Sale of Opium Act* 1897. After searching for a permanent site for Palmerston in 1867, Cadell had explored the Gulf of Carpentaria and discovered the Roper River mouth. Next he was whaling in New Zealand waters, trading between Fiji and neighbouring islands; in 1874 he was recruiting labour from the Dutch East Indies for the pearling fleet on the Western Australian coast. He got into difficulties with the government for ill-treating his Malay employees, and with the Dutch authorities for kidnapping natives. Cadell moved to the Arafura Sea and so back to the Arnhem Land coast again, but several mutinies occurred on his luggers because of ill-treatment. Late in 1878 ten Aboriginal men, including Wandy Wandy, and four women stole a boat from Cadell and found their way back to Port Essington. At about this time a warrant was issued for his arrest for kidnapping Queensland Aborigines. He disappeared in 1879 and was later reported to have been killed by one of his crew off the Kei Islands, near the West Irian coast.

David Morgan, who was now running two hundred head of buffalo as well as cattle and ponies on the Cobourg station, had tried to come to some understanding with E. O. Robinson and T. H. Wingfield (who had taken up part of Croker Island) about the employment of Aborigines. Morgan had proposed that neither party should employ or entice away Aborigines employed by the other party; but Robinson would not agree and seemed to be unneighbourly. Foelsche advised Morgan to make out an agreement between himself and his employees, ensure they fully understood it, have it witnessed by a European and send a duplicate to the Protector of Aborigines at Palmerston. Morgan was advised also to inform Robinson and Wingfield of this and the names of his employees in writing and to caution them not to employ those named unless they produced a written discharge of services. Foelsche advised Lewis to have Morgan appointed a sub-protector of Aborigines, as this would give him some influence over the local people and power to intervene on their behalf if not properly treated by others who might employ them. Also, this would protect them from being taken away by vessels working along the coast. The first settlers on Cobourg Peninsula had taken it upon themselves to issue rations to the Aborigines there, Levi had been given a small sum of money for this purpose and it had been suggested that he be made a sub-protector, but it seems this was not adopted. Foelsche also proposed that he be sent along the coast in the government cutter *Flying Cloud*, to explain such an arrangement to the Aborigines, taking interpreters from Port Essington and other places; 'nearly all the natives know that I am some authority', he added. Eventually the *Flying Cloud* was used to make annual inspections of the coast with Foelsche on board, but the purpose was more to issue licences and collect fees from the trepang fishermen than to protect the Aborigines.[6] Foelsche's suggestion that written labour agreements between Aborigines and Europeans be introduced seems to be the first such proposal in the Territory. They would have had little legal value, as was later found, but Foelsche was moving in the direction later taken by legislation proposed at the end of the century.

The Cobourg Peninsula was not the only area along the north coast of interest to pastoralists. By May 1877 the government resident had had several applications for runs of about four hundred square miles each on Melville Island. Price would not recommend them as he believed the applicants had no capital and were speculators. The minister, Ebenezer Ward — who had been a chief clerk at Escape Cliffs during B. T. Finniss's expedition — agreed and commented that the Aborigines on Melville Island were known to be numerous and formidable and that bloodshed would almost certainly follow an attempt to establish 'a mere station settlement there'.[7]

Back in Palmerston, Foelsche's relations with Price improved. In March 1879 they were 'to all appearances the best of friends' and Foelsche did all he could to please the government resident, so that Price had no reason to find fault with him. But, Foelsche told Lewis, he never expected from the government resident any help that would advance his interests. Price had never recommended that the government recognize his service in the Northern Territory, although he had done so for Donaldson, who had not been there half the time Foelsche had. All the government officers but Foelsche received higher salaries in the Territory than they would in South Australia. If he stayed another twenty years, he wrote, he would not be able to save enough money to send his family on a trip down south. From this time Foelsche took an increasing interest in Lewis's affairs in the Territory, becoming an agent for the Cobourg Cattle Company. In March 1879 he advised that, although Morgan continued to work hard at Cobourg, he could not see that money could be made from buffalo and ponies there, not even to pay expenses. People would not eat buffalo meat if they could get any other and they would be supplied with that as soon as the cattle, which had arrived on the Roper from Queensland, reached Palmerston in a few months. In July Foelsche was reporting that he had sold meat from Cobourg on the local market at fivepence a pound and arranged for the hides to be shipped to W. H. Brook, Lewis's brother-in-law and secretary to the Cobourg Cattle Company in Adelaide. But he advised Lewis to get rid of the station if he could.[8]

By December 1879 Foelsche was complaining to Lewis that he could not be expected to act on behalf of the company unless he was given funds to do so. He said he declined to act any longer, objecting to being stopped in the streets of Palmerston, as had often happened, and asked when he intended to pay its debts. He had incurred expenses on the company's behalf, but he had not the slightest chance of making a penny in return. In January 1880 Foelsche was angry:

Nothing would please me more than to be in Adelaide if only for half an hour to enable me to meet the Coburg [*sic*] Cattle Company and their secretary face to face and tell them a bit of my mind ... You get me to look after your affairs at Port Essington, and now you want me to find the money too. You know perfectly well now that there is no sale for dried meat, hides and horses, that there is nothing else at Port Essington to bring in a revenue. Ponies would sell but how are they to be got in?

On Croker Island disaster had befallen Wingfield. He (a middle-aged Victorian) and Robinson had started a trepang station there in March 1878. Little is known of Wingfield but Robinson, an Englishman, had been born in Oxford in about 1850 and had come to Australia to go pearling on the Western Australian coast, had been speared in King Sound and had gone to Port Darwin to recover from a wound in a thigh; then he had joined Lewis's expedition to find Permain and Borradaile. Robinson believed that these two men had failed because of their desire to 'do the niggers some good'; a Bible and a bag of flour were their weapons, but the desire of 'the niggers was anti-pathetic' and they had killed Permain and Borradaile near Tor Rock. 'The niggers got the flour anyway and they didn't want the Bible', he said many years later. According to Robinson, Wingfield was a splendid chap but he had no 'nigger craft'. Robinson left him in charge of the place while he went to Port Darwin in a lugger for stores. When he got back on 23 December the place was strewn with broken spears. Everything in the hut was gone and the fowls were pecking at his 'poor mate's body in the sand'. Wingfield had been speared in the back and wounded in the head.[10]

The *Flying Cloud* was sent to Croker Island with two troopers but the Aborigines had 'cleared out' and Foelsche believed there was no use in trying to catch them until the wet season ended. He said that the Aborigine who had cut Wingfield's head open with a tomahawk was one of those whom Cadell had taken away from Mount Norris Bay and the one who had killed Cadell's mate, named Price, in Torres Strait. Foelsche hoped that the government would afford him the opportunity to try to bring the fellow to justice. Two Port Essington Aborigines, Bob White and Jack Davis, were out after him, but Foelsche doubted that they would bring him in. Bob White had guided Leichhardt to Port Essington; Jack Davis, brother of Flash Poll, was one of the old Port Essington people who spoke English 'remarkably well', according to John Lewis, and had been on a trading vessel to Hong Kong. He and another Aborigine had been picked up there by a Royal Navy captain, Crawford Pascoe, who had been at Port Essington in 1838 and had arranged for them to be repatriated. Davis later told Lewis that when he went away his name was Aboriginal but when he came back he had forgotten a great deal of his native language and went by the name of Jack Davis, and his people 'did not believe he was the king or heir to the throne'.[11]

Foelsche was back at Port Essington in June and found that 'boys' who were on Croker Island when Wingfield was killed were afraid to come to Lewis's station. He had sent Jack Davis to fetch them and

Davis had returned with his sons, Jim and Harry. Foelsche also had Bob White and his people brought from Raffles Bay. His objective was to ascertain whether he could get sufficient evidence to secure a conviction of Wandy Wandy and Big Jack, both implicated in the murder of Price in Torres Strait. He told Lewis he would recommend the government spend a little money to secure the offenders and bring them to justice, adding: 'you know it will not do for me to shoot them unless I feel anxious to be tried for murder'. He said the Cobourg Cattle Company could assist by urging the government to provide him with the means of securing the murderers and making an example of them. He also wanted the *Flying Cloud* with police on board to make 'judicial' visits to Port Essington two or three times a year. Robinson was now the manager there, assisted by a boatman named Kite, but they were afraid for their lives. Wandy Wandy had sent word to Port Essington that some day he would kill all white fellows and have plenty of flour, rice and tobacco. An Aborigine had informed Robinson that Permain and Borradaile were killed at the back of the Tor Rock, that the local people speared the ponies first and ate them, then killed the two men, cooked them on a fire and devoured them. Relating this tale to Lewis, Foelsche said: 'I wish the government would authorise me to deal out summary punishment to these tribes. I fear if something is not done "Wandy Wandy" and his gang [will] become bolder and bolder and kill every European they have a chance of'.[12]

Two witnesses to the murder of Wingfield came to Port Essington a few days later and from them Foelsche learned that an Aborigine obtained tobacco from Wingfield and then wanted more and more. For some unknown cause, Wingfield had shot him. The blacks then sent for Wandy Wandy and Bob White's sons who were camped about six miles away. They had come up that day and Wandy Wandy had gone to the hut, found Wingfield asleep and killed him. Other Aborigines had then speared him, hammered him with sticks and buried him, then stolen a lot of rice and rum and cleared out. Foelsche said it was perfectly useless for him to try to catch Wandy Wandy. He did not have to do so: the wanted man was brought to Port Essington by some of his own people and others, but not as a prisoner. Robinson had Jack Davis bring Wandy Wandy to the house, where he handcuffed him; he was sent by a boat to Port Darwin and committed for trial. Foelsche sailed back in the *Flying Cloud* to bring in the witnesses. Foelsche now pointed out a problem: the highest judicial officer in the Territory was a magistrate, who could not try capital cases.

The Government are now in a fix; if he is to be tried for murder, the case has to go to Adelaide; if only for manslaughter he can be tried here; the depositions go down by the mail for the law officers of the crown to decide what charge is to be preferred against him.[13]

Edward Price had been conscious of the legal difficulties presented to him as a magistrate. In February 1878 he had pointed out to the minister that under the 1875 Act for the better administration of justice in the Northern Territory, no crime punishable by death could be tried in the Territory. This meant, he said, that in the case of murder by an Aborigine, the prisoner and all witnesses would have to be sent to Adelaide. If convicted, he would have to be returned to the Territory for execution if the government wished to prevent similar crimes in future. Price added that, as this situation was known to the whites and 'some of the more intelligent blacks', it was probable that if a black murdered a white, the Europeans would take the law into their own hands rather than make the long trip to Adelaide. In most cases it would be difficult to prosecute any white man for this crime, because most potential witnesses would be unwilling to give evidence or go to Adelaide. At present, he said, this was likely to happen because of the strong hatred against the blacks arising from their recent 'treacherous' crimes. Price believed that, if the whites knew that an Aborigine could be tried in the Territory for murder, they would probably not take the law into their hands. The minister agreed and advised that a Bill would be prepared giving effect to Price's suggestion, except that in the event of any conviction for murder, the depositions and judgment would be considered by a judge of the Supreme Court before the sentence could be carried out.[14] The government in fact did nothing. When Wandy Wandy was arrested for Wingfield's murder, Price was told by the then minister that if committed for trial on the capital charge, the prisoner was to be sent to Adelaide for trial. An administrative problem for Price was solved when Wandy Wandy was found guilty of the lesser charge of manslaughter.

Price had also mentioned the murder by Aborigines of R. E. Holmes, landlord at Collett's Creek hotel, seventeen miles from Southport, in March 1880. Holmes's application for renewal of his licence had been opposed at the annual meeting of the licensing board in Palmerston because, it was alleged, he had chained a black woman in his house. Holmes denied this and, as the allegation could not be proved, the licence was renewed. Staying at the house was an Aboriginal woman, Mary, and her mother and a boy. Two blacks had been hanging about the house and, after Holmes returned, four strange ones appeared with goose eggs and asked for drinks and slept in the stable. Next day Holmes sent the Chinese cook on an errand and, when he returned, the cook found Holmes near to death. Mary told him that the blacks had attacked the publican and run away, taking a bag of flour, tins of meat, tobacco, a tablecloth and some blankets. Foelsche was sent there to investigate but decided that the police could not follow the murderers' tracks in the swampy ground. Three Aborigines were later arrested and gaoled for Holmes's manslaughter.[15]

Cadell was not the only freebooting mariner to plunder labour from the Territory's coast. In September 1881 Foelsche noted that a three-masted ship had been in Raffles Bay and enticed a number of people away, apparently to Torres Strait. He said he would not be surprised to hear of more murders. The government, he believed, should pass an Act compelling vessels which employed Aborigines to go to the nearest port to have them properly signed on, as was done in Western Australia.[16] This concern for a proper system of Aboriginal employment, both at sea and on land, was the closest Foelsche ever came to expressing support for some measure of protection for them. He appears to have been the first European in the Territory to have voiced such concern but his later record was less impressive, because he left such issues to others and only gave his opinion when requested. Perhaps by this time his personal disappointments were souring any humanitarian impulses towards the Aborigines which he may have had.

Foelsche's relations with Lewis improved a little after he was sent £100 by the Cobourg Cattle Company in April 1880, apparently as compensation for expenses incurred while acting as its agent. Also, he had some hope of getting away from the Territory. There was talk of transferring him down south, he told Lewis in September of that year, but he did not know whether it would come to anything, especially now that the Territory seemed to be getting a fresh start. Besides, the government had put his salary in the second class in the estimates of expenditure for the next financial year, and this was 'a better screw than the Inspectors get in S.A. but, of course, this will have to be passed by the House yet. You may give any members you know a hint not to oppose it'. In September 1881 his hopes had been dashed and it looked again as though he would never leave the Territory. There had been another change of government and his expected pay rise had not been approved. Foelsche was now taking root, having purchased 320 acres on the Barry River near Lake Dean. The railway to Pine Creek had been started and the surveyors had reached that lake. Foelsche, however, had got himself into a legal bind when purchasing this land from Joshua Jones, who had gone to New Zealand. The land grant was in the name of Jones's son who was under age and therefore could not transfer it. Foelsche asked Lewis to seek the advice of their friend, the Chief Justice, on whether the transfer could be made on a judge's order. He had not been to Port Essington for some time but he knew that the old garden there had been abandoned. Robinson was living there with only a Pacific Islander for company but was getting tired of it.[17]

Lewis had been thinking of selling the Cobourg run. Fisher and Lyons, who had formed a station on the eastern side of the Adelaide River opposite Fred's Pass would, in Foelsche's opinion, be interested in it if he did not ask too much. But Lewis did ask too much. 'You made a mistake', Foelsche told him later, 'not to sell the place when you had a chance to clear out with a profit'. In August 1883 Fisher and Lyons were still anxious to buy Cobourg but were waiting for Lewis to 'let it slide', when they would buy it at auction for a 'trifle'. Fisher and Lyons, who now had 20 000 head of cattle in the Territory, were stocking the Alligator Rivers region, and Foelsche thought Port Essington was just the place they would like to have. In 1884 the Duke of Manchester, on a visit to the Territory while looking for investment possibilities in Australia, had told Foelsche, still acting as agent for Lewis, that he intended to purchase Cobourg if he could arrange the necessary finance in Sydney. The duke was unsuccessful in Sydney but still hoped to raise the money in London. Lewis's greed, however, was getting the better of his judgement, as Foelsche angrily told him in January 1885: 'I think you made a mistake in sticking in another £1,000 but I expect the truth of it is you are afraid I [will] succeed in disposing of the property and you [will] have to pay me a £1,000. If you don't want to sell, why the devil don't you say so?' Foelsche considered that if Lewis got £9000 for the property he might consider himself lucky. Once more he was angry with his old friend. He said the property had not increased in value by £1000 since he was in Adelaide 'but as soon as you saw that I had a chance of disposing of it you must stick on another thousand'. In the end Lewis failed to sell Cobourg and had to hand it back to he government because he had not fulfilled the conditions of the lease.[18] Lewis may not have cared very much. He had his own pastoral property, Kooringa, near Burra where he was the local representative of the stock and station agents, Liston and Shakes, and he was investing in the new mines at Broken Hill. One of his sons, Essington, became head of the Broken Hill Proprietary Company in the next century.

Because of its inherent self-contradictions, Foelsche's strict moral code sometimes brought him into public ridicule. In June 1881 the *Northern Territory Times* published a report on prostitution among Aboriginal women. Foelsche and seven other citizens of Palmerston wrote to the *Times* protesting against the 'disgraceful article and indecent allusions in your paper today, and its general mismanagement', and cancelled their subscriptions. Foelsche and his friends were subsequently dubbed the 'Octagonists' and became the butt of much banter. Douglas Lockwood wrote: 'One reader reported that the offensive article had at least caused the police to remove the blacks from Palmerston'.[19] On the other hand, when the southern outcry developed in mid-1885 after details of the white retaliation following the Daly River murders became known in Adelaide, Territory residents rallied around their chief of police. Sixty-one residents of the mining districts wrote to Foelsche, testifying to his 'untiring efforts in bringing the crime home to the Daly River murderers'.

We most sincerely sympathize with you in the matter of the treatment you have received at the hands of certain parties and give you our unanimous opinion that in all particulars pertaining to this very difficult duty, you have exhibited both judgment and ability, and, in our estimation, are deserving the thanks of us (the interior residents of the Territory) most personally interested in and acquainted with such work as you have performed.[20]

In December 1883 Foelsche at last got away from the Territory on six months' leave. Charlotte and the girls, Mary and Emma, went with him and he expected 'something might turn up' while he was in Adelaide. He had thought of applying for a magistrate's post at Blinman in the north of South Australia but Lewis had talked him out of it, saying it was a miserable place. Foelsche's family would not hear of going there, preferring to stay in the Territory. He expected the railway from Palmerston to Pine Creek, when constructed, would result in great changes and 'put new life into the place'; if so, he would 'almost as soon stay here'. Foelsche had now been photographing developments, scenes and Aborigines in the Territory for ten years and in 1883 he was preparing plates to be sent to an exhibition in Calcutta. His paper on the Aborigines of North Australia had been read on his behalf to the Royal Society of South Australia in August 1881 and in that year he had sent notes on the 'Larrakia' of the Palmerston district and the Unalla tribe of Raffles Bay to E. M. Curr, who included them in his *The Australian Race*, published in four volumes in 1887. Foelsche's notes generally describe the appearance, distribution, numbers, customs and vocabularies of the two tribes; some suggest the effects of contact with Europeans on the Larakia and of the Malay trepang fishermen on the Unalla. There were 500 Larakia in 1881, according to Foelsche—100 men, 120 women, 150 youths of both sexes and 130 children—and the total had not decreased since the arrival of the Europeans. Twenty years previously smallpox, which they said had come from the east, had afflicted the Larakia. Six still alive, aged between twenty-five and forty, bore its marks. So many had been affected that the dead had been left unburied. Foelsche believed that the smallpox had been carried overland from Port Essington, where it had been introduced by the Macassans in 1866. He informed Curr that the Larakia practised cannibalism, normally eating children under two years of age. He had taken the roasted body of a child from some members of the tribe. Foelsche had nothing to say of the effects of European contact upon the Unalla. The same smallpox epidemic introduced by the Macassans in 1866 had ravaged the tribe, which called it *mea-mea*, and in 1881 four Unalla bearing the marks of the disorder were still alive.[21]

This was Foelsche's heyday, the peak of his career. He had returned to Adelaide as a veteran of northern colonization, a respected enforcer of the will of the government and an accepted expert on the Aborigines. He was probably the most urbane of the Palmerston pioneers and the most enduring. He represented sobriety, sensibility and diplomacy in a troubled province where not all South Australians were sure they belonged. Grave doubts about the wisdom of the whole colonial venture were beginning to arise in South Australia, where some doubted that the early promise of the Territory would be realized. While government residents and other officials came and went, Foelsche seemed to embody certainty, permanence and civilization. He was the tangible evidence of success in the face of unrealistic expections.

Chapter 7

Pastoral Invasion

While Aboriginal reaction to European intrusion in the Northern Territory until 1872 had sometimes been hostile, the frequency and the pattern of response rarely suggested determined resistance. There had been violent incidents, such as those on Melville Island, at Raffles Bay, Escape Cliffs, Attack Creek, the Woolna threats to Palmerston in 1870, the attacks on Lewis's party in the East Alligator region, the Barrow Creek incident and the murders of Johnstone, Walker and Ellis. These, however, appear to have resulted from traditional opposition to any strangers, black or otherwise, passing through tribal lands, from desire for European goods, and sometimes from vengeance for European transgression, often unintentional, of Aboriginal law. Only the Tiwi on Melville Island and the Warramanga at Attack Creek showed any sustained rejection of the intruders. Some people, such as the Cobourg Peninsula tribes and the Larakia in the Palmerston district, generally accepted, even welcomed, the Europeans. Organized attempts to drive them out of tribal lands were rare, probably because even the unfriendly tribes were little disturbed by the newcomers — except on the goldfields where the population of foreigners rose rapidly after 1872. Nonetheless, the foreigners there were confined to small pockets of land and, although some tribes, especially the Woolwonga, were affected, conflict was uncommon. The only other intruders in this period were telegraph construction workers and station staff, but they were confined to even smaller pockets than the miners, they made no demand on traditional resources except a little water and, because of Todd's instructions, soon constituted centres of supplementary resources for local peoples. The first decade of white settlement was one of localized antagonisms and hesitant but general adjustment by the newcomers and natives to each other. It is quite possible that, if there had been no change in existing conditions — apart from a gradual increase in the number of foreigners — the Aborigines and

Europeans might have reached a fairly amicable and lasting accommodation, in which the worst features of colonization might have been avoided. All this was changed by the coming of the pastoralists with their herds of cattle.

In 1878 Roderick Travers and his partner, Gibson, sent 1200 head of cattle overland from their Aramac station in western Queensland to stock Glencoe station which they were establishing on the Adelaide River. They were among the eastern pastoralists persuaded by A. W. Sergison to take up land in the Territory, following his visits to the Daly and Katherine districts. The party of seven including W. Travers, who was a nephew of Roderick Travers, was led by Nat Buchanan whose job was to ride ahead of the party and find water for each night's camp. Buchanan had explored western Queensland with William Landsborough in 1859–60; he had blazed a stock route from Port Denison (Bowen) to Bowen Downs in the Gulf Country, where he became the first manager; he had piloted cattle to the head of the Georgina River in the 1870s; and in 1877 he and Sam Croker had ridden from Rocklands station on the Georgina River, near the site of Camooweal, to explore the Barkly Tableland, and then to the overland telegraph line. On the 1878 trip Buchanan followed the coastal route taken by D'Arcy Uhr in 1872. From the Nicholson River they drove the cattle to Redbank Creek in the Territory, where one night Aborigines, 'who had been hovering around', killed a horse. Thirty or forty miles farther at Calvert River another horse was killed. From the top of some cliffs local people threatened the droving party, who became nervous. That night Buchanan fired a shot into the darkness around the camp, hitting a stump. At Snake Lagoon a third horse was speared but managed to survive. Now, as they moved westwards out of tribal territory, the attacks on stock ceased.

Buchanan's party crossed the McArthur River a few miles upstream from the future site of Borroloola and moved on to the Limmen Bight River, where it was decided that, because supplies were running low, Buchanan and Wattie Gordon should ride on to obtain supplies from the telegraph station at the Katherine River, which they reached on 15 November 1878. On 13 December all the party still at Limmen Bight River were mustering stock except Travers, a man named Bridson and some blacks who had been allowed into the camp. Bridson left to search for a missing horse and on his return two hours later found Travers dead. The young man had been bending over a dish mixing a damper when he was struck from behind with an axe, his head almost being severed. The axe had been stolen from the camp and most of the meagre supply of flour, some of the tools and the contents of some boxes had been taken. A day or two later the attackers attempted to rob Travers's grave but were driven off with riflefire. Next day the four whites still in the party followed their tracks intending to punish them, but they had taken refuge in nearby mountains. Just as Hugh Gordon (Wattie's brother), now in charge of the party at Limmen Bight River, was deciding to abandon the cattle and waggons and strike out for the telegraph line, Buchanan and Wattie Gordon arrived with rations and Sam Croker, who had joined them at Elsey Creek. Before resuming the drive, 'a punitive expedition was organized against Travers' murderers, who met with just retribution. At the same time a rifle and other stolen articles were recovered from the blacks' camps'.[1]

No details of this retribution are given in a book by Buchanan's son, Gordon. Quite possibly the severe action of the Aborignal people at Limmen Bight River was itself a retribution against Europeans in general for Uhr's aggressive style six years beforehand. Although John Millner had been killed at Attack Creek when he was a member of a party overlanding cattle, the circumstances in that case suggest a personal problem between Millner and his attacker over the Aboriginal woman Fanny. Bands of Warramanga had confronted his brother's party several times but their motives appear to have been to persuade the whites to leave their country. The Warramanga did not attack a Millner camp. On the other hand, Buchanan's party had not been harassed or confronted by the local people before the attack on Travers. No stock had been killed. No grass had been burnt in an attempt to drive them out. Nor had there been any tentative approach by people curious to understand the whites and perhaps obtain goods from them, as had usually happened on the route from South Australia. The killing of Travers suggests revenge by people with an old score to settle. Killings of whites in similar circumstances were soon to become a feature of Aboriginal–European contact along this route used by the Queenslanders bringing their cattle into the Territory.

In March 1879 the party was still stuck on the Roper River because of heavy rain but, with the passing of the wet season, they were able to press on and reached Glencoe a few months later without further incident and with increased cattle numbers due to births along the way. The Gordon brothers remained for a year on Glencoe, while Buchanan and Croker went south to explore country south-east of Daly Waters. In 1880 Nat Buchanan and his brother William established Wave Hill station in the Victoria River district and Croker became their manager. Next year Buchanan was hired by C. B. Fisher and Maurice Lyons to lead a drive of 20 000 head of cattle from Queensland to Glencoe, which they had bought from Travers and Gibson. Some 16 000 came from three stations near St George in southern Queensland, and the whole mob went along the same track as was used in the 1878 expedition. As Gordon Buchanan later observed, the cattle invasion was then in full swing. Another 5000 head of Fisher and Lyons cattle were on the trail to the Top End. Buchanan's 1881 expedition was successful and his son mentions no troubles with the Aborigines along the way. In 1883, the Gordon brothers joined Buchanan at Wave Hill station on the headwaters of Victoria River. Hard on the heels of Buchanan in 1878 had come Ernest Favenc, the Brisbane journalist who had been offered by his employer, Gresley Lukin, editor and part-owner of the *Queenslander*, leadership of a party to explore the country between Blackall on the Barcoo River and Port Darwin. Its intent was to find a route for a proposed transcontinental railway line and to ascertain the value of the country for agricultural purposes. Leaving Blackall in July 1878 they crossed Buchanan's tracks at a creek which Favenc named after the pioneer overlander, pressed on to the sheet of fresh water now called Anthony Lagoon and in January 1879 reached Powell Creek telegraph station.[2]

Favourable reports from the Buchanan and Favenc expeditions came at a time when Sydney pastoralists were being advised of the considerable advantages of establishing cattle and horse stations in the Northern Territory to supply Java, where cattle were said to fetch £40 a head, and India where there was expected to be a market in horses for the Indian Army. In 1879 Edward Price in Palmerston expected an early opening of a cattle trade with Java and Japan, while incoming pastoralists also pinned their hopes on India and Malaya. Land in Queensland had become expensive, whereas Territory land was still cheap. All this encouragement coincided with a revival of the Queensland economy in 1877–78, which stimulated investment in pastoral expansion in 1878 and 1881–82. Nearly 64 000 head of cattle entered the Territory from Queensland in 1882, 1884 and 1885. The Top End pastoral industry was in this way developed largely as an extension of the Queensland pastoral industry.

The movement from the south was not so large but some of the expeditions were just as spectacular. Alfred Giles, who had driven cattle northwards in 1873 and 1875 to supply the telegraph stations, was engaged in December 1877 by a wealthy South Australian pastoralist, Dr W. J. Browne, to take cattle to the Top End. The 2500 head were already on their way from Chowilla on the Murray River when Giles took charge of them at Browne's station, Booborowie, in the Canowie district. He reached the Katherine River, eight miles down-stream from the telegraph station, more than fourteen months later, and there established Springvale station. In his memoirs Giles does not say when he began the trek nor when it ended. He does claim that Springvale was the first cattle station in the Top End; as Buchanan was still stuck on the Roper in March 1879, he is probably correct. These were the first true cattle stations in the Top End — as distinct from John Lewis's buffalo-hunting enterprise on Cobourg Peninsula — and the third was Elsey, which was formed and stocked with 2700 head of cattle and 100 horses by Abraham Wallace in 1881. Giles later stocked Newcastle Waters, Delamere, Price's Creek and Flora stations for Browne.[3] Speculation in Northern Territory runs had been as common throughout the 1870s as had gambling in gold-mining shares. By 1877 there had been 1087 claims for pastoral land in the Territory but in that year only 102 were still held. Only some half-dozen were stocked in 1877, including the Central Australian runs, and in 1880 only six runs, totalling 2965 square miles, were established. By the end of 1886 there were 49 genuine stations, varying in size from 96 to 21 500 square miles.[4] Even though the number of stations was then small compared with Queensland and South Australia, the pastoral industry had arrived, and serious disruption of Aboriginal society in several large regions of the Territory had begun.

Aboriginal resistance to foreign invasion is difficult to quantify, largely because of the absence of known motives for individual attacks. For instance, an attack motivated simply by desire for European goods is not resistance and may be the opposite; the attackers may, like brigands, welcome passing victims. Also, violence arising out of misunderstandings over offered women or expected favours is not resistance. On the other hand, attempts to dissuade Europeans from passing through, camping in or settling on tribal territory is resistance. And, having resisted violently, a tribal group might also plunder any European possessions available. Indeed, resistance and profit from European presence often occurred together. While it would be fair to say that Aboriginal resistance increased markedly after the cattle invasion began, we should bear in mind the above qualifications when attempting to measure its strength.

In June 1881 two men, Brodie and McNamara, in a party droving cattle from Queensland, rode on ahead of the others with pack horses to Rosy Creek near Limmen Bight River, and camped. After breakfast next day, McNamara lay down and Brodie went after the horses. On returning to the camp, Brodie found McNamara speared through the head and all the rations gone. The drovers had to live on beef until they reached the next settlement. This incident was one of a series in that area and led Foelsche to write to the Acting Commissioner of Police, W. J. Peterswald, in Adelaide that all the murders of whites travelling overland from Queensland had been committed by the Limmen Bight Aborigines. In no case were the guilty ones known nor could they be identified. It was 'perfectly useless', he said, to do anything lawful to stop the murders. He claimed to have great influence over the Aborigines in the settled districts, who brought him any offender he wanted. But the Limmen Bight district was seven hundred miles from Palmerston and 'the dread of Police is unknown' there. He wrote:

The only thing that will in my opinion check these tribes from continuing their murderous attacks on travellers is to inflict severe chastisement if the Government will legalise it. If this is not done in all probability travellers will shoot the natives on the overland route which in my opinion makes matters worse. Measures such as I propose will be the most merciful in the end.[5]

Price sent to the minister a report from Foelsche in which the inspector said there was not the slightest chance of arresting the murderers of McNamara. There was no white witness to the murder and it would take five weeks for a police party to reach the area, by which time none of the stolen property would be left. Foelsche added: 'The whole will entail considerable expense without any good resulting unless I am empowered to punish the guilty tribe without trying to arrest the murderers which I am confident cannot be accomplished'. Price agreed with Foelsche. 'It is hopeless to get anyone convicted', he wrote, 'and the only punishment must be similar to the manner in which men of war punish savage natives in the South Seas . . . If the government will sanction the summary punishment of the guilty tribe it will be a severe lesson'. Price quoted the advice of Wallace, founder of Elsey station, who had just travelled with cattle through the Limmen Bight area. Wallace said that white troopers would be of no use in such a case as McNamara's murder, and he urged the adoption of a force of 'regular native constables', as done in Queensland.[6] The minister was John Langdon Parsons, who was not persuaded by these arguments. He telegraphed Price that nothing could be done.

The first cattleman killed on a station in the Territory was Duncan Campbell on Elsey in 1882, as distinct from young Travers who was *en route* with cattle. First word of Campbell's death was brought to Elsey in July by Sam Croker, saying a native had told him that Campbell, who was with two Queensland Aboriginal stockmen mustering cattle sixty miles east of Elsey, had been murdered. The two Queensland stockmen were said to be still alive but were to be murdered at a corroboree. The persons responsible were believed to be now at Mole's Hill, home of the people who had attacked Johnstone's party in 1875. Reporting this to Adelaide, Price said he had directed Corporal George Montagu and a constable to start at once in pursuit. The result of this police action is not known. A man named Bourke had arrived at Elsey, having met another named Hann returning to Queensland. Aborigines had attacked Hann who had been forced to fire, repelling them with great difficulty. Bourke believed that these people had killed Campbell. Price urged that legislation be passed to try Aboriginal offenders in the Northern Territory and, if found guilty, to execute them at the scene of the murder. Outrages by blacks were increasing, he said; they seemed to think they could only be imprisoned. Montagu and his party apprehended a party of Queensland Aborigines on whom they found Campbell's gun and blanket. One named Peeri told Montagu that Paddy had confessed the murder to him and that a Territory Aborigine named Charley had assisted. Paddy was committed at Katherine for trial for murder. Charley was shot dead by police near Chambers Creek in October 1885. Mounted Constable Cornelius Power and trackers, accompanied by J. A. Palmer of Elsey station, located Charley with the assistance of Goggle Eye, the man who had seen Augustus Gregory and his party of explorers arrive on the Elsey Creek in 1856. Goggle Eye had been compelled to pilot the police party to Charley's camp and identify him. Charley refused to surrender but threw a spear at Palmer, a boomerang at Power and a woomera at one of the trackers. The trackers then shot him dead. Paddy was tried at the Circuit Court in Palmerston in December 1884 but was reprieved after giving evidence against Charley.[7] Price's advice on trying capital cases in the Territory was again rejected and local jurisdiction in such cases not permitted until Mr Justice T. K. Pater was sent to Palmerston after the Daly River murders in September 1884.

In May 1884 John Costello began transferring his pastoral activities from Queensland to the Northern Territory. He already had Lake Nash on the Georgina River, a few miles west of the border, and had recently bought leases to new runs stretching from the McArthur River to north of the Roper. He sold his properties in the Emu Park district near Rockhampton and moved his stock via Burketown, where he encountered the Duracks already on their way from Thylungera in south-western Queensland to the Kimberleys in Western Australia. At Skeleton Creek, Costello's party experienced the same hostility met by Nat Buchanan and most other overlanders since then. Two horses were speared at night. Next night, while keeping watch, Costello fired at someone moving in the dark and heard a cry, but did not know whether he had hit anyone; nevertheless, the Aborigines did not return. He formed a station on the Limmen Bight River, eight miles upstream from the crossing point on the track, and called it Valley of Springs. In his first wet season the Aborigines took advantage of the sodden state of the land and attacked cattle which could not get away from them. The results were a disastrous loss of stock. Although they attacked many times, Costello and his men never saw the marauders. Many beasts were speared to be eaten, many died from wounds and some appeared to have been slaughtered for 'sport and devilment'. Many small mobs were cut out and then 'scattered so far and wide that it was impossible to muster them again'. No attacks were made on the rough homestead built at Limmen Bight River. In the dry season the Aborigines destroyed the pastures of Valley of Springs by a succession of bushfires. Sometimes a 'score' of these were blazing at the one time and often Costello and his men had to battle to save the homestead from fire. It is not clear from Michael Costello's biography of his father which tribes were responsible for this resistance. According to Norman B. Tindale, Valley of Springs was on the border of the Wadere and Mara tribal lands and near that of the Ngewin. Whoever they were, their attitude towards these strangers who had 'sat down' on their land seemed to change with the arrival of Costello's wife and children by chartered schooner from Rockhampton. They made their first approach, a small group camping in a gorge near the homestead. Costello had fenced this at both ends to form a stockyard and in this compound the Aborigines held nightly ceremonies.[8]

A big stockman at Valley of Springs, Jim Ledgerwood, a man of 'simple and trusting disposition', on occasion went unarmed to these 'native concerts'. One night at full moon the local people were 'most cordial' in their welcome of him and carried no weapons. Ledgerwood was standing against the wall of the gorge watching a dance, when some of the tribe beckoned him to come closer. As he was about to do so he looked up and saw four men with spears raised. He sprinted back to the homestead dodging spears. A day or two later Jack McCoy, travelling alone from the McArthur River to Limmen Bight River, was speared in his night camp, decapitated and robbed. Two fencers, Watson and Bird, engaged by Costello were attacked on a new station, Wickham Park on the Wickham River. Watson escaped but, according to information obtained from Aborigines later, Bird's body was thrown into the crocodile-infested river; no trace of him was found. The attackers robbed the fencers' camp, taking food and cooking utensils, axes, tomahawks and knives. Beyond the immediate coastal range, on the headwaters of the Limmen Bight River, Amos Brothers and Broad had formed Broadmere station, staffed by two white stockmen and a Chinese cook, as an outpost of their McArthur River station. One day the stockmen were confronted by a large group of Aborigines who attacked, spearing a horse and then its rider. Both galloped away but the wounded man fell. The other had to abandon him, riding for Broadmere where he picked up the cook and fled to McArthur River. There the manager organized a party, which went to Broadmere and found the mutilated body of the fallen stockman. The attackers had disappeared. A lone traveller, who wanted to preach the gospel to the Aborigines, was killed near Valley of Springs homestead by Murrimicki, described by Michael Costello as 'a treacherous and bloodthirsty old warrior who let no white man pass who could be killed with safety'; being something of a strategist, he always chose his point of attack near a favourable ground for retreat.[9]

In September 1884 D'Arcy Uhr, who still made his living droving stock from Queensland into the Top End, said the attacks by blacks were getting worse each trip he made. During his last journey the Aborigines rushed the camp of a man named Fraser, killing him and one of his 'black boys' and leaving a second 'boy' for dead. When he heard of the attack, Uhr went out to muster his horses and found that five of his best hacks had been killed; the blacks then attacked his camp. Several murders had been committed in this area and the perpetrators had not been punished. In November 1884 two pastoralists, Creaghe and Hay, were attacked on the Hodgson and Roper Rivers. The blacks had set the whole country afire, they said, and they asked for native police to protect the four stations formed on the coast and 20 000 head of cattle *en route* between Burketown and Elsey for Territory runs. J. L. Parsons, now government resident in Palmerston, commented to the minister, R. C. Baker, that the low rents received for pastoral country would not enable him to provide police all over the Territory, but a station at Elsey Creek appeared urgent. In December 1885 Stephen Payne of the Calvert Downs Cattle Company wrote to the then minister, J. A. Cockburn, that its station in the Gulf Country had been stocked at very heavy outlay and under adverse circumstances. He was discouraged to learn that the Aborigines were sweeping away the company's cattle and imperilling the lives of its employees. 'If the natives are not checked we will be forced to abandon the station, causing the loss of many thousands of pounds', he said. Payne suggested that a police station be established at the Robinson River or some adjacent station. Cockburn simply ordered that Payne's letter be filed. The township of Borroloola had been proclaimed in September 1885 and early next year the residents were complaining of the lack of police protection. A surveyor, W. K. Cuthbertson, reported to Parsons that the district was the 'resort of all the scum of North Australia', who stole clothing hung out to dry, got men drunk and then robbed them of their cheques, took the first horses they came across and killed what beef they required. 'These men are also very cruel to the natives', he said. The blacks along the McArthur River were treacherous, Cuthbertson added, the storekeeper at Borroloola, William McLeod, having suffered several losses to them while bringing stores the forty miles up the river from its mouth:

On the last occasion they stole about three hundred pounds worth of drapery etc and afterwards they were all seen going about in new Bedford cord trousers, tweed coats, new shirts, rugs, towels etc. One who had been carrying water and firewood for my camp for a few days, stole in one night and took a Snider carbine, 100 rounds of Cartridges, ½ lb. of lampblack and a gridiron, evidently intending to go and live on fresh beef for a while, but [I] don't think he will make much use of it. They also stole some rifles from Mr McLeod at the same time as the clothes.

Cuthbertson said that the Aborigines on the Barkly Tableland, however, were quite the reverse and gave no trouble.[10]

By 1888 the situation along the lower Roper had become so serious that, under pressure from squatters in the McArthur River–Limmen Bight areas, a police station was established at Leichhardt's Bar. Murder, horse and cattle killing by the Aborigines, and horse and cattle stealing by whites, were common. Another was requested for Anthony Lagoon for the same reasons, but not granted.[11] During the great drought and economic troubles of the 1890s John Costello abandoned all his Top End properties, transferring the stock back to Lake Nash and losing more than a quarter of a million pounds. His son does not specifically state that Aboriginal aggression was a cause of this retreat. McArthur River station was stocked with 14 000 head of cattle in 1883 and in no subsequent year was a greater number sold than branded, while in several years none was sold. Yet by the beginning of 1902 the herd did not exceed 10 000; the government resident attributed the decrease almost entirely to Aboriginal depredations. Such attacks did influence decisions to abandon stations—Tempe Downs in the Centre, Frew River north-east of Barrow Creek and Florida in eastern Arnhem Land—but the number so affected was small. The chief reasons for relinquishing stocked runs in the 1890s were the economic conditions. Rather than threatening the Northern Territory pastoral industry with extinction, as implied by some commentators, special factors combined to force the Aborigines, with their cheap labour, to save the industry from total collapse at that time.

The first magistrate located in Borroloola, Gilbert McMinn, arrived in 1886, when it had achieved a reputation as a rowdy town. The arrival of the first policemen, Mounted Constables Michael Donegan and William Curtis, on 4 October appeared to have a sobering effect on the town, leading McMinn to observe that 'there is not a quieter or more orderly township in South Australia'. Outside the town, however, the frontier conflict continued. Alfred Toms, master of the cutter *Smuggler* had been killed on 12 July that year by Aborigines who had stolen aboard the ship at night while moored off Vanderlin Island at the mouth of the McArthur River. The crew had been sleeping below when, hearing a noise on deck, Toms had put his head up through a hatchway only to be 'tomahawked'. The others managed to fight off the attackers. Only a few days beforehand, John Morrison had been speared on board another cutter, *Alice Gray*, near the Robinson River. Noting these events soon after arriving in Borroloola, Donegan, who was the senior officer, wrote that the blacks were said to be very troublesome on the Robinson, McArthur and Calvert Rivers. A few days later still, Donegan was asking Foelsche for two additional constables, because the blacks were 'very numerous and troublesome and have already killed men, horses and cattle'. His request was refused. Another sailor was murdered in May 1888. Captain Francis Marrin of Townsville, master of the *Spry*, invited some of the Aborigines, who appeared when his ship arrived at Carrington's Landing at the mouth of the McArthur River, aboard his ship, gave them tobacco and asked them to 'make him a present of a gin'. Passengers on the ship cautioned him against the blacks but he took the ship's boat and rowed up the river looking for timber to use as ballast. Immediately a black followed in a canoe and others ran along the bank. Passengers and crew whistled and called to Marrin, urging him to return, but he took no notice and soon was out of sight. He was never seen again. Donegan learned later from local Aborigines that Marrin had landed but was immediately attacked and his body thrown into the river where, apparently, it was taken by crocodiles. His boat was taken by the blacks.

There were troubles also inland. In the same month, Donegan was reporting that the Aborigines were 'very numerous here & treacherous, and it seems the more civilized they get the more treacherous they become'. He said that 'blackboys are daily running away from the Cattle Stations and joining their tribes', who they instructed to kill cattle and men, 'which they seem to be doing pretty freely lately'. Donegan told Foelsche that a number of cattle and horse stealers had been camped for the past six months on the Queensland border. These men, he believed, would soon start stealing again on a large scale, 'as they have no other means of living'. To cope with the savage blacks and lawless whites of the district, another constable and a force of trackers should be stationed at Borroloola. Trackers were provided but one of them, Jack, soon deserted. He did not, however, make for his own country but went to Calvert Downs station where in August 1888 he was working. Donegan believed that Jack had been enticed there by the manager, a man named Gorman, alleged by Donegan to have been in league with the cattleduffers. Gorman had induced Jack to desert in order to weaken the police strength at Borroloola and to assist the outlaws, he said.[12]

Life for a policeman in the Territory was hard at any time, but at Borroloola it was probably harder than normal because of the lawlessness and endemic disease. In April 1887 Foelsche saw a report in the Palmerston *North Australian* that Donegan's horse, Ruination, had been the star of the New Year race meeting, and had 'fleeced the multitude at odds of 20 to 1'. It was further alleged that Donegan had bet fifty pounds on his own horse. Foelsche accused Donegan of impropriety. Donegan was indignant, telling his superior that horse racing was the 'only source of amusement we have in a place where we live in a chronic state of fever & ague & suffer occasionally from famine'. In January 1888 Donegan requested a transfer to South Australia from 1 July, when his three-year term in the Territory would expire. He said that since he had arrived at Borroloola he had suffered severely because of fever and for nine months of the previous year had been almost unable to move about. He feared that a repetition of last year's illness would be fatal for him. Later, he wrote that Curtis had been 'very little good' and his replacement, Mounted Constable Biddell, had been laid up with fever almost continuously since arriving, unable to perform any duty. No magistrate was in the town at that time, McMinn having become acting government resident in Palmerston; all official duties, including customs-collection, had fallen on Donegan's shoulders. As a result he had seldom been able to get out of the town. When he had taken a party of volunteers down the McArthur to search for Marrin, he had had to leave more than £700 in customs levies, and some police horses, at the mercy of anyone who came along. A murder had been reported at the Calvert River but it was 'useless myself & tracker trying to do anything among a lot of savage blacks'. Donegan offered to stay after his term had expired so that Biddell could be transferred sooner. Biddell's replacement, Wheatley, arrived on 19 August feeling unwell and next day it was clear he had fever. His condition slowly worsened and Donegan decided to send him back to Palmerston by the next boat, but on 4 September, while Donegan and another newcomer, Mounted Constable Edward Smith, were absent from the police station, Wheatley cut his own throat with a razor, dying next day. As a result, Donegan had to remain in Borroloola until the next mail boat arrived.[13]

The use of trackers at Borroloola was never satisfactory. Another one, Fred, who came from Newcastle Waters, ran away in mid-1889. Lance-Corporal Cornelius Power, now in charge of the police at Borroloola, reported that Fred had run away without any provocation and had taken two blankets, a tomahawk and clothing supplied to him. The remaining tracker was recruited from the local tribe and Power considered it 'positively unsafe to travel with him, as he may at any time lead or entice the bush blacks to attack us when asleep'. At Power's request, Foelsche sent a tracker from the Palmerston district, but the problem of Aboriginal depredations on the stations was not solved, cattle being killed on every station in the district. In December 1889, Power noted that large numbers of blacks were coming into Borroloola, some having been there for six months. He suggested that the government send to W. G. Stretton — the former trooper who had arrived in the Territory with Foelsche in 1870 and was now sub-collector of customs and sub-protector of Aborigines at Borroloola — a 'good supply of rations and other articles usually issued in South Australia to Aborigines'. If these were issued to the old, the sick, and women with children, the Aborigines would be induced to remain about the town, which would 'materially lessen the annoyance to station holders by the natives'. He believed that this would reduce the Aborigines' hostility and that their contact with Europeans in the town would tend to civilize them. At the same time it would give the police a better opportunity to supervise and protect them.[14]

While investors and speculators had begun to select runs from the Northern Territory map as early as March 1864 when the first land sales were held, the first permanent pastoral settlement in Central Australia did not begin until 1876, when Owen Springs and Undoolya were declared to be stocked. The original application for Undoolya was made in 1872 by E. M. ('Ned') Bagot, pioneer pastoralist in the Kapunda district and builder of the southern section of the overland telegraph line; the first two leases in the Centre, for Undoolya, were issued on 14 June 1876 to Andrew Tennant and John Love. The next four leases, for Owen Springs, were issued to Joseph Gilbert soon afterwards. Undoolya and Owen Springs are the oldest continuously occupied runs in the Territory. In 1877 Glen Helen and Henbury stations were stocked and the Hermannsburg mission station, which also ran cattle, was founded; Mount Burrell was stocked with sheep in 1879. In the same year the government surveyor, Charles Winneke, discovered gold at Arltunga, at the eastern end of the MacDonnell Ranges. Miners were not interested in this field until alluvial gold was found there in 1887 and even then it was slow to develop, the first battery not being erected until 1898. The first miners in the Centre were more interested in garnets, thought at first to be rubies, which the surveyor, David Lindsay, had discovered in 1883. Here Aboriginal women were drawn into the European economy — and the personal relationships, which drovers' 'boys' had experienced already. At a field of 'Australian rubies' at Castle Hills in the MacDonnell Ranges in 1888, some ruby pickers had Aboriginal women companions, whose rations were an additional charge upon the company employing the men, the Hatton Garden Gem Company. Constable J. J. East, who reported in that year on the MacDonnell Ranges for the minister controlling the Northern Territory, described the work. A white picker would drag out shingle in a creek, sift out the small particles and scatter the larger ones before the 'squatting form of his sable partner'; some of the women developed 'surprising acumen in distinguishing the better stones'.[15]

By September 1884 thirty-two pastoral stations were operating in the Territory, running more than 96 000 cattle and more than 26 000 sheep, but only a handful of these were in the Centre. In 1884 both Erldunda and Barrow Creek stations were stocked. Next year Tempe Downs station, south-west of Alice Springs, was formed by John Lewis, Charles Chewings and S. and John Drew. Later they were joined by D. W. H. Patterson, W. Liston and J. Shakes, and in 1889 the seven partners formed the Tempe Downs Pastoral Company. Lewis, Liston and Shakes had become connected in 1888 through the creation of the joint-stock company, Bagot, Shakes and Lewis Limited, formed after the death of 'Ned' Bagot. This interlocking of pastoral interests was to assist Lewis and his associates in securing government protection for Tempe Downs when Aboriginal resistance to the cattle invasion developed. This protection may, however, have provoked some of the violence it was intended to control. Resistance was stronger, more damaging and lasted longer on Tempe Downs than on any other station in the Centre.

The one tribe which offered consistent, uncompromising resistance to European intrusion, from first contact with the Dutch until the end of the nineteenth century, was the Tiwi of Melville and Bathurst Islands. White settlers occasionally expressed interest in obtaining runs on the islands, but each time they did, reports from the government resident of the time were most discouraging. Late in 1881 Price was asked for a report on the extent of water supply, vegetation, timber, landings,

stone and lime to be found on Melville Island, together with estimates of
numbers of natives and cattle. He replied quite firmly that he was unable
to obtain the information sought. The Aborigines, he said, were so
hostile and fierce that no party, however well armed, had ever penetrated
any distance on the island. Both his predecessors, Bloomfield Douglas
and G. B. Scott, had failed to do so. The Aborigines, tall, powerful men,
attacked both alone and in numbers and had been able to prevent the
landing of any whites. Even the mainland people were afraid to attempt
to land there. An armed force of fifteen to twenty men would be
necessary to exterminate the inhabitants and gain possession of Melville
Island.[16] In 1895 the buffalo-hunters, Joe and Harry Cooper, set up a
buffalo-hunting camp there; when Harry was killed two years later Joe
was forced to flee with two kidnapped Tiwi women. In 1900 Joe Cooper
returned with the women, a strong force of Iwaidja from Cobourg
Peninsula, horses and abundant supplies. He succeeded in establishing a
permanent camp on the island, which remained until Father F. X. Gsell
established a mission on neighbouring Bathurst Island in 1911.

Other people along the northern and eastern coasts of Arnhem Land
were equally hostile but less successful in preventing European
penetration. In 1884 Florida station was established on the Goyder
River by John Macartney, one of the wealthiest of the Queensland
pastoralists. Aboriginal attacks of the kind suffered by the pastoralists
in the Limmen Bight region were a constant problem at Florida until
Macartney abandoned it in 1893. Gordon Buchanan remarked of it
that: 'Hostile blacks and sour, unsuitable country wiped out most of
the cattle and scattered the remainder far and wide'.[17] This was certainly
the period of the greatest Aboriginal resistance to European intrusion,
but it is a mistake to attribute too much to this resistance. Arnhem
Land was so unsuitable for cattle that even without Aboriginal hostility
it would have been abandoned. Even by this time resistance was waning
and, although Aboriginal violence continued in the Victoria River
district and south-east of Alice Springs, overwhelming circumstances
now favoured the intruders rather than the original people of the
Northern Territory grasslands.

The most visible contemporary evidence of Aboriginal resistance
to the pastoralists was violence, but of course this was not its only
form. The chief reaction after initial contact was generally an
accommodation, in which Aborigines accepted their presence and their
goods rather than be driven out of their homelands, and the Europeans
used Aboriginal services, such as labour, knowledge of local resources
and the sexual favours of their women. It was an inequitable
arrangement, in which the whites had most of the advantages. This was
non-violent resistance, in which Aborigines made concessions in order
to preserve essential elements of their culture. Unfortunately, because
of the lack of reliable evidence from that period, it is not possible to
show in any detail the full measure of this non-violent resistance.

Chapter 8

The Daly River Murders

The murder of four whites on the Daly River in September 1884 was one of the worst cases of violence against Europeans in the history of the Northern Territory. The lack of control of the police and others sent to the scene of the crime, the violence of their actions, the reaction of the public, including the press, in Adelaide to this severity, and the mishandling of the subsequent trial demonstrate, more than any other single event, the failure of South Australian Aboriginal policy and practice in the Northern Territory. In particular, the incident shows the wide gap between southern civilized attitudes and northern frontier attitudes.

The copper lode at Mount Haywood on the Daly River had been discovered in 1883 and five Europeans were working it when one of them, Harry Houschildt, left on 15 August 1884 for Rum Jungle. By 3 September nothing had been heard of him and the men at the mine had started to become anxious but, even so, took no special care for their own safety. On that morning Johannes Noltenius, John Landers and Henry Roberts were working at the face of the lode and Thomas Schollert, the Danish cook, was attending to kitchen chores. The party had been assisted for some time by members of the so-called Woolwonga tribe on the edge of whose territory the mine was located. Suddenly Landers cried out, attacked by eight or nine Aborigines. Four others were with Roberts as he worked and, as he jumped aside to escape attack, he was struck on the right temple and lost consciousness. Noltenius, seeing Landers speared, dropped into a cutting and ran for the camp but was speared before he could get there. Regaining consciousness Roberts, who was apparently left for dead, went to the store to get arms and then extracted the spear from Landers's side and most of the one in Noltenius's side. Both were jagged wooden spears and difficult to remove. Schollert was dead in the kitchen. Seeing they had lost the initiative when Roberts obtained weapons, the Woolwonga had retired. That day Roberts, Landers and Noltenius left the camp for

Glencoe, the Daly River cattle station of Fisher and Lyons, but Landers could walk only four hundred yards and had to be left behind. Noltenius managed to walk eight or nine miles before Roberts was forced to leave him by a billabong. Pressing on, Roberts encountered an Aborigine known as Bob Patrick, who had left the mine with Houschildt and was now leading two of his horses. Patrick told Roberts that Houschildt was now lying sick at Poett's landing on the Daly and had sent him back with the horses. Roberts rode the rest of the way to the station, accompanied by Patrick. When they reached it, he sent Patrick back on one of the horses with food and other supplies for Noltenius and requested him to remain there until assistance arrived — which apparently he did not. The station manager, named Sachse, another white man and a station black went to Noltenius's assistance, soon followed by two Europeans from the Howley mining camp who had arrived at the station. Sachse and the others found Noltenius and Landers dead. They buried Noltenius where they found him but Schollert's body had been thrown into the mine workings and could not be retrieved, so it was covered with mullock and rock. The camp had been plundered.

On 7 September, James Love, a stockman on the Daly River station, rode into Yam Creek and reported the murders to Corporal George Montagu, officer in charge of the police on the goldfields. With Mounted Constable James Foster Smith and the goldfields surgeon, Dr Percy Wood, Montagu went to the Daly River station, interviewed Roberts, whose wound was dressed, then rode to the mine. Montagu found that Landers had been speared and shot with a pistol. Next day three constables arrived by the steamer *Palmerston*, on which Dr Wood returned to the capital. The police rounded up nine horses belonging to Houschildt and took them to the Daly River station. With one of the policemen and a Queensland Aborigine employed at the station, Montagu set out to find Houschildt but failed at first and so returned to the cattle station. Until this time Montagu and his parties had not seen one Aborigine. Next day two Woolwonga arrived with a note from a stockman living at Jigjigla; from one of them, Tommy, Montagu learned that Houschildt had been murdered by a man named Nammy. Accompanied by two troopers and his informant, whom they secured by means of a trace chain around his neck and handcuffs to prevent escape, Montagu went to the east side of the Haywood Range. On 19 September they found Houschildt's body by a creek, wrapped in a mosquito net and almost entirely buried in sand. Apparently he had been attacked when asleep, speared and then shot with his own revolver. After burying the body, the police proceeded up the Daly, crossed to the south side and came upon an Aboriginal camp. On seeing the police, Aborigines fled into scrub. 'As they did not stop when called on, they were fired on, with what result is not known', Montagu later reported. In the camp the police found European goods, supposed to have been taken from the mining camp. Next day the police came upon another camp; the Aborigines fled and they too were fired upon. At this stage, the informant Tommy escaped. Back at the station, Montagu found that a party of whites led by a man named Masson were preparing to 'go out'. On 24 and 25 September the police returned to the Howley and Yam Creek.[1]

The government resident, John Langdon Parsons, who had succeeded Price in May 1884, thought the Woolwonga were assisted by a few Woggites. Tribal names used by early Europeans in the Territory were often incorrect. There is no Woolwonga tribe although there is a Wogait tribe at the mouth of the Daly River. The term Woolwonga appears to have used by the first whites to cover several tribes along or near the Daly River. The Aborigines working at the Mount Haywood copper mine, if in their own territories, were either Pongaponga or Ngolokwanga. Parsons informed the minister, R. C. Baker, that after inquiring into the matter he had concluded that the miners were victims of over-kindness, over-confidence and a want of distrust of the blacks indicated by their not always carrying firearms 'which is the white man's only safety and protection in life'. Parsons claimed that the miners were kind to the blacks in their gifts of food and tobacco — but not liquor, because they had none — and that they lent the blacks guns to shoot game for them. They were completely off their guard. The Aborigines had lured Houschildt away with a story of another big copper lode, offering to show it to him, but had killed him on the first night away from the camp. Referring to southern criticism of subsequent actions by the police and civilians, Parsons said those far from the scene without knowledge of the miners or the circumstances had been indulging in 'mealy mouthed philanthropies' about what had been done and what ought not to have been done. No doubt there had been many outrages upon black men and women but there was no suspicion in the case of the five copper-miners. The sole cause of the murders, Parsons said, was desire for loot and for 'tucker', the constant sight of which 'excited an irresistable passion to possess and eat it'.[2]

Parsons's reaction to the Daly Creek murders was typical of a newcomer from the south who immediately identified with the Europeans for whom he was responsible and not the Aborigines of whom he knew nothing. His attitude was to change with acquaintance. Born in Cornwall in 1837, Parsons had studied for the Baptist ministry in London and visited South Australia in 1863 before moving on to New Zealand, where for a few years he was in charge of a church in Dunedin. He returned to South Australia and served as Baptist minister at North Adelaide before forsaking the ministry for a commercial career. He entered parliament in 1878 as one of the representatives for Encounter Bay before switching to the seat of North Adelaide in 1881, when he became Minister of Education in J. C. Bray's first government. He was also appointed minister controlling the Northern Territory, which he visited in 1882, apparently being fired with enthusiasm for the province because, when his term expired in 1884, he was appointed government resident.

Parsons had sent Foelsche in the *Palmerston* on 21 September to meet Montagu at Owston's Landing on the Daly. A party of Larakia had been sent a week before from Palmerston in the hope that they would pick up clues. Parsons's intention was to capture 'old men' of the guilty tribe and force them to identify the killers. Foelsche failed to meet Montagu's party which had turned back to Yam Creek but, with assistance from two parties of surveyors sworn in as special constables, and the *Palmerston*'s crew, Foelsche captured five Aborigines, two of whom were later identified by Roberts as being present during the attack. It was claimed that one, Long Legged Charley, had been connected with every outrage by Aborigines in the Territory. Foelsche used a ruse to make the capture, informing Aborigines in the mine area that he was a sugar and coffee planter who was offering work to Aborigines. He said he had plenty of 'tucker', 'bacca' and possibly grog on his ship anchored downstream. This drew Charley and several others. Foelsche then gave Charley a letter to Captain Carrington on the steamer, supposedly authorizing him to issue rations and tobacco. One of the surveying party leaders, W. K. Cuthbertson, even took Charley, Tommy and Jacky in a survey boat to the steamer. Immediately they went aboard they were clapped in irons. Subsequently Foelsche arrested two others, Jimmy and Daly. All five were taken to Port Darwin in the *Palmerston* and charged in the magistrates court. Tommy, Jacky and Daly were committed for trial for the murder of Noltenius, Landers and Schollert; and Charley, Jacky and Tommy for the murder of Houschildt. The fifth, Jimmy, was remanded for a fortnight on both charges while more evidence was being gathered.

In the meantime two parties of teamsters had been attacked at Argument Flat near Rum Jungle. Charles Bridson with his mate, Charles Maliff, was taking a waggonload of supplies to the goldfields, while George Stanley was returning with an empty waggon to Southport. In an early report to Adelaide, Parsons said that towards sundown on 26 September Aborigines came to the whites' camp and obtained flour. At about 9 p.m. two Aborigines went to the Rum Jungle Hotel. One of them was Neddy Lewis, who had travelled with John Lewis to Port Essington, and the other, named Louis, had worked at the Powell Creek telegraph station. Both were Woolwonga. Louis asked how many whites were in Rum Jungle and neighbourhood. He said a large body of blacks had gathered on the Finniss River, three or four miles away, and that food was scarce in the bush. He and Neddy Lewis left the hotel at about 11 p.m. During the night Bridson heard natives about the camp but did not intervene. Early next day he and the others rounded up their horses and, returning to camp, noticed spears planted in the bush. They got their firearms ready. Bridson had been present when Walker was killed on the Blue Mud Bay expedition, and may have been in Buchanan's expedition when young Travers was killed, and so had reason to be apprehensive. While the three teamsters were at breakfast, about thirty blacks suddenly rushed towards them, seized concealed spears and began attacking. The whites ran behind their waggons and began firing, dispersing the attackers, who left behind many spears, a rug and watch supposed to have belonged to Houschildt and some knives and forks believed to have come from the copper mine. After the affray, Bridson and his mate proceeded up country and at Adelaide River Bridson told J. A. G. Little that Louis, Neddy Lewis, a man named Boco Jacky and three others unknown to him had been shot. Stanley proceeded to Southport where he reported the matter to the police.[3]

Parsons advised that the best way to deal with the five arrested for the Daly River murders would be to bring them to a speedy trial and, if found guilty, to execute them as near to the scene of the murders as possible.[4] This, he told the minister, would deter many a savage from crime. To execute them in the gaol would lead others to conclude that they had escaped and 'whitefeller could not catchee'. The two recent outrages expressed the Aborigines' 'irresistable love of plunder' and also their perception that their hunting grounds were going to be taken from them and their old, free, nomadic life rendered impossible. This was a strange coupling of assumed motives but his second one was the first official recognition of the process which was now seriously affecting the Aborigines of the Top End — the depletion of natural resources was forcing Aborigines to take desperate measures to obtain food. Louis and Neddy Lewis may well have correctly intimated the reason for the Argument Creek attack when they said food was short in the bush. Both the Daly River and Glencoe stations, with their thousands of head of cattle, were only a few miles away.

Parsons reported that although 'deep and strong' feelings were expressed by the European community in the Territory following the Daly River outrage, the community never 'lost its head'. In ambiguous words he said it was unanimously felt by the community that 'all that could be done must be done', but that there was no clamour for 'wholesale slaughter and reprisals'. The Duke of Manchester, who was twenty miles from the copper mine a day after the murders, had said at a dinner at the government residence before he left Palmerston that no 'rage of revenge' had been shown, 'but simply the desire to teach the natives that they cannot perpetrate outrages of that kind on the whites with impunity'.[4] When Parsons wrote this on 1 October 1884 he did not have the reports of Montagu and others — another policeman named Wilson and two civilians, Phil Saunders and Augustus Lucannus.

Following the attack on the teamsters, Montagu led a small police party to Rum Jungle, arriving on 30 September, and found the remains of five Aborigines, which had been burnt by troopers Wilson and Summers. Finding that Saunders's party of civilians had gone westwards, Montagu crossed the Adelaide River and rode eastwards without seeing Aborigines, then northwards to Marakai cattle station where he learned that Woolwonga had been threatening the Europeans there. Work had been suspended and the manager had gone to Southport for assistance. The police, however, saw only a few friendly Woolna who were working on the run. Hearing that a large group of Aborigines coming from the direction of the Daly had crossed the main road near the Howley and most likely had headed for the ranges along the Mary River, 'a great place of resort for blacks', Montagu and his troopers rode up the Mary past Mount Bundey. While on the Mary plain they destroyed an Aboriginal camp, implements and spears, but did not see the occupants. From its junction with the Mary they followed the MacKinlay River to Mount Wells, and on the afternoon of 11 October came upon Aborigines encamped on a lagoon on its east side. The following extract from Montagu's report is the only clear indication by him that he and his men killed Aborigines in the aftermath of the Daly River and Argument Flat incidents:

The women and children ran away, but the men, taking their spears and woomeras, retreated to the water. Some of them were recognized as known Woolwongas — Bob Murray, Charley Brooks, etc. One of them, while in shallow water, was in the act of throwing a double wooden spear at Mounted Constable MacDonald, and it was only his quickness in firing that saved his life. A spear passed through the top of Mounted Constable Cox's singlet, and grazed his neck. Three men managed to get away at first, as Mounted Constable Luck could not get his horse to follow them, as it would not leave the others. None of those who took to the water are known to have got away. It is supposed that there were between twenty and thirty men in the camp.[5]

The police found a large variety of European articles in the camp, including some knives and handkerchiefs, a chisel later identified by Roberts and a knitted jacket like one owned by Schollert. Also in the camp they found a large portion of a young bullock, supposed to have come from the herd on Glencoe station. Montagu's party continued up the MacKinlay and returned to Yam Creek on 14 October. Reporting three days later to Foelsche in Palmerston, Montagu wrote that he did not know what the other parties had done, 'but I believe that the natives have received such a lesson this time as will exercise a salutory effect over the survivors in the time to come'. Then he remarked: 'One result of this expedition has been to convince me of the superiority of the Martini-Henry rifle, both for accuracy of aim and quickness of action'.[6] In the public outcry which followed release of Montagu's report next year, even the defenders of 'condign punishment' agreed this last remark was most injudicious. Late in October 1884 Montagu asked to be transferred to South Australia, saying he had been in the Territory eleven years. Foelsche recommended transfer.

Constable Wilson failed to catch up with the other parties on the Daly, so he went to Argument Flat and found the bodies of two Aborigines who had been shot in the attack on the teamsters. Saunders had nothing to report except that he did not think Woolna or Alligator Rivers people had been involved in the murders. Lucannus, a former Queensland Native Police officer, led seventeen white civilians and 'two blackboys', which split into three groups. On 5 October one of these groups, led by Lucannus, attacked an Aboriginal camp, dispersed the occupants and destroyed their spears; later they destroyed spears in another camp but at no time found property belonging to the copper-miners. Another of these groups, led by Charles Winn, came across 'niggers', found a lot of blankets, handkerchiefs and tobacco in their camp, and dispersed them. The reference by such a man as Lucannus to dispersing Aborigines almost certainly meant killing them.[7]

The propriety of Parsons's instructions to the persons in charge of the search parties, and the actions of some of them, especially Montagu, became a public issue in South Australia. Montagu was given strict instructions by Parsons. He was to ascertain if possible the names of the offenders, endeavour to capture them and, if they resisted, 'they do so at their own risk'. These instructions were quite conventional and if carried out with normal restraint may have resulted in some deaths but would not have resulted in culpable homicide. On the basis of Montagu's report, between seventeen and twenty-seven Aboriginal men were killed by police on the MacKinlay River. Montagu's report does not indicate that a serious attempt was made to arrest any Aborigines, such as those who had thrown all their spears. On the contrary, his report suggests the police deliberately killed Aborigines who could not escape. The only reported police casualty was a scratch to Constable Cox's neck. The whole episode smacked of vengeance-killing. If Montagu and his men killed at least seventeen in the MacKinlay, it is likely that they killed others during the previous skirmishes. In a telegram to Baker ten days after the mine-murders, Parsons said the 'up country' party was to be under Lucannus, whom he merely described as an 'ex Mounted Constable'. To anyone who did not know Lucannus's background, this might suggest he was a former mounted trooper in the South Australian police force. Parsons then informed Baker that the 'up country' party was 'willing to promise not to shoot Blacks except in self defence but cannot be under police'. Parsons recommended that the government provide only rations for this party. He then quoted part of a telegram from it saying that its purpose was 'simply to ascertain the fate of Houschildt and our movements must be untrammelled. If govt will not assist on these terms must rely solely on private help'.

Baker approved Parsons's plans, agreeing to the 'bush party' not being placed under police command.[8] The whole question of what happened in the aftermath of the Daly River murders was kept from the South Australian parliament and people for a year, when rumours reaching Adelaide forced the government to table Montagu's report.

In Adelaide, initial public reaction to news of the Daly River murders was similar to that following the Barrow Creek attack — angry and punitive. The *South Australian Register* on 9 September 1884 said it was useless to make a perfunctory search for the perpetrators of outrages weeks after they had taken place, to catch two or three persons believed to have been implicated, send them to Palmerston and have them tried and sentenced to a few years' imprisonment. 'The men who murder and rob travellers and settlers must be pursued forthwith, and as soon as their complicity in the crime has been sufficiently established they should be shown no mercy. There and then the majesty of the law should be vindicated,' it stormed. Perhaps with the *Maria* massacre of 1840 in mind, the *Register* urged that the 'rough-and-ready processes of trial and conviction must be followed by the equally primitive process of executing justice on the spot'. It claimed that, unless the government provided effective police protection in the interior of the Territory, the attempt to extend settlement and to develop the natural capabilities of the country must be abandoned. Economic necessary, it seemed to argue, was more important than natural justice. Three days later, after the deaths of Noltenius and Landers were known, the *Register* went farther: 'It should be possible to find out the guilty tribe and mete out condign punishment'. On the frontier itself, the *Northern Territory Times*, which had been established in November 1873, fully reflected local passions. On 4 October, a month after the murders, it, like Parsons, claimed that the victims had been 'too kind, and had far too much confidence in the harmless nature of the blacks'. They had suffered the most horrible of deaths 'at the hands of a race of creatures resembling men in form, but with no more trace of human feeling in their natures than the Siberian wolves'. The *Times* added:

Sickly sentiment and Exeter Hall humanitarianism should be valued at their true worth, our European settlers must be allowed to till the soil, and extract the wealth from the land which they have made their home, free from the murdering raids of these savages. Backward the tribes must move before the tide of civilization, or, if they will not give place peaceably . . . so must the hand of every man be raised against a tribe of inhuman monsters, whose cowardly and murderous nature renders them unfit to live . . .

The paper also urged that legal technicalities be dispensed with and said a 'sharp lesson' would do more to ensure the safety of settlers than the slow and circuitous processes of the law. It implied what actions the search parties were taking when it said the 'right class' of men were now on the tracks of the Daly River blacks, 'but we do not expect to hear many particulars of their chase; the less the better, in such cases as the present, it is far more sensible to avoid complications by the exercise of judicious reticence'. While the Territory press and some officials may have been happy that the actions of this 'right class of men' not be made public, rumours eventually reached South Australia and led to demands for an inquiry. In the meantime, however, Parsons was discovering that the due processes of the law could not be manipulated and hastened even by a government resident.

The long-vexed question of trying capital offences was apparently resolved in 1884, when the South Australian parliament passed the Northern Territory Justice Act, which provided for a judge to be appointed in the Territory. Mr Justice T. K. Pater was chosen. Soon after his arrival in October he suggested that the only lawyer in Palmerston, R. D. Beresford, should represent the Crown in all the murder cases, including the Daly River murders, awaiting hearing. Parsons pointed out that Beresford was already engaged as the defending counsel in the other cases; he suggested that J. G. Knight, an architect by profession but also a magistrate in the Territory, should prosecute in the cases defended by Beresford. The protector of Aborgines, Dr R. J. Morice, had already suggested to Parsons that part of the annual vote for Aborigines be used to pay for the defence.

Judge Pater, in the meantime, had changed his mind; he told Morice to engage Beresford for the defence and set a fee — apparently to be paid by the government, as the defendants had no means. Pater also approved Beresford representing another Aborigine, Paddy, and a Chinaman, Ah Kong, awaiting trial in two other cases. When he heard of this, Parsons was furious. The judge, protector and lawyer, he told Baker, had acted together to defeat the government's instructions. He recommended that Morice be deprived of his offices as protector and visiting justice at the gaol. 'Such proceedings', he said, 'are subversive of discipline, and brings [sic] government into contempt'. Baker accepted Parsons's recommendations and went farther: Morice's position of colonial surgeon was abolished on 10 December as part of a government campaign to cut costs in the Territory.[9] The goldfields surgeon, Dr Percy Wood, was appointed protector of Aborigines. It appears that Parsons did not wish that the accused be defended, especially by a lawyer, for the reasons implied in his letter to Baker on 1 October. He wanted a 'speedy trial' and to execute them at the scene of their crimes as a lesson to others. A defence lawyer might impede such expedition, even frustrate the government's intentions, by raising objections which the Crown could not answer, especially as the intended prosecutor, Knight, was not qualified in law.

In the event, Beresford did defend the Woolwonga 'with signal ability', according to an Adelaide newspaper in the following year.[10]

On 22 December three of the accused were found guilty of the murders of Noltenius, Landers and Schollert. Pater and Parsons recommended that they be executed as near as possible to the scene of the murders and be left hanging as a warning for some time. As it happened, the sentence of the court could not be carried out — it was discovered that the proceedings had been irregular. The government proposed that this problem be overcome by 'legalizing the conviction and hanging the men by act of parliament'. The ministry changed in June 1885 and Baker was replaced by J. A. Cockburn in the Downer government, which 'declined to endorse this unique method of procedure' but legislated to retry them, contrary to British legal practice which discouraged retrials, especially in capital cases. In June one of the prisoners, Jacky, also known as Nammy, confessed to Dr Wood that he and six others, whose names he gave, had killed Houschildt while asleep. Houschildt had come to their camp and asked for the wife of Wallah, who gave her without objection but later 'growled' because the woman slept with Houschildt in the night. Wallah wakened his wife and then Nammy and six other Woolwonga speared Houschildt while asleep. Another of the accused, Tommy, stated that Nammy's spear was found in Houschildt's arm. Noltenius, Landers and Schollert, he said, had been killed because the Woolwonga wanted their 'tucker'. A man named Nango speared Landers and Noltenius and another named Lancoe knocked down Schollert and he, Tommy, speared him. Another man, Dabal, struck Roberts. Tommy also said one of the prisoners, Daly, was not present, was not a Woolwonga, had no 'growl' against the whitefellers and was angry when he arrived and found them killed. Another prisoner, Jimmy, had made a separate statement supporting Tommy's, including the names of the culprits; he named Nango as the ringleader. The case was retried in December, when Nango pleaded guilty to spearing Noltenius and Schollert. Jimmy and Tommy were found guilty and Daly was acquitted. A few days later Jacky (Nango) was sentenced to death. The sentences on all three convicted men were later commuted to life imprisonment.[11]

The administrative problems of this case had considerably embarrassed Parsons. As one Adelaide newspaper commented in October 1885: 'It would seem as if blunders would never cease in connection with the trial'. Morice, it said, had fallen a victim to the 'most arbitrary conduct on the part of those who rule over the destinies of the Northern Territory'.[12] On 2 and 4 June, Morice, exasperated by the government's delay in compensating him for retrenchment as required under the public service regulations, wrote to the *South Australian Register* criticizing the Colton government's policy towards Aborigines. He said that, while Foelsche and a police party were securing the actual Daly River murderers, another party of non-official persons, armed and provisioned by the government, 'were let loose to act as they thought best'. He alleged that this party insisted it not be accompanied by a single policeman; the minister was reported to have hesitated about consenting, but yielded to pressure from the government resident. He went on:

What this party did has never been made public, but the officers on the S.S. Palmerston, which was lying in the Daly River ... say that all one night they heard a constant discharge of firearms. There was good moonlight at the time. The general belief in the Territory was that they simply shot down every native they saw, women and children included. While this was going on three teamsters reported that they had been attacked by the natives at Argument Flat. The teamsters resisted, and shot five or six of them. There were three weak points in their tale. None of the teamsters was wounded; it is unusual for natives to attack in the bold way described; and, lastly, it was admitted that there were women with the natives (one of the killed was a lubra, I think). Now it is well known that natives when they mean mischief always keep their women out of the way ...

Morice added that as soon as he heard of this affair, Parsons sent out another non-official party. When it returned, its members reported that they did not meet any natives; 'Of course the party were not asked to account for the Government ammunition they took away; and a few days after some of the men were boasting over their cups that they shot forty-seven, including women and children'. Morice said this may have been a lie but 'everyone' believed them. It was difficult, he said, to say how many Aborigines had been killed as a result of the Daly River outrage, 'but from all I have heard from different sources, I should say not less than 150, a great part of these women and children'.

In parliament on 10 June the Premier and Chief Secretary, John Colton, denied Morice's claims, saying: 'No party to make reprisals in the N.T. was ever sent out by the Government, nor did any such party ever go out'. He agreed that a private party was organized, but he said that the government had no power to prevent it going nor wished to do so. Rations only were provided by the government on the distinct promise from each member that he would not fire upon the blacks unless required to do so in self-defence. Colton said there was no reason to suppose that they did not keep their promise. One of the party, A. P. Baines, a justice of the peace, had stated: 'Our party did not shoot one native'. Other members of the party had said Morice's claims were untrue. Captain Carrington, master of the *Palmerston*, said that his officers denied having heard firing at night or saying they had. Carrington said that, as far as he knew, no party was within thirty miles of the ship. He was on board the steam launch when it was up the river and he had not heard any firing at night nor had heard of any one doing so. This appeared to quash Morice's allegations, but rumours began to spread in their support, particularly one that Montagu had made a report which had not been made public. The

Colton government had fallen six days after the premier's statement, although not because of the Daly River affair. When a member of the Legislative Assembly moved on 12 November that Montagu's report be tabled, the Assembly agreed.The *South Australian Register*, which had been so severe in its reaction to news of the Daly River murders was, on 14 November, unreserved in its condemnation of what the Europeans had done to Aborigines in the Territory:

Down in South Australia good men try to civilize them with the Bible; elsewhere we civilize them with the Martini-Henry rifle... the cold-blooded manner in which Corporal Montagu and his associates murdered these unhappy wretches is a disgrace to him, a disgrace to the community, and an outrage on the civilization about which we boast. The story of the expedition reads like an extract from the history of the Spanish conquest of Mexico... [Montagu's] was a butchering expedition, and the unfortunate victims were mere targets. They have been taught the value of civilization. It is civilization which has despoiled them of their territory, which has deprived them of their freedom, which has armed their enemies with the Martini-Henry rifle.

The former trooper, James Foster Smith, who had accompanied Montagu on the Daly River expedition but apparently not on the one to the Mary and MacKinlay Rivers, wrote to the *Register* on 28 November 1885 saying that he was in the police barracks when Montagu's party returned. Among the incidents related by the troopers was one which appears to be the killing in the MacKinlay River. He said the police came upon many Aborigines who took refuge in a waterhole; 'The police at once surrounded it, Corporal Montagu going on one side with the horses, and they commenced carefully firing upon the natives, who were all killed but one'. Smith said he remarked to one of the troopers that he thought they had been guilty of murder, but was told: 'It is all right; we only acted under orders'. Smith was told that the orders were to call upon the natives thrice in the Queen's name to surrender and, if they did not surrender, to shoot them. The orders came from Inspector Foelsche, he was told.

The Aborigines' Friends' Association waited upon J. A. Cockburn, then Minister of Education and minister controlling the Northern Territory, and presented a memorial requesting an official inquiry. Cockburn agreed, pointing out that he would have ordered an inquiry previously if he had known of Montagu's report, but that it had been sent from Palmerston a year ago, filed and not brought to his attention when he became minister. In some defence of Montagu's action, however, Cockburn reminded the deputation that in each of the camps attacked property of the murdered men was found and that this was prima facie evidence of guilt. One of the deputation, C. B. Young, pointed out that this property had been discovered after the slaughter had taken place. It may appear strange that Cockburn, who was not minister at the time and therefore not responsible for what happened, should have offered some defence of Montagu, but ministries changed on average once a year during the South Australian period of administration of the Territory. Also, there was a measure of common membership of ministries and so continuity of government. Cockburn may have feared that the whole body of South Australian politics was under threat. His action appears to have been a case of the establishment closing ranks, but it merely stimulated more criticism.

The *South Australian Register* of 8 December 1885 spoke of Cockburn's 'audacity' in defending the horrible murders perpetrated by Montagu. It also attacked Parsons over his private remark to Baker in October 1884 about 'mealy mouthed philanthropies'. Philanthropy, it said, was not mealy mouthed when it raised its voice against wholesale murders. Then it added: 'The perpetrators are not only those who shot down the wretched blacks, but the officials who authorized and concealed this disgraceful deed'. In Palmerston, Parsons refrained from more incautious remarks and, if Foelsche was feeling nervous about his future prospects, he did not comment on the Daly River incident to his confidant, John Lewis.

The Territory press was not contrite in the face of the recent revelations. The second newspaper, the *North Australian*, which had begun in Palmerston in 1883, scorned the 'pretty little pieces of "Christian" criticism being circulated through the Adelaide weeklies'. In its issues of 24 December 1885 and 8 January 1886 it dismissed the critics as having no practical experience of the Aborigines who grew up with the idea that to kill was part of a just creed. In matters of life and death, the paper believed in 'an eye for an eye, a tooth for a tooth'. It added that the one mistake Montagu had made had been to refer to the superiority of the Martini-Henry rifle: 'There is a symptom of boasting about this that might tend to convey a wrong idea. As to the shooting of blacks, we uphold it defiantly'. The *Northern Territory Times* of 26 December 1885 said that Montagu and his party were entitled to the hearty thanks of the whole community for the prompt manner in which they suppressed what was 'undoubtedly a carefully organized rising of a numerous tribe of natives, having as its objective the utter annihilation of a handful of white settlers for the sake of loot'. On 23 January 1886 it said that Montagu's action was 'the only rational method of dealing with blood-thirsty savages, in spite of all the arguments of the Aborigines' Friends' Society'. Alfred Giles, now owner of Springvale station, wrote to the *Times* of 6 March 1886 saying that the Aborigines had no moral laws, their festive dances and corroborees were lewd and disgusting, their songs, rites and ceremonies revolting and fiendish and the idea of chastity among their women preposterous.

Not less preposterous is the idea of the black women being outraged, unless it is by stopping their supply of tobacco. As to the numerous murders being attributable to the white man violating the moral laws of the tribe, I have already shown [it] to be impossible when such laws do not exist.

The board of inquiry set up by the government in December 1885 was not picked for impartiality, as the *South Australian Register* of 23 December 1885 inferred. The chairman was A. P. Baines, who had been a member of one of the armed parties. The other members were H. W. H. Stevens, Foelsche's son-in-law; Dr Percy Wood, promoted colonial surgeon after Morice's dismissal for 'doing his duty in defence of the blacks'; 'Mr McMinn, an architect drawing a handsome salary from the government'; and Mr Hillson, a bank manager 'known to be friendly to the Government Resident'. The *Register* claimed that the board sat behind closed doors and heard testimony only from invited witnesses and, instead of gathering evidence from the scenes of the killings, took evidence only from the constables involved. In Adelaide, an auxiliary board comprising Cockburn and F. W. Cox, chairman of the Aborigines' Friends' Association, was to take the evidence of Montagu who had been transferred from the Territory. Apparently no effort was made to obtain evidence from Morice and J. F. Smith; the report issued by Baines in Palmerston on 17 January did not mention receiving any evidence from them. The *Register* of 18 January 1886 carried the Board's findings. The Board decided that a 'grossly exaggerated view had been taken of what took place between the police and the natives both at the Daly and Mary Rivers'. It said Montagu's report was incorrect and misleading. Montagu had told the board that he had received subsequent information that most of those who took to the water on the Mary escaped. From the evidence of the constables with him on the Daly, there was no proof of any natives having been shot; from the evidence, there was no doubt the blacks encountered on the Mary were involved in the copper-mine outrage; and only two blacks had been shot in self-defence. The board unanimously held that the Aborigines were treated with leniency and that 'there is no evidence to show that slaughter or cruelty was practised by the police'. Foelsche and Parsons could breath more easily after a finding like that. It meant that police and settlers in the Territory could now take the law into their own hands with impunity, provided that they acted discreetly.

Chapter 9

Native Police

On the day after the news of the Daly River murders was received in Adelaide the government was asked to establish a native police force along the lines of the one operating in Queensland. A memorial signed by fourteen men with interests in the Territory was presented to R. C. Baker, minister controlling the Territory. They claimed that unless better police protection was afforded, development of the Territory would be seriously retarded. An effective black police force would deter the Aborigines by its mere presence and would be the best means of repressing their outrages. They claimed that in Queensland it was quite safe to venture anywhere from the eastern seaboard to the western boundary. The member for Flinders, J. Moule, who introduced the deputation, stated that unless the blacks were deterred from committing such outrages as the Daly River murders the white residents would be obliged to take the law into their own hands and shoot the blacks whenever they came across them. In response Baker said the government had to consider the proposal very carefully because it knew the actions of the black police in Queensland had given rise to a 'great deal of unfavourable comment'. He believed that recent outrages in the Territory were tribal affairs and it might be wise to seize any members of a tribe and hold them as hostages until the guilty ones were 'obtained'. Possibly referring to the *Maria* massacre, he said this had been done in the past with great effect. He believed that establishing a black police force and treating any outrage as a tribal affair would be the best course to adopt.[1]

Baker's reticence in forming a force which might emulate the Queensland Native Police Force was understandable. At its peak this paramilitary force had 250 white officers and black troopers and operated separately from the colonial police, although under the control of the Commissioner of Police and the Colonial Secretary who, in Queensland, was also responsible for Aborigines. Between 1849 when it was introduced and 1897 when it was abolished, at least 5000

Aborigines were killed in clashes in Queensland, mostly at the hands of the Native Police, who did not take prisoners but simply 'dispersed' gatherings of Aborigines without having to account for their actions in a court of law. Alfred Giles, a man of undisguised contempt for the Aborigines, opposed the introduction of such a force in the Territory because of its reputation for killing the innocent. Giles proposed that Aborigines be used only as trackers.[2]

These events might suggest that South Australia and the Northern Territory had not previously had native police. As we have seen in the Introduction, Aboriginal constables had been employed in South Australia as early as 1842 and a black police unit was stationed on Eyre Peninsula in 1850. As the frontier moved away from Adelaide to the far north and west of the colony the black constables, or trackers as they were now called, moved out of sight. R. M. and C. H. Berndt have noted that these trackers were often used to intimidate and oppress tribes in the northern districts at the time settlers were moving into the Territory from the south. It was not surprising that Foelsche should have tried to use trackers soon after arriving in 1870. At Charlotte Waters telegraph station on his trip northwards with cattle for Springvale in 1878, Giles received a message from Foelsche asking him to obtain three 'black boys' to be used as trackers in the north. Foelsche said the Port Darwin blacks were not good at tracking whereas the southern ones were adept at it. Giles obtained three 'good young fellows' who proved helpful in tracking lost stock on the way north. Camped at Temple Bar, just south of Alice Springs, one night, 'wild mountainous blacks' decoyed two of these recruits away to their camp. Giles and the remaining man tracked them next morning and found them in the local tribe's camp. They had been speared and battered to death because, he assumed, the local people had a grudge against their tribe. Giles and the stationmaster at Alice Springs protested about the lack of police protection there and as a result the third police post in the Centre was established at Alice Springs in 1879. Early in 1882 Mounted Constable William Willshire arrived at Alice Springs to replace the officer who had been transferred to Barrow Creek.

After the Daly River massacre, Baker ordered that a force of native police be raised, but Foelsche and Parsons argued against a native police corps. Also, they did not want locally recruited trackers, saying such men would not 'discover' their friends and were poor trackers. 'We want trackers from Central Australia or Queensland', Parsons told Baker; 'We do not want a black police for the Queensland black force goes out and disperses and shoots natives'. The government sought the advice of the Queensland Commissioner of Police, D. T. Seymour, who said native police were most effective when used as a body rather than when distributed among police stations. Baker accepted this, saying the native police would be more useful and more likely to stay if kept in a body and moved from place to place as required. The South Australian

Commissioner of Police, George Hamilton, suggested getting Willshire's opinion. Willshire's advice is not known, but Baker's view prevailed.[3]

Willshire apparently recruited men from the Arabana, in whose territory the Peake station west of Lake Eyre is located. Then, leaving Mounted Constable Erwein Wurmbrand in charge at Alice Springs, he rode with six of them to Palmerston late in 1884 and handed them over to Mounted Constable Cornelius Power in January 1885. Parsons sent the detachment to Pine Creek for the remainder of the wet season and from there they operated on the Daly and Roper Rivers. Foelsche drew up guidelines, approved by Parsons, for the officer in charge of native police. In the event of an outrage by Aborigines being reported, the officer would endeavour to capture the offenders. If resistance were met, firearms might be used to secure the arrest of the offenders and in self-defence. But, Foelsche stressed, 'it is to be borne in mind that the system termed "dispersing the Natives" which simply means shooting them is not to be practised and for this the officer in charge will be held strictly responsible'. A full report of any action against Aborigines was to be sent as soon as possible to the inspector's office, and the officer in charge was to visit blacks' camps occasionally to make them understand that if they committed depredations they would be brought to justice. Willshire returned to Alice Springs, accompanied by one of the troopers, Jack Harrison, who had wanted to return to his home country on the Peake River in South Australia. He died 'of some internal complaint' two days after they reached Alice Springs. In 1885 the police station was moved from the telegraph station at Alice Springs four miles south to Heavitree Gap. Willshire raised another detachment of Aboriginal troopers, comprising six regulars and a number of auxiliaries. It is not clear where he raised them, but he was instructed to patrol the country from the Peake River to Barrow Creek, which suggests he again recruited in the Peake district. Willshire said about two hundred Aranda camped at Heavitree Gap and, although he was often absent on long rides of hundreds of miles, nothing was stolen from the police stores, 'it being sufficient to leave a blackfellow in charge'.[4] This may indicate either an amicable relationship between the Central Aranda and the black police, or fear of the imported blacks — it is not now possible to know which.

By May 1886 Parsons and Foelsche were dissatisfied with the Aboriginal troopers in the Top End. Parsons urged the new minister, Cockburn, to disband the force and keep one tracker at Palmerston — and to send some to Borroloola and also to Katherine or the Elsey if a telegraph station were opened at Elsey. Parsons said Katherine was a great rendezvous for squatters and that blacks were troublesome and dangerous between there and the Roper and were killing cattle. Cockburn agreed that the force be disbanded and its members redeployed as suggested. By December 1886 only three of the six recruited by Willshire remained in the Top End, but they were homesick and unsatisfactory as trackers. They were replaced by three others who early in 1887 were dispersed — one each to Palmerston, Katherine and the new police station at Borroloola. The native police as a corps thus ended in the Top End, Aborigines being used only as trackers for the remainder of the South Australian administration. In the Centre, the force raised by Willshire on his return in 1885 continued for some years with deadly effect.[5]

According to Giles, only the Aborigines north of the MacDonnell Ranges were hostile in 1875. Apparently he was referring to the actions of the Kaititja in the Barrow Creek area. This peaceful situation seems to have continued until at least 1879 when the first policeman was posted at Alice Springs. Giles proposed this to protect Europeans and foreign Aborigines working for them, not as a reaction to the spearing of cattle on the runs. Little is known of reaction before 1880 but it may be regarded as a period of tentative approach. The first stations had been stocked by 1876, and by the early 1880s attacks on European stock had become frequent and on several occasions homesteads were attacked. In 1881 Charles Chewings noted a general atmosphere of fear among settlers on the upper reaches of the Finke River. They considered the Aborigines to be 'unsafe out from the stations' and wore revolvers on their hips wherever they went; 'Soon the missionaries reported that their neighbours complained of cattle killing by the Aborigines and it was not uncommon to hear that an offender had been shot'. Cattle-killing had become so prevalent on Owen Springs, Undoolya, Glen Helen and the newly formed Anna's Reservoir stations that in August 1884 the officer in charge of the far-northern division of the South Australian police spoke of the 'present emergencies'. Mounted Constable Brookes, sent from Barrow Creek to Anna's Reservoir, 120 miles north-west of Alice Springs, organized a party of black trackers and station hands, located a group of Unmatjera suspects and fired on them when they resisted arrest. Some were wounded but all escaped.

While Brookes was hunting one band of Unmatjera, another attacked the homestead at Anna's Reservoir, burning it down and destroying property valued at about £1600. Only the cook, Thomas Coombes, and another man, Harry Figg, were present at the time. The blazing rafters and thatched roof fell on Coombes and Figg who were badly burned and speared. Each time they opened a door to try to get out they met a volley of spears. At the same time, the fire detonated hundreds of cartridges, the station's supply. Eventually Figg put his arm out of the partly opened door and, firing indiscriminately with a Colt .38 revolver, hit one or two of the attackers and forced the others to retreat. Figg and Combes were permanently injured. Willshire, now the senior constable in Central Australia, then led a party of native police and settlers to apprehend the offenders. On 29 August they surrounded a camp of about sixty Unmatjera before dawn and, according to Willshire, shot two who

An Aboriginal camp at Palmerston, one of Foelsche's many ethnological studies

The first police office in Palmerston, *c.* 1889

Police officer, William Kelly, with chained Aboriginal prisoners at the Roper River, *c.* 1908

resisted arrest, and wounded three others. Before returning to Alice Springs on 17 September the party shot two others resisting arrest. Locals believe that at least fifty Unmatjera were killed at Italinga, on the northern edge of Hart's Range, by a party of whites in the 1880s. It is not clear whether this story derives from Willshire's action in that area. Twelve years later Willshire wrote that the government told him to 'go out and do as the law provides in such cases'. He said he worked hard for ten months, sometimes with seven or eight white men and finally with trackers, and as a result he could say: 'All's well that ends well'. Willshire gave no cause for the attack on Anna's Reservoir station, but Erhard Eylmann, a Berlin doctor who travelled through the Northern Territory in 1899, says the immediate cause was 'that drovers had had sexual intercourse with a girl who was still a child'.[6]

To the south, Willshire's own camp on the Finke River was attacked and one of his trackers killed. He and his black police tracked the offenders westwards, each man in the detachment riding half a mile apart, aiming to drive the quarry together at one spot. Willshire encountered one Aborigine who attacked him with spear and woomera. Willshire fired at him with his 'shooting iron' but claimed not to know what became of that 'greasy native'. He went back to the camp and 'some of my lads came home next day with a fine collection of spears and boomerangs — they had evidently been amongst them'. In others words, without their officer being present, the black police had killed Aborigines and taken no prisoners. Lack of control over black troopers, and failure to state later exactly what happened, now approximated the Queensland practice Parsons and Foelsche had preferred to avoid. But they had no authority over Willshire. At this time Willshire's superior at Port Augusta, Sub-Inspector B. C. Besley, instructed that there were to be no 'Queensland style' dispersals, but this had little effect on Willshire's attitude. In 1896, after he had left the police force, Willshire described how Native Police followed up an alleged crime by Aborigines in the Centre:

The Native Police start from the scene of the murder or from the carcase of a slaughtered beast — as the case may be — on tracks that are generally days old. The offenders may be quite unknown to the black troopers but once they had seen and scanned the tracks, they can identify by them the natives who made them; and if any offender is known, his track at once reveals his name. The tracking goes on, day after day, from water to water, until the 'spoor' becomes fresher, and at last appears only one day old. The ranges are carefully scanned with field glasses for the smoke of camp fires, or other indications of aboriginal life ... Next day a few old lubras appear in sight ... The route taken by these old women indicates the locality of the offenders, and the pursuing party abandons the tracks and divides, one section galloping off at full speed to get around the fugitives and cut off their retreat, while the other section spreads out and closes in. This is called 'rounding up'; and when the operation is complete, and the natives are effectively 'bailed up', they commence the usual string of lies and evasions... But sometimes the 'rounding up' process cannot be accomplished; the natives take to the ranges, and a hot pursuit follows... The blacks for a hundred miles both east and west of the Alice will fight like demons at first, and it behoves the pursuers to keep a sharp look out for flying spears, both on their own and their horses' accounts.[7]

In October 1884 fifteen cattle were speared on Glen Helen station and the manager and two of his men attacked in a gorge by Western Aranda people. Wurmbrand arrested three suspected cattle-killers at Glen Helen and passed through Hermannsburg with them in chains on his way back to Alice Springs. Soon afterwards the missionaries heard that the captives had been shot and, on investigating, discovered the bodies heaped together and still in chains. Wurmbrand claimed they were trying to escape. There was a loud outcry in the newspapers and the protector of Aborigines investigated the matter, but no action was taken. Soon after this incident, the police shot four others in a camp who were resisting arrest. In April 1885 the Aranda surrounded Glen Helen homestead and attempted to burn it down, but the attack failed. Wurmbrand again went out with a party and in four or five weeks officially killed two Aranda and wounded two others. A station-hand who accompanied him later told the missionaries at Hermannsburg that seventeen were shot. At the end of 1886 cattle-killing broke out again on Undoolya and at least four parties under Willshire and Wurmbrand responded, but no Aboriginal deaths or arrests were reported. At the end of 1886 the only resistance came from the Western Aranda at Glen Helen and the Unmatjera north-west of the MacDonnells.[8]

In 1888 Willshire published a summary of Aboriginal violence at the principal stations in Central Australia. At Owen Springs, owned then by Elder and Company, the Aborigines were 'much addicted to cattle killing and are otherwise "bad"'. At Anna's Reservoir the blacks were 'very bad on this run... very fond of beef'. At Glen Helen, 115 miles to the west, blacks were spearing a good many of the station's cattle in the ranges. Erldunda, a cattle and horse run 160 miles south of the Alice, was in a district where the blacks were 'very bad indeed, occasionally attacking runs'. A few months previously Erldunda had been 'stuck up' by the natives, who were repulsed by the manager, R. E. Warburton, with gunfire. The attack on Erldunda in May 1887 was followed by more cattle-killing. Two expeditions by the native police shot three Matuntara and captured two, suppressing crime at Erldunda until the drought set in a few years later. Willshire said that Tempe Downs was troubled by native cattle-killers, thirty head having been speared recently. On the other hand, Henbury, about a hundred miles south, was a 'quiet' neighbourhood — why, he did not say. This picture may have been painted by Willshire to suit his own antipathetic attitude towards the Aborigines, presenting them as wanton criminals — but, as the senior police officer in the district in 1888, he was in the best position to see what was happening. His account moreover, is supported by other evidence.[9]

In August 1888 a deputation of pastoralists, including three of the partners in Tempe Downs and F. Krichauff of Hermannsburg mission station, waited on the South Australian Chief Secretary, J. G. Ramsay. They asked for additional police protection because of the destruction of cattle on Tempe Downs, Hermannsburg and other stations. A letter from the manager of Tempe Downs, R. F. Thornton, was presented, stating that all of his time was taken up by the activities of the blacks. He and a party of whites with a 'black boy' had been out after Aborigines who had been killing cattle on the Walker and Petermann Creeks at the same time. On entering a gorge to drink they found themselves trapped and were lucky to get out. Thornton had been complaining about this situation for two years and things had become so bad that, if something was not done about it, the owners should abandon the run, 'as it is only throwing money away trying to breed cattle'. Thornton said a black police force capable of constant patrolling was needed. The police at Alice Springs had been to Tempe Downs but had achieved nothing — their numbers were too small and they did not have sufficient horses to do the work. One deputation member claimed that the enlarged black police force requested was not intended for reprisal but simply to let the natives know they would be punished if they continued to damage the properties. Three such deputations had been made to the government on this matter, and so far it had done nothing. Another member said many capitalists were coming to the conclusion that it was impossible to occupy the outside country profitably. Recently some stations in Central Australia had been offered for sale at prices less than the value of the store cattle imported for stocking them. Yet another said blacks had been shot down by the settlers because neither party was properly protected, and that the situation would end in a kind of war between the whites and blacks. Ramsay promised action and police strength in the Centre was increased. Willshire was soon assisted by Mounted Constables Daer and Wurmbrand and at least six native constables.[10]

Undoubtedly parties of whites, without police being present, had already taken the law into their own hands. Obviously Thornton's party intended to, before the Matuntara turned the tables on them. Whereas there is fairly reliable evidence of unofficial punitive raids in the Top End, the evidence is very circumstantial in the Centre. For some years the Lutheran missionaries at Hermannsburg had been concerned at the local practices of white men cohabiting with Aboriginal women, known as 'comboism', and the shooting of Aborigines. In 1889 their public allegations led to an official inquiry which in turn achieved nothing. The missionaries could not prove their allegations and the cattlemen called to give evidence refused to incriminate themselves or others.

Attacks on stock began at Tempe Downs early in 1887, two years after the station had been formed. As a result of pressure from the

Tempe Downs Pastoral Company and other Central Australian pastoral interests, Willshire was instructed to organize a stronger corps of native police, this time on Queensland lines. Whereas he had previously been answerable to the officer in charge of the far-northern police division at Port Augusta, he was now appointed Officer in Charge Police Patrol Party for the Interior and instructed to form his own headquarters at Boggy Waters, six miles from Tempe Downs homestead. In the meantime a third policeman had been posted to Alice Springs. Even though police resources were now concentrated on Tempe Downs, the frequency of attacks increased. One thousand cattle died there between the year of its founding and 1892, including six hundred in the latter year, although many may have died as a result of drought. Attacks on cattle resumed at Erldunda in 1892–93, when police parties again scoured the country; as a result, Aborigines killed few cattle after that period. Willshire believed that blacks from Hermannsburg were the worst cattle-killers. In January 1890 he asked for more trackers to cope with the 'most cheeky and daring tribes in Central Australia'. Another deputation from the Tempe Downs Pastoral Company in February 1890 asked for extra police protection. The minister, J. H. Gordon, the Strathalbyn lawyer who had spoken out against hasty action after the Barrow Creek attack in 1874, was now a partner in Bond Springs cattle station in the Centre. Gordon sympathized with the company but pointed out that two more trackers had been added to Willshire's force at Boggy Waters, which was now costing £500 a year, the same as the rent paid by the company. Willshire was removed from the Centre in 1891, and cattle-killing resumed on Tempe Downs. In January 1893 John Lewis wrote to his old friend, W. B. Rounsevell, now Treasurer and minister controlling the Northern Territory, that twenty head of cattle had been killed in a month and complaining that the police at Charlotte Waters had not answered the manager's call for help. As a result three more Aboriginal constables were recruited at Alice Springs, apparently from Central Aranda, and a new police post was opened on Tempe Downs, manned by Constable Daer and four native police. The Native Police Corps in Central Australia now included fourteen Aborigines: six at Alice Springs, four at Barrow Creek and four at Tempe Downs.[11]

Drought began in the Centre in 1889, and a shortage of traditional food may have been a reason for increased cattle-killing as the drought worsened in the early 1890s. As in the case of violence on the overlanding tracks from Queensland to the Top End, it is necessary to consider Aboriginal need for food and desire for European goods when considering these attacks as evidence of Aboriginal resistance in Central Australia. It would be wrong to assume that all attacks — on cattle and on homesteads — were motivated only by attempts to drive out the Europeans. Even so, the methods used and the number of cattle killed suggest that in some areas and periods the chief aim of the

Central Australian attacks was to force out the Europeans and wanton destruction was the chief method. In 1894 a white constable and six native police were sent to Illamurta, 150 miles south-west of Alice Springs and 36 miles from Tempe Downs. By the end of that year ten of the leading cattle-killers had been arrested and gaoled, including Racehorse and some of his band who had for years cut down the Tempe Downs and Glen Helen herds. By late 1894 attacks on cattle had ended on all pastoral runs in the Centre except Tempe Downs, Glen Helen and Frew River.

The establishment of cattle stations in the arid lands between the Centre and the Top End began with Frew River and Elkedra stations in 1888–89, southeast of Tennant Creek. In June 1891 about sixty Wakaja attacked the stockaded Frew River station early one morning but the manager, three men and dogs, forewarned by an Aboriginal woman, succeeded in driving them off. Their intention to burn it down and murder all their 'oppressors' was thwarted only by the vigilance of a large number of kangaroo dogs and bloodhounds inside the stockade. Two more attempts were made on the homestead before 1895 as harassment of stock increased. As the drought worsened Kaititja and Wakaja tribesmen killed or 'perished' three hundred cattle in three weeks. In March 1894 the manager, Coulthard, reported six hundred cattle had been speared in a few months. In 1895–96 both stations were abandoned. Eylmann, who visited Frew River, said it was abandoned because so many cattle had been 'waylaid' by the Aborigines that it was no longer profitable. He said the station inhabitants had always treated the Aborigines with the greatest severity and 'any cattle thieves who fell into their hands were unmercifully shot down'. He saw there two skulls which had each been 'penetrated' by a bullet. He heard from a 'reliable' 20-year-old Aborigine that the whites had once captured a large number of women, including the mother of two of his sisters, and held them for some weeks before releasing them. In retaliation for this act, all the men of the local tribe had besieged the station for some days in June 1891.[12]

Aboriginal resistance to the European invaders lasted longer and was more intense in the Centre than elsewhere in the Territory because of decided advantages in their favour. The small number of cattle stations, their enormous sizes and the great distances between them all made it difficult for the pastoralists to offer protection to each other as had happened in the closely settled pastoral districts of Queensland. The whites therefore had to depend more upon punitive parties and preferably a police presence to deter the cattle-killers, but the small number of police compelled the Europeans to rely more on their own resources than settlers in the Top End, where there were more police but fewer trackers. The heavy scrub and ranges of the McArthur River — Roper River stretch of the Queensland track certainly afforded cover to marauding Aborigines, but so did the gorges of the

MacDonnell and other ranges in the Centre. Such stations as Glen Helen, Tempe Downs, Erldunda and Frew River were on the best permanent waters in Central Australia, and during droughts the Aborigines were forced to withdraw to these resources and so to the stations. The two droughts, beginning in 1889 and 1897, which affected the Centre more than the Top End, therefore further stimulated cattle-killing.

The lack of a superior court in the Centre was a serious impediment to the administration of justice. The magistrate's court at Alice Springs could deal only with minor offences for which the maximum penalty was six months imprisonment. But the maximum penalty for unlawfully wounding a beast was four years with hard labour and the maximum penalty for killing cattle with intent to steal the carcase was eight years imprisonment with hard labour. This meant that any Aborigine arrested for cattle-maiming or killing had to be sent to Palmerston or Port Augusta for trial. As in the Top End in 1878, settlers would rather take the law into their own hands than make the long trip to a distant court as witnesses. Probably for this reason Willshire and Wurmbrand killed 'escaping' prisoners. Offences against Aborigines went almost unpunished. In the whole period of settlement to 1894 only three Europeans were tried for such causes — one in 1887 for using threatening language, one in 1890 for common assault, and in 1891 Willshire was charged with two counts of murder.

On 22 February 1891 two native constables, Jacky and Thomas, shot and killed two Aborigines, Donkey and Roger, on Tempe Downs near the homestead during a visit by Willshire and four troopers. An inquiry into the affair was held late in April by F. J. Gillen, telegraph station-master and justice of the peace at Alice Springs. Willshire claimed that Donkey and Roger had been shot in self-defence by the troopers at a native camp upon which the patrol had come at daylight. Jacky and Thomas told Gillen that they had been instructed by Willshire to shoot the victims. Gillen visited Tempe Downs and interviewed a number of Aborigines there. Having completed his inquiry, he telegraphed the Attorney-General, R. Homburg, saying the case was 'serious and revolting' and the police should be instructed to arrest Willshire. Gillen reported that Jacky and Thomas were not shot in a native camp as alleged by Willshire but one hundred yards from the kitchen of Tempe Downs station; that Donkey was shot while asleep; and that Roger, on hearing the shot, was killed as he rose to flee. Willshire had claimed that the blacks had removed and burned the two bodies, but he was now said to have had them removed and burned. Willshire had influenced the black trackers to corroborate some of his statements concerning the affair which on investigation, Gillen said, were disproved. Willshire said he had gone to the camp with the troopers to arrest Donkey and Roger on a warrant issued by a magistrate, C. Gall, but Gall denied having issued the warrant. Homburg accepted Gillen's advice, and Willshire was arrested and charged with the murders of Donkey and Roger. Mounted Constable William South, who arrested Willshire, thought his action at Tempe Downs 'most unaccountable, unless the result of insanity, as surely no sane man, however wicked he may be, would go into Native's Camps within 200 yards of a Head Station and shoot them'.[13].

During a seventeen-day journey, including nine days in leg-irons, Willshire was taken eight hundred miles to Port Augusta, where he was locked in gaol. He spent thirteen hours each night in a small cell by himself before being released on £2000 bail. His case was heard in Port Augusta before Mr Justice Bundey and a jury on 23 July, when he pleaded not guilty. The Crown Solicitor, J. M. Stuart, told the court Willshire had reported to Besley at Port Augusta on the affair at Tempe Downs, but he did not claim that Donkey and Roger were cattle-killers until he sent a second report. He had not mentioned in either report that their bodies had been burned. Jacky told the court he was ordered by Willshire to go to Tempe Downs and shoot Roger and Donkey. He said another trooper, Larry, had shot Donkey and Thomas had shot Roger who had nothing in his hand at the time. Roger was lying on the ground but not dead. Willshire then ordered him, Jacky, to shoot Roger, which he did, killing him. After breakfast he, Larry and Thomas took the two bodies to a sandhill and burned them. He said Willshire and another white man, William Henry Abbot, an Alice Springs prospector, were present and made one of the fires. Later he had told two white men on camels on the road to Alice Springs that he had shot Roger. He said he had lied to Gillen later because he had been told by Willshire to do so. He said Donkey and Roger had stolen cattle and had killed an old man, Naimi, who was Larry's father, at Willshire's camp. Roger had also killed Thomas's brother. Thomas also told the court he had shot Roger because Willshire had told him to do so. Donkey and Roger had killed his brother. Larry corroborated the evidence of Jacky and Thomas. One of the trackers, not named in the press reports, said Donkey and Roger had been shot because they had taken Willshire's 'lubra'. No other reference was made to this woman in or out of court, but Willshire's *Thrilling Tale of Real Life in the Wilds of Australia*, published in 1895, was dedicated to a 'light-hearted girl' who assisted him to 'record items of Aboriginal lore, that will be handed down to posterity', and later in the book he inferred that he wandered 'through the bush of Australia, with a black gin for a guide'. He called her Chillberta, a name meaning 'falling rain', and said she came from the Lake Amadeus area. She had stuck by him when he was 'threatened by villainous foes' and had returned with his party to 'civilization' on the Finke River and 'died as she had lived'.[14]

Willshire was defended by Sir John Downer, QC, member for Barossa, a former Attorney-General and Premier (June 1885–June 1887) and a leading conservative. Downer did not call witnesses for the defence but, after cross-examining the Crown witnesses, told the jury the evidence was flimsy. He said this was one of the most disgraceful cases ever brought into court. He played on the sympathies of the jury by painting Willshire as a man of high character and responsible position, performing arduous and dangerous duties, practically carrying his life in his hands. An officer of noted integrity and ability, he had been brought down from the far interior, hurled into gaol and put into the dock to answer on peril of his life a charge of murder, 'because he had thoroughly done the difficult work entrusted to him'. He said some parts of the evidence were 'impudent'; there was no proof that Willshire had killed the blacks but he risked being hanged on the testimony of 'two self-confessed murderers, whose statements were of the most extraordinarily contradictory character'. Downer claimed that Gillen's inquiry was 'carried out in the good old Star Chamber style in the absence of the accused'. The murders had resulted from a tribal vendetta, he said. The jury took only a quarter of an hour to acquit Willshire, who was 'conducted by an enthusiastic crowd to his lodgings' and received over the next few days nearly fifty congratulatory telegrams from friends in the northern districts, most of them from Central Australia. Willshire had suffered considerable hardship because of the case, especially in raising bail. When he sold seventeen horses he received only seventy pounds. He said later that the 'working men in Alice Springs at that time treated me well'. Friends rushed into print to support him, including one who used Downer's confusion of duty and murder charges, when he said: 'The Government employ M. C. Willshire for a certain duty, they supply him with revolvers, rifles and ammunition in abundance, and immediately the time arrives for these weapons to be used for the benefit of the country the officer in charge becomes a felon'.[15]

This epitomized the twisted reasoning of the frontier: a man was employed by the government to perform a certain duty, such as protection of European lives and cattle, and so he should perform that duty without being responsible for any actions not contrary to European interests, including unprovoked murder of Aborigines. This is not to say that Willshire was guilty as charged; even an impartial jury well away from the frontier may have felt impelled to give him the benefit of the doubt on the evidence presented. The case was important not so much for what happened to Willshire but for the attitudes expressed by Downer and Willshire's supporters. In 1846 a white man had been hanged for the murder of an Aborigine in the south-east of South Australia, but that was in the time of Colonial Office control. Plainly, at least in up-country South Australia in the early 1890s, popular sentiment would not permit the hanging of a white man for the murder of an Aborigine. This was no different to the attitude in Queensland, where no European was hanged for the murder of an Aborigine in the whole colonial period.

Willshire was reinstated but transferred to South Australia. In January 1892, Goldsborough, Mort & Co. Ltd, owners of Victoria River Downs, urged the government to establish a Native Police post in the district to control the Aborigines, who had given a lot of trouble in the past few weeks, having attacked one or more of the stockmen. Foelsche, still opposed to the use of native police, said this would be too expensive and suggested a white constable with one or two trackers. Nothing was done for more than two years; in the meantime W. S. Scott, manager of nearby Willeroo station, was killed by Aborigines. Foelsche now said no men were available to go to the Victoria River, but the government, under pressure from Goldsborough Mort, solved that problem by sending Willshire up from the south. In May 1894 he established a post at Gordon Creek between Willeroo, Victoria River Downs and Auvergne stations and close to Jasper Gorge, haunt of marauding Aborigines. Funds were so short that Goldsborough Mort was asked to provision one policeman and two trackers.[16]

Aborigines had been killing cattle on Wave Hill and Victoria River Downs stations, when Willshire and his black troopers came upon some of them in August 1894, camped in a gorge near the Wickham River:

The war cry sounded through the tribe, and they picked up their spears and commenced climbing the precipitous sides. As there was no getting away the females and children crawled into rocky embrasures, and there they remained. When we had finished with the male portion we brought the black gins and their offspring out from their rocky alcoves... There were some nice-looking boys and girls among them. One girl had a face and figure worthy of Aphrodite...

Willshire was very partial to the black beauties he and his men captured, but hotly denied that such actions as implied above were the cause of Aboriginal violence against Europeans. The 'oily, soapy hypocrites in towns, who know nothing about it, will tell you "It is done because white men take their lubras" '. He wished these 'canting snufflers' placed in some of the predicaments he had known; 'Religion won't aid you then; nothing but a good Winchester or Martini carbine, in conjunction with a Colt's revolver. They are your best friends, and you must use them too'.[17]

In May 1895 two teamsters, Mulligan and Ligar, were attacked by Aborigines in Jasper Gorge but held them off for three days before escaping on horseback to Auvergne station. Next day the attackers were still looting the waggon when Willshire and one trooper came upon the scene. They fled, and Willshire and the trooper mounted guard on the waggon until next day when two parties of whites and 'black boys' arrived. According to Willshire some stolen property and three 'gravy-eyed old gins' were captured. He does not even infer that any Aborigines died as a result of this action. Aboriginal oral history sources claim that Mulligan and Ligar had been attacked by Ngaliwuru and Ngarinman tribesmen because they had captured two of their women.

Some weeks later, it was said, two girls of the Bilignara tribe, working at the Gordon Creek police station, were sent into the bush to persuade their people to come to the station to build a yard. The Bilignara agreed, but when they arrived they were chained by the trackers, lined up and shot; the bodies were heaped and burned in a creek bed. There is no physical evidence today of the alleged massacre, and the Gordon Creek police station diaries do not mention anything untoward happening there at that time.[18]

In January 1895 Willshire had applied for transfer to South Australia to be near his aged parents and sisters at Norwood. This was approved, the transfer to take effect from 1 November. On 8 May, however, six days before the attack on Mulligan and Ligar, the minister controlling the Northern Territory, F. W. Holder, saw a newspaper report that Willshire and his trackers were pursuing the murderers of two stations blacks on Victoria River Downs. The report, which referred to Willshire's 'native police', appeared to be innocent enough, but Holder was angry. He wrote to the Chief Secretary and Premier, C. C. Kingston:

I earnestly request that M. C. Willshire may be immediately removed from the Northern Territory. His reputation is such that in my opinion he is the last man in the world who should be entrusted with duties which bring him in contact with the aborigines. The honourable the Chief Secretary will no doubt agree with me that if it is decided to comply with my request for his recall no time should be lost.[19]

It appears that the government knew a lot more about Willshire's actions in the Territory than was made public at the time of his trial or later. He was recalled and was living on the northern outskirts of Adelaide when his romantic and bitter memoirs, *The Land of the Dawning*, written while he was still at Gordon Creek, were published in 1896.

Despite the odium created by the Willshire affair, abuses by the native police towards Aborigines continued, especially in settling personal accounts. Following the shooting of an Aborigine named Ookilly by a native constable in Central Australia in September 1898, Holder recommended to Kingston that black police should not be armed with carbines or rifles. He was not convinced the police had acted in self-defence in this case. Two months later the Commissioner of Police ordered that in future native constables were to be issued only with revolvers, considered to be sufficient for self-defence.[20] This appears to have marked the end of the native police on 'Queensland lines' in the Northern Territory.

The period from the arrival of Willshire early in 1882 to the restrictions placed on the Aboriginal troopers in 1898 was one of minimal control over police activities in Central Australia. While the period from 1874 to 1884 in the Top End included several incidents of European revenge against Aboriginal violence, such incidents were exceptional in the normal course of Aboriginal–European relations.

The presence by 1885 of humanitarian administrators such as Langdon Parsons, and the strengthening of administrative control at least as far south as the Roper, meant that the period of frontier law and order passed quickly in the Top End. In the Centre, where the government resident in Palmerston had no influence and the lines of communication and administration were longer and weaker, the power of local officials was stronger and policemen such as Willshire and Wurmbrand had greater discretion, backed by big pastoralists with political influence in Adelaide. Even the appointment of F. J. Gillen as sub-protector at Alice Springs in 1892 did not materially improve the situation, because of his undisguised allegiance with the pastoralists. The chief influence for change was the growing concern of humanitarians in Adelaide, but this was not to be fully effective until the turn of the century. In the meantime, the Aborigines' main hope of protection lay with the missionaries.

Chapter 10

The Missionaries

The South Australian Legislative Council's select committee on the Aborigines in 1860 concluded that the Aborigines were doomed to extinction and that any measures taken to assist them would only be temporary. The South Australian government accepted a responsibility to provide rations to them as some form of compensation for what they had lost, but it was loath to accept a heavy burden of administration. Apart from re-establishing the office of protector — whose chief duties were to supervise the distribution of rations and to report any abuses of the Aborigines — the government looked to private benevolent organizations to deal directly with them. For this reason the upsurge in missionary activity in the 1860s was officially welcomed. So successful did the missions appear to be in relieving the government of its obligations that the office of South Australian protector was abolished in 1868 and not restored again until 1881. Of course, successive protectors had been appointed in the Northern Territory since the first attempt at settlement at Escape Cliffs in 1864, and this office, later expanded by the appointment of sub-protectors, continued throughout the South Australian period. As with other aspects of Territory administration, the protectors based in Palmerston could not traverse the whole Territory; so Aboriginal affairs in the Centre were without supervision until 1881, when E. L. Hamilton was appointed sub-protector for the far north of South Australia and in the next year protector of the whole colony. In 1884 Sub-Inspector Besley at Port Augusta was made a sub-protector. Because of his direct responsibility for the police in Central Australia, it is likely that Besley rather than Hamilton dealt with any complaints of abuses against the Aborigines in the first instance. Any such complaints concerning policemen could, of course, have placed Besley in a conflict of interest.

Into this situation came the Hermannsburg Mission Society of Germany with the objective of saving the souls of the Aranda. The society had founded a mission station at Killalpaninna on Cooper's

128

Creek just east of Lake Eyre in 1866, but the Dieri people there were hostile and the society's efforts fruitless. The Immanuel Synod of the Lutheran Church in Adelaide took over Killalpaninna in 1872. The Hermannsburg Mission Society, in conjunction with the Evangelical Lutheran Synod of Australia, decided to find another site and sought the opinion of the Surveyor-General, G. W. Goyder. Subsequently the Commissioner of Crown Lands granted ninety square miles of land on the Finke River, ninety miles west of Alice Springs. It was later expanded to nine hundred square miles, and three missionaries, G. A. Heidenreich (supervisor), W. F. Schwarz and A. H. Kempe, together with five colonists, arrived on 4 June 1877. Unlike the Dieri east of Lake Eyre, the Aranda were friendly and good relations were established from the start. Some assisted the missionaries to build the station in return for food, which was largely provided by the government. At first this did not induce the Aranda to stay on the station but, as pastoral settlement proceeded in the district, they were forced increasingly to depend upon mission food to supplement their traditional diet. By 1879 most open rangeland in the district had been invaded by herds of cattle, and the Aranda were being forced out of their traditional hunting grounds. Only a few Aranda were residing at Hermannsburg late in 1879, when two waggons loaded with government supplies arrived. Immediately more than a hundred settled there and within eight months had exhausted all the supplies. This has been described as the beginning of the intelligent exploitation of the whites by the Aborigines at Hermannsburg. The number of permanent residents dropped after the supplies were exhausted but as resources improved increased to about a hundred in 1889 and remained at about that level. Tension between the mission and the settlers soon developed. The pastoralists criticized the usefulness of the Hermannsburg station and the provision of government rations. Some claimed police protection was more important than a mission, because the Aborigines were killing their sheep. In 1879 the government instructed the telegraph stationmaster at Alice Springs, E. E. C. Flint, who had survived the Barrow Creek attack, to make an unannounced inspection. Flint did so, reported favourably and recommended continuing government support. The missionaries were increasingly concerned by the effects of European contact on the Aranda. In 1884 Schwarz wrote to the protector about the ill-treatment the Aborigines were receiving from the settlers, which, he said, was arousing their hostility. He also alleged that 'continual fornication with the Aboriginal women by the settlers was a constant source of trouble'.[1]

By 1889 the missionaries were strongly criticizing the settlers and police in reports to the Lutheran Synod in Adelaide. They said the settlers lured the young Aborigines away from the mission with generous promises. They dressed the women in men's clothes, got them to drove cattle and had intercourse with them. These women were better dressed and fed than those at the mission. The missionaries regarded this practice as an attempt to undermine their efforts and asked that it be stopped. Soon relations between the missionaries and the cattlemen were rancorous. During a visit to Adelaide in January 1890, Schwarz addressed a meeting on the Aborigines called by the missionary, C. Eaton Taplin, a son of George Taplin, the founding missionary at Point McLeay, to urge a complete change in government policy. Schwarz severely criticized the Central Australian settlers, saying the object of many actions taken against the Aborigines was to exterminate them, especially the men. He claimed to know of many occasions on which settlers had shot them. Schwarz said: 'It was a question of cattle versus blacks, and if the squatter wanted the country the blacks had to go'. He criticized the police and said that Aboriginal women were kept for 'shameful' purposes on almost every station. Syphilis, he said, was widespread and the mission girls were generally led astray by white men. He demanded that something be done to protect the Central Australian Aborigines.[2]

At this time Willshire reported that Aborigines on the mission were the worst cattle-killers and used the mission as a refuge. When the deputation of pastoralists with interests in Tempe Downs waited on the minister, J. H. Gordon, in February 1890, seeking more protection for the station, Gordon quoted Willshire's claim. The published report of this meeting prompted Kempe and another missionary, L. Schulze, to write to Taplin, who sent their letter to the *South Australian Register*.[3] Kempe and Schulze said the Aborigines were 'shot like wild dogs' and 'immorality' was rife in Central Australia. Willshire responded by saying that not only did the missionaries harbour cattle-killers and encourage them, but they tied up young Aborigines, threatened them with firearms and fetched absconders back by force. Soon Central Australian settlers were writing to the newspapers supporting Willshire and defending their own way of life. Gordon decided that the claims by both sides should be investigated, although he appears to have identified himself with the settlers. He swore to close the mission if Willshire's accusations proved to be true, but apparently he did not swear to do anything if the missionaries' allegations proved to be true. A board of inquiry comprising a magistrate, H. C. Swan, and Taplin (nominated by the Lutheran Synod) was formed in June 1890 and asked to investigate the claims made by both sides and recommend steps to be taken for the better protection of the Aborigines.

Swan and Taplin visited the area, interviewed missionaries, settlers, goldminers at Arltunga and police, and reported in September. They claimed to have 'met with' five hundred Aborigines and verified the existence of five hundred more. Swan and Taplin said that, owing to the scarcity of waterholes in the interior and because cattle would not approach water beside which blacks were camped, the cattlemen ordered the Aborigines off their hunting grounds; but there was no reason to suppose that any violence had been used. On the contrary, it was evident the blacks were persuaded to move without any trouble. As for Schwarz's claims about Wurmbrand taking away three captives who were later found shot dead and still in chains, they were satisfied there was nothing in this charge. They disagreed with Schwarz's claim that Aboriginal boys who were useful were well treated but that the older men were maltreated, and said Aborigines had every opportunity to leave stations if they were severely handled by the whites. They believed that Schwarz's claim that young Aboriginal women were kept on stations for immoral purposes was calculated to give the wrong impression of Central Australia. Although recognizing that considerable immorality did exist, they found the claim not proven, as the women on stations were employed in housework, milking etc. Allegations that Willshire had shot blacks he had been sent to arrest and had brought in two girls with whom he had lived were found not to be supported by the evidence. Nor were allegations that three girls from the mission had run away and were living with Willshire. The girls had run away with some Afghans, who had gone to the mission for a load of wool, and been recovered by the police. Schwarz had alleged that halfcastes were numerous, but Swan and Taplin had not seen or ascertained the existence of a dozen halfcastes in the district over which they had travelled. Claims by Kempe and Schulze that settlers had shot down the blacks like wild dogs and had used their wives and daughters for immoral purposes also were unsupported by the evidence. As for Willshire's claims, Swan and Taplin found that the missionaries had shown a lack of judgement on one or two occasions, chains being used to detain certain Aboriginal prisoners and thrashing used as a punishment, but that this did not amount to cruelty. They believed the Lutherans had been prompted by the kindest motives. In only one case had an Aborigine employed on the station as a shepherd taken to cattle-killing; the mission was no more a harbour for cattle-killers than any other station. Witnesses had agreed that the police did their duty well and, as long as native troopers were required, Willshire was confirmed as the right man for the job. But, because he and the missionaries were 'at variance', Swan and Taplin recommended that his camp be shifted from Boggy Waterhole to somewhere between the boundaries of Tempe Downs and Erldunda.

They recommended also that the old and infirm Aborigines be encouraged to make the mission their home by being supplied regularly with rations; that Aborigines on the mission be decently clothed; that dormitories be supplied for the girls and boys; and that after two years the government subsidy be discontinued. By then, they believed, the mission should, with proper management, be self-supporting. As for the future protection of the Aborigines, they recommended that reserves of five hundred to a thousand square miles in area and not less than two hundred miles apart be created. They should be stocked and placed under the care of a manager and schoolmaster. As this policy would be expensive, they advised that only one such reserve be established at first, at Crown Point station, with others to follow after a year or two. They believed a system of reserves would allow the Aborigines to be entirely self-supporting.

As the *Adelaide Observer* commented: 'In effect the report white-washes the accused all round', and 'the fact that the natives have made no organized resistance to the usurpation of their country by the white man ... affords a strong argument in favour of dealing generously with them'. All experience, it said, pointed to the Aboriginal race becoming extinct in a generation or two but, meanwhile, it was incumbent upon those who had dispossessed it of its natural hunting grounds to deal liberally with it. Swan and Taplin's report supplied a strong argument for dealing with the Aborigines with far more rational and systematic methods than then existed. Such press comments as this suggest that the condition of the Central Australian Aborigines had touched the conscience of South Australia, yet none of these recommendations were fully implemented: Willshire remained at Boggy Waters until his arrest in April 1891 but his successors were sent to Illamurta; the government subsidy was not stopped in 1892 but reduced to £100 a year; the mission constructed dormitories for the children and substantial 'wurlies' for the adults, and issued more clothes but not more rations. A reserve was proclaimed by excising ninety square miles from the Crown Point lease but this was revoked after nine months on petition by the leaseholder. The missionaries' complaints, however, did eventually bring about a protectorate in the Centre when F. J. Gillen was appointed sub-protector for the Alice Springs district.

Even with the continued support of the government and the apparent end to the feuding between them and the settlers and police, the Hermannsburg missionaries by this time could see their mission heading for failure. The Lutherans had attempted to found a mission soundly based on local industry, such as wool and cattle, where nomadism would be abolished by attracting Aborigines to those industries. They would study the local language and teach the Aborigines to read and write it so that they might more easily understand Christianity; and the young and old would be given regular religious and secular instruction. Unlike the settlers the missionaries did not at first believe the Aborigines were doomed to extinction or unduly treacherous and murderous; nor did they have contempt for the Aborigines' capacities or persons. They had begun their mission convinced of the blacks' capacity for moral improvement and to receive God's grace, but the more they became acquainted with Aboriginal culture the more their contempt for it increased. Their faith in the Aborigines' capacity for salvation was shaken. No compromise should be made with this heathen culture; all adaption should be made by the Aborigines. By the mid-1880s all hope of converting the adults had been abandoned. The Lutherans concentrated on the young and attempted to segregate them from the adults, especially the old men, and became convinced that the blacks were fated to remain the servants of the whites. At this time they had come to believe the Aranda were doomed to extinction. Even so, they managed to make their first converts in 1887 and by 1891 nearly fifty Aranda had been baptized. Disease among the Aranda, including typhoid, appears to have risen sharply after 1887, and Schulze believed that almost all suffered syphilis. Illness was gradually affecting the missionaries themselves and Schwarz was forced to leave. Schulze followed him soon afterwards in October 1891 and when Kempe's wife died he also left. Two other missionaries replaced them but they could not speak Aranda and achieved little. When the Horn scientific expedition called at Hermannsburg in July 1894, the director of the South Australian Museum, Dr E. C. Stirling, found no evidence among the Western Aranda of 'an abiding improvement, either mentally, morally or physically'. Similar observations were made by another member of this expedition, Professor Walter Baldwin Spencer. The Hermannsburg Mission Society's effort on the Finke River had failed and in September 1894 the Immanuel Synod of the Lutheran Church in South Australia, which still operated a mission at Kopperamanna on Cooper's Creek, purchased it and took over activities there. Hermannsburg was retained as a place name, and the Immanuel Synod continued to operate the mission well into the twentieth century.[4]

In 1882 the Jesuit order in South Australia asked the government for land near Palmerston on which it could begin a mission to the Aborigines. The government resident, Edward Price, when asked to comment had little to say but obtained a report from Foelsche which he sent to Adelaide. This report by Foelsche, together with another he was to make to Judge Dashwood in 1898 when Dashwood was framing his abortive Aboriginal legislation, are his two major official statements on the Aborigines. The 1882 report reveals something about the condition of Aborigines in the Top End after twelve years of permanent European settlement. It does not refer to conditions in Central Australia, for which Foelsche had no official responsibility, nor does it directly refer to the pastoral industry of the Top End, suggesting that as yet he knew little about what was happening on the pastoral frontier. It represents contemporary official knowledge of and attitudes towards Aboriginal–European relations in the Top End.

Although it was a painful fact, he wrote in his report, cannibalism and infanticide were still practised secretly by all the tribes, but Aborigines were nevertheless capable of being civilized and made useful members of the civilized community, if proper means were adopted. It would be no easy task to eradicate the vices they had acquired from many nations with whom they had been in contact and by whom 'they have been demoralised to a fearful extent'.

Many crimes have been committed by them in this Territory since its settlement... but it is hard to say what were the provocations that led to the greater part of them; from my own experience and communications received from Natives, I have reason to believe that during the period that this Territory has been settled, more Natives have been murdered in cold blood by Europeans, than Europeans by Natives, and it is a well known fact that the latter are not always the first aggressors.[5]

Of course, Foelsche added, the Aborigines were savages and proper precautions must always be taken, when meeting them in their native haunts, not to give them an opportunity to take advantage of one's lonely position, 'for invariably they will follow the dictates of their savage minds and kill intruders on their native soil'. Even so, with kind yet firm treatment they soon comprehended the superiority of the white man, respected his higher position and submitted to his ruling. They became tractable and many made good servants, especially the women. They mastered English quickly and acquired a sense of right and wrong. In the Port Darwin neighbourhood the 'rising generation' seemed disposed to abandon their old customs and to adopt the habits of the Europeans. Many young ones were employed in the stores and assisted in loading cargo and did all sorts of manservants' work. Young and middle-aged women made good washerwomen and some ironed clothes as well as Europeans. The young women made 'capital' nursegirls and became very fond of their charges. Remuneration was chiefly food and clothing and sometimes sixpence or a shilling.

In Foelsche's opinion, contact with Europeans had in some measure civilized the Aborigines and raised them to an outward appearance a little above their original position, but on the other hand it was the painful truth that these associations had demoralized them and had taught them vices previously unknown to them, such as smoking tobacco and drinking intoxicating liquor. The large proportion of male to female Europeans—thirty-one to one at the last census—had led most Aboriginal women in the settled districts into prostitution, encouraged by their own men, to obtain tobacco and liquor. The absence of halfcaste children indicated that the progeny of this illicit intercourse was 'put aside as soon as born'. The protector of Aborigines, Dr R. J. Morice, did not keep records of Aboriginal births and deaths but there was no perceptible change in the population. Foelsche believed, however, that vices acquired from the Europeans would slowly undermine their constitutions and reduce their numbers. He made these estimates of the number of Aborigines who had come into contact with whites: Port Darwin and neighbourhood, 150; goldfields, 200; Port Patterson and Daly River, 200; Adelaide River, 100; Alligator Rivers, 200; and Port Essington and neighbourhood, 200; total, 1050. The tribes along the east coast as far as Blue Mud Bay were somewhat civilized as a result of many years of contact with the Macassan trepang fishermen. The Aborigines had been employed by the Macassans to fish for trepang but they were slaves to the drinking, smoking and other vices introduced by these visitors and as a result suffered venereal disease.

Throughout his report Foelsche was detached, expressing an interest in and knowledge of the Aborigines unusual among his contemporaries, but never expressing any concern. While he noted the deleterious trends resulting from European contact, he did not suggest what should be done to stop or reverse these trends. In his detached way he commented: 'By the majority of the [European] population the Aborigines are looked on as beasts, destitute of reason, and are treated as such'. In forwarding Foelshe's report, Price merely agreed the Aborigines were not so degraded as supposed and he believed it quite possible to bring the younger ones into a 'fair state' of civilization, especially if a mission were established under the Jesuits, 'who are well known for their successful efforts as missionaries'. Clearly Price and Foelsche had no idea how to deal with the perceived present and future problems of the Northern Territory Aborigines, other than to hope that private organizations such as the Jesuit order could solve them. This was also the position of the government which, on the basis of Foelsche's report and Price's advice, granted 320 acres of land at Rapid Creek near Palmerston.

The Jesuits had been commissioned to undertake this mission after Father Duncan McNab, a Scottish missionary who had laboured in Queensland in the 1870s without success, visited Rome in 1880 and urged that a religious order work among the Aborigines of the Northern Territory. The first Jesuits, led by Father Anton Strele, arrived in Palmerston from South Australia on 24 September 1882 and immediately set about constructing buildings and planting tobacco, bananas and pineapples with the help of the Larakia. They moved into the mission, called St Joseph's, on 10 October that year. The Larakia were soon enticed to the mission by small gifts of food, but nine weeks after its founding they returned to Palmerston where they 'lived by begging and sin'. Even so, in January 1883 a large number were camped nearby and began working for the Jesuits. The mission area proved too small and the government increased it to a thousand acres, later adding another two hundred. In 1883 Strele informed the government that he now had sufficient staff for another mission and said the Daly River district seemed to be fit for such an undertaking. Great numbers of Aborigines lived there and it would be easier than at Rapid Creek to keep them separated from the whites. While he intended that Aborigines on the Daly would help the missionaries to cultivate the land, they required room for hunting and fishing, 'as they cannot break off at once all their former habits without running great risks for their very preservation'. Strele asked for complete control of the reserve and the exclusion of all whites.[6] In 1886 the total Jesuit staff was ten, including three at the supplementary station now established on the Daly River. At Rapid Creek a school with regular lessons was operating in 1885, the Larakia being taught in their own language. But in 1888 the acting superior, Father Donald McKillop, reported to the government that the Rapid Creek mission had failed. The Jesuits' plan, like the Lutherans' in Central Australia, had been to induce the Aborigines to settle down in a self-supporting agricultural colony, along the lines of the Jesuit *reducciónes* in Paraguay. In this way they hoped the Aborigines would abandon their nomadic way of life, cultivate fields, settle down and become British citizens — but there was no compelling reason why they should. The Larakia came and went as they pleased. Palmerston was close and tobacco could be obtained there by easier methods, such as begging and prostitution, than by hard work at Rapid Creek. In nine years there the Jesuits baptized only one adult Aborigine, a Woolna.

After a clash between the Larakia, Woolna and Alligator Rivers tribes in May 1887, McKillop decided to concentrate all efforts on the Daly River and he began moving resources there. Next year active missionary work had ended at Rapid Creek, which was maintained only as a farm and place for building up herds of goats, horses and cattle. It closed in June 1891 after the last missionaries there were sent to the Daly River. Named as the Queen of the Holy Rosary, the Daly River mission was usually known by the Aboriginal name Uniya. The Jesuits had failed to understand the real reasons for the failure of Rapid Creek, believing them to be the distractions of civilization at Palmerston and interference from eastern neighbours; in fact, there was a basic incompatability between Aboriginal culture and the Jesuits' idealistic agricultural colony. They thought the answer to the problems encountered at Rapid Creek was to start afresh with another tribe, far removed from the temptations of white contact. On the Daly they set out to establish a number of small stations, each staffed by three or four missionaries, still on the Paraguayan model. But they were ignorant of conditions there, such as Aboriginal aggressions, flooding of the Daly and unsuitability of the land for agriculture. As to the last factor, they had probably been misled by the government and settlers in the Top End, who for years steadfastly believed the Daly was ideal for agriculture. On arrival they found the Aborigines friendly and by September 1887 two Aboriginal men and their families were resident at Uniya and cultivating their own plots. Several buildings had been erected and small gardens were apparently flourishing. In that month the first religious instruction was given to ten Aborigines and next day the first school class was held. Uniya was at the junction of territories held by tribes called, by the Jesuits, the Woolwonga, Mulluk Mulluk and Agaquilla, about sixty miles upstream from the mouth of the river. In 1888 about thirty Aboriginal families had settled at Uniya, forty Aborigines were hired as workers, thirty-one children attended the school, the colony had goats, fowls and a tobacco crop which was doing well, and rice had been planted on the flood plains. The mission was at its high point.

An epidemic, apparently whooping cough or influenza, introduced by Europeans and Chinese working on the Daly River copper mines, struck the Aborigines of the area. This abated but malaria followed. The rice crop failed and malaria returned, 'incapacitating the natives and reducing the staff, now five, to wretchedness once again'. In April 1889 the first adult Aborigine was baptized and by June eleven had been christened. The copper mines closed in that month and so one of the missionaries' many problems — contact between the local people and the whites and Chinese — was removed. In March 1891 food crops again failed at Uniya; McKillop decided to close it down and move all resources to Serpentine Lagoon, about twenty miles west of the river, which had already been selected as the major mission site. The lagoon station was also called Uniya and was just as unsuccessful as the first. The soil was poor for imported plants but native food was abundant, so the Aborigines had little incentive to work at the mission. Doggedly the Jesuits stuck to the Paraguayan agricultural ideal and do not seem to have considered alternatives such as cattle production. After two years they abandoned Serpentine Lagoon and moved to a third site, also called Uniya, about twenty miles downstream from the first one. The government had granted three hundred acres there in August 1891, and all three other stations, Rapid Creek and the two original Uniyas, were formally closed. Despite the setbacks, human resources were not lacking. The third Uniya had eleven Jesuits — four priests and seven brothers — and Aborigines from the first Uniya and some from the second followed them there. At the end of 1891 about fifty were permanently residing at the third Uniya. Stock had increased, several acres had been cleared, and erected upon them were a temporary house, a small chapel, dormitories for the boys and girls, a store and work shed, a forge, stables and a windmill for irrigation. In the financial crisis which hit Australia in the early 1890s, donations from Australia and the Jesuit order in Austria, from which the first Jesuits in South Australia had come, dried up. Crops at the third Uniya would not bear in the first year and food was seriously short in 1892. Influenza struck again in June that year, forty Aborigines being afflicted and twelve dying. As early as 1888 the Jesuits had come to believe the only hope for a mission was in a place where total segregation of the Aborigines was possible, as on an island. They asked for Melville or Bathurst Island, but this was not granted to them, so they continued to labour on the Daly.[7]

To obtain funds McKillop and another missionary spent twenty months away from the Territory in 1892–93, taking two Aborigines with them. They raised £800, enough to save the mission from destitution, and in 1893 the crops began to yield and the herds to thrive. From 1893 to 1898 the Daly River mission was apparently successful, the number of Aboriginal colonists, pupils, apprentices and workers there being about two hundred at times but declining to seventy or eighty at the end of the period. The largest number of Aboriginal colonists was fifteen in 1897. They were Christian and tended two-acre farms but it seems they received nothing but tobacco for their labours. Although the Daly rose forty feet in March 1898 and flooded the fields, normal life soon resumed and the mission made its first profit in that year. Next March it experienced greater floods. Despite all these difficulties the Jesuits on the Daly looked as though they were going to succeed. Then they were forced to close down completely, because of factors outside their control. As early as June 1895 they had been told by the order that this might happen. The Austrian Jesuits were no longer able to send men and funds to Australia; a merger with the Irish Jesuits in eastern Australia (mainly in Victoria) was proposed but the Irish were unable to support the Northern Territory mission; the Jesuit leader, Father Anderley, who had supported the mission strongly from its inception, had died at the end of 1891; his successor was not committed to it and petitioned *Propaganda Fidei* in Rome to close it. After McKillop left in 1896 no official superior was appointed to replace him. In March 1899 the crops were again flooded, completely ruined this time, and the settlers' huts were washed away. On 20 June 1899 Father Milz, the order's *visitator*, arrived at Uniya and closed the mission. Valuables were packed up, buildings dismantled, Aborigines dismissed, stock sold to local pastoralists and the Jesuits sent back to Europe or South Australia.[8]

In 1881, before the Jesuits opened their first mission in the Northern Territory, Father Duncan McNab had written to Strele and advised him that 'the tribal law must be broken and the family compact applied instead'. In the late 1870s McNab had attempted to obtain homestead blocks for Queensland Aborigines, hoping they would become families of agricultural settlers and thus break the hold of the tribe on individuals. His plan failed but, nonetheless, he tried to foist it on the Jesuits. Despite all their setbacks the Jesuits did attempt to establish family farms on the Daly and it seems that by 1898 they had succeeded. They had in effect converted some Mulluk Mulluk, the main tribe with whom they dealt there, to the European ideal of individual capitalists and agriculturalists. Also, they succeeded in converting a large number of Aborigines to Christianity, whereas McNab converted none. Their success may have been illusory in that the Aborigines may have accepted the new lifestyle and roles required of them in order to obtain European food and goods. It is just possible they were so impressed with these men who laboured with such sincerity and self-deprivation, almost to the point of death at times, and wished to emulate them, believing their own culture to be under no direct threat. The Jesuits did not break the hold of tribal law, as McNab had urged. Their religion and regime apparently had no destructive effects upon the Daly River people. They did not forbid many traditional practices. Although they required the Aborigines to wear clothes, they did not otherwise attempt to force them to become black Europeans. Unlike George Taplin at Point McLeay mission in South Australia, who was a man of his time, they did not set out to destroy Aboriginal culture as soon as possible. Nor did they remove tribes from their territories, as had happened with the South Australian missions and was then happening in Queensland under the new Aborigines' protection legislation. The Jesuits were remarkably tolerant and patient, realizing that any permanent change would take generations and would come only when the Aborigines wanted it. It is ironical that one of the truly successful missionary efforts in Australia in the nineteenth century was terminated not by failure but by its own church for largely internal reasons.

The Lutheran mission at Hermannsburg and the Jesuit missions in the Top End were the two major attempts to convert Northern Territory Aborigines to Christianity in the South Australian period. The Lutherans suffered hardships on the Finke River but no more than the Jesuits. The Lutherans received considerable government supplies through their period, except for 1876–78 when they did not request them; whereas the Jesuits received only meagre government assistance, depending heavily upon church and private assistance. Like the Lutheran missionaries in Moreton Bay, Queensland, 1838–1850, the South Australian Lutherans despaired of the Aborigines, eventually dismissing them as inferior beings beyond salvation; but the Jesuits never lost hope. The Hermannsburg experiment, 1877–94, was a failure and the mission station continued only because another branch of the church took it over; whereas the Jesuit mission was terminated when about to succeed. At Hermannsburg the unofficial South Australian policy of segregation and assimilation was practised, with the objective of eliminating Aboriginal culture; whereas on the Daly the Aborigines were not segregated, retaining contacts with their own people and traditions and, apart from certain codes of dress and behaviour, were invited by example to adapt themselves to Christianity. At Hermannsburg acculturation of the Aranda resulted as much from mission policy as from contact with the whites whom the Lutherans tried to keep away from them; on the Daly, as W. E. H. Stanner noted many years later, 'With the close of the Mission, the period of white contact marked by tolerance and sympathy had ended, and a devastating "acculturation" was about to take its course among the tribes'.[9]

In 1898 the Church of England began seeking to establish a mission on the South Alligator River. A permit to do so was granted in April 1901 to the Northern Australian Industrial (Church of England) Mission on a hundred square miles of land at Koparlgo between the Manassie reserve (on the West Alligator River) and the South Alligator River. The mission trained Aborigines in cooking, housework, fishing and carpentry but it soon failed and the government resident's report for 1908 refers to the 'late mission' at Koparlgo. In 1906 the Bishop of Carpentaria, the Right Reverend Gilbert White, proposed that a mission be established on the Roper River and worked in conjunction with the Anglican mission at Mitchell River on the eastern side of the gulf. The government resident at that time, Charles Herbert, opposed the selection of a site, saying it should be placed nearer to the centres of settlement, 'where an attempt could be made towards combatting the evil effects which civilization carries with it among the aborigines'.[10] The bishop got his way and the mission station was opened a few miles upstream from the Roper mouth in 1908. The Reverend J. F. G. Huthnance, who was in charge, was appointed a sub-protector of Aborigines. In his report for 1911 the Acting Administrator of the Territory, S. J. Mitchell, said this mission had passed through its initial difficulties. He also said the Plymouth Brethren had a small establishment in Darwin (the name adopted by the Commonwealth when it took over responsibility for the Territory), where eight to ten young Aborigines had found a home. This, he said, was not an educational institution. In September 1910 W. J. Denny, a minister in the Verren Labor government, had dedicated all of Bathurst Island less 50 000 acres for Aboriginal purposes and granted 10 000 acres in the south-east corner for a Roman Catholic mission. The following year Father F. X. Gsell, who had been in Palmerston since 1906, established a mission there. The Northern Territory did not prove to be a rich field for missionary work compared with other regions of Australia. Of the missions established before 1911 only Hermannsburg, Roper River and Bathurst Island survived.

The lasting effects of missionary work and presence among Aborigines of the Northern Territory during the South Australian period has not been studied fully and any indications are usually enmeshed with non-missionary effects. Perhaps the most valuable assessments have been made in the Daly River district because of the work of W. E. H. Stanner in the early 1930s. In 1982 Michaela Richards reviewed these early influences as a preliminary to an unpublished study of Aborigines and settlers on the Daly River, 1912–1940. The first European enterprise on the Daly was a sugar plantation established by W. Owston in 1881, but by May 1883 he had abandoned it. Copper was discovered in 1882 and mining flourished in 1886–90 but had been abandoned by 1894. Chinese gardens had supplied the mines but none remained in 1894. Fisher and Lyons' pastoral station

station on the Daly, which had run more than 4000 cattle during 1883–86, and other, smaller, holdings were all abandoned by 1890. The Chinese reopened the mines in 1899 and in 1904 the government erected a reverberating furnace and began smelting on the Daly; but in 1908 this was closed, although a handful of Chinese worked the mine until 1913. A man named Niemann worked the abandoned 'New Uniya' site, presumably the third site, in 1903, using Aborigines to trap animals, mine silver and cultivate crops. In 1910 W. Roberts and D. Thomas established a tobacco plantation and with Aboriginal assistance cleared and cultivated twenty-five acres in less than two years. Their apparent success was used by government officials as an object lesson in what could be done with Aborigines in agriculture. The Aborigines seem to have lived well off the produce of this plantation, which produced cereal, fruit and vegetable crops, but Roberts's and Thomas's main hope, tobacco, was never commercially successful. The non-Aboriginal population on the Daly appears to have reached fifty or more in short periods and, while this was a small number compared with the heavy Aboriginal population in the district, the evidence suggests that the immediate and even the long-term effects on the local people were significant. Aborigines acquired a taste for European goods, particularly tobacco, which was used as a form of payment — by the Jesuits as much as any other Europeans. Stanner has pointed out that although native food was abundant in the district, Aborigines deliberately moved to the Europeans' settlements in order to acquire their goods. This contrasted strongly with the experience in Central Australia where the biggest movement to ration depots occurred during periods of drought.

Stanner estimated that the Jesuit missions suspended the normal economic lives of about fifty Aborigines each year although, as G. J. O'Kelly has indicated, the number may have been higher. There is little evidence of Aborigines being employed in mining before the end of the nineteenth century, although some were employed there at the time of the murders. After 1904 Aborigines were consistently employed by the Chinese and Europeans, as many as twenty-four in 1906. Roberts and Thomas had eight on their plantation in 1911. Payment appears to have been always in kind — food, tobacco and sometimes alcohol, opium, clothes and material goods. Aboriginal labour was the cheapest and almost the only labour available to the end of the South Australian period. The movement of outside tribes into the Daly River district was evident long before 1911. McKillop estimated that some Aborigines living and working at Uniya in 1892 had come as far as sixty miles, and large numbers of visiting Aborigines camped about the mission station in the hope of receiving trade goods. Disruption of traditional life was evident by 1911, when medical officers visiting the district reported a low standard of health, low fertility and opium-addiction among Aboriginal women and a consequent absence of children from

Aboriginal camps. By the early 1930s Stanner found that acculturation had been 'devastating', but McKillop, reporting in 1896, had found that the Jesuits' persons were 'wani' or sacred to the Daly tribes. The old men taught that they were not like other men and that their teachings were 'wani' and belonged to the truths originally taught by their fathers.[11] The long-term effect of religious contact with Europeans has not yet been fully studied.

Chapter 11

The Humanitarians

Coincidental with the seeming failure of the Hermannsburg Society
mission in Central Australia after 1885 and the admitted failure of the
Jesuits at Rapid Creek in that year, some Europeans became concerned
for the Aborigines' material welfare. This concern flowed from an
awareness of the material losses and physical abuses the Aborigines
had suffered as a result of European colonization. Any actions resulting
from it were not aimed at changing their religion or even converting
them into black Europeans. The aim was at least partial redress for
wrongs and was purely humanitarian. The humanitarian movement in
South Australia and the Northern Territory was slow to begin and had
little support, official or public, for many years. Apart from the
establishment of ration depots — in most cases introduced in the
Territory in the hope of inducing Aborigines not to kill cattle rather
than any concern for their welfare — there was no organized assistance.
Throughout the South Australian period humanitarianism in the
Territory was little more than sentiment. Whereas individual whites
were strongly critical of government policy in Queensland as early as
1861, there was little public comment on the condition of the
Aborigines in the Territory before the 1890s. Of course, everything
happened later in the Territory than elsewhere in Australia but, even so,
remoteness helps to explain South Australians' early indifference to
events on their northern frontiers.

After two decades of self-government, thousands of Queenslanders,
largely untouched by frontier attitudes, had sufficient knowledge of
the situation on the western and northern pastoral frontiers of
their colony to make their concern plain to the government of the
day. They were not separated from the objects of their concern by
a thousand miles of desert. In 1880 the influential journal, *The
Queenslander*, ran a campaign condemning the methods of the
Native Police Force, and humanitarians attempted to solve the
Aboriginal problem, as they saw it, by means of direct aid, sometimes

with government support. No such campaign occurred in South Australia, which had been self-governing longer than Queensland and had prided itself upon its liberal ideals since foundation. The citizens of Adelaide and its environs, living in areas long ago cleared of Aborigines, had little knowledge of, or interest in, what was happening in the Territory. Certainly, there had been public protests against alleged ill-treatment by punitive expeditions in 1878 and 1884–85 and the Lutherans had criticized the settlers and police in 1889–90. Yet, it was not the ill-treatment of Aborigines which finally stirred southern feelings, but rather the 'immorality' of Aboriginal sexual relations with other races, the increasing number of halfcaste children, and incidence of disease and opium-smoking. Victorian morality rather than humanitarianism was the motivation.

Even so, there were a few genuine humanitarians at this time, the two most important being J. L. Parsons and C. J. Dashwood, both government residents. Parsons' and Dashwood's administrations both began with indifference, and at times antipathy, towards the Aborigines. Parsons had arrived in May 1884 and during the immediate aftermath of the Daly River murders was weak in his handling of public passions, offering insufficient restraint to those who wished to take revenge. His immediate wish was to apprehend the guilty, try them quickly without the benefit of counsel, hang them at the scene and let the bodies dangle for some time as a grisly warning to others. But by January 1885 his attitude had changed. He was the first to recognize that, in the seizure of their lands and the consequent deprivations, the Aborigines had a real grievance. He understood that they must necessarily strike back in an attempt to protect their rights. He did not allow the administrative and legal muddle, into which he had got himself over the question of counsel in the Daly River case, to distort his perception of the Aborigines' condition.

By January 1885 Parsons was starting to have serious doubts about what really happened at Argument Flat in September 1884. In the aftermath of the Daly River murders, Charles Bridson's claim that Woolwonga had attacked the teamsters' camp had been accepted without question. Now it was rumoured that one of the Aborigines killed had been a woman, but an attack by Aborigines accompanied by women was so unusual that Bridson's story did not ring true. Bridson had claimed that he and his two mates were 'stuck up' by about twenty blacks who demanded tucker and, when this was refused, showered them with spears without warning, but subsequent evidence showed the whites were armed and waiting behind prepared positions. Five Aborigines were killed and several wounded, whereas none of the whites was even scratched. A second report by police, written on 31 January 1885, said the Aborigines had visited the teamster's camp on the previous day and had said they would return next day. It sounded improbable to Parsons that the Aborigines would have announced their intention to return if they also intended to attack. One of the injured Aborigines, Boco, had given information, not now available, which caused Parsons to decide to prosecute the teamsters and he sent Foelsche 'up country' to find more evidence. Late in February Foelsche returned after interviewing Boco and told Parsons he had no doubt his statement was quite correct, but all his own endeavours to gain additional evidence had failed. 'I do not see the slightest chance of getting a committal against the three Europeans implicated on the evidence of a single native', he said, and suggested the prosecution be abandoned, 'in as much as the matter is almost forgotten'.[1] What Parsons thought of a policeman who was prepared to treat five murders as 'almost forgotten' after only five months is not known, but reluctantly he had to agree.

In August 1885 the protector of Aborigines, Dr Percy Wood, wrote to Parsons on the condition of those in the Palmerston district. He was concerned because he believed violence would break out between the Larakia and the Malay pearlers who had come to Port Darwin after pearlshell was found in the harbour in February 1884. Larakia women had gone to live with the Malays who spent their money on them and sometimes took them to sea in their boats. Wood used this occasion to recommend several measures designed to protect Aborigines against abuses and to improve public morals. He proposed that Aborigines be kept out of Palmerston unless registered as servants; that no Aboriginal woman be allowed in the town between sunset and sunrise; that none be allowed in a boat on coasting trips; that all Aborigines in town be decently dressed; that the protector sign all agreements between Aboriginal servants and employers so that any disputes could be settled under the Masters and Servants Act; and that no agreement be binding for more than one year unless specifically fixed at the time of agreement. Wood believed imprisoning Aborigines for long periods for theft was ineffectual, because it was no disgrace to them to be living in gaol in the same conditions as Europeans. He proposed instead short imprisonment on bread and water and a flogging. He expressed concern for Aborigines brought from other colonies, especially Queensland, by Europeans to help them while droving stock into the Territory. Some had been abandoned when the stock had been delivered and the drover had returned by ship. They usually became ill, went to the Palmerston hospital and became a liability upon the protector or, before it closed, the Jesuit mission at Rapid Creek. Wood wanted any European arriving in the Territory with Aborigines in his employment to give to the nearest magistrate or police officer their names, sexes and home districts. No such Aborigine should be younger than twelve years of age. This latter provision would stop the practice of kidnapping Aboriginal women and children on the road, some of whom, he believed, were sold to other whites. He further proposed that no white should be permitted to leave an imported Aborigine in the Territory without the consent of the protector, and that anyone wishing to employ an Aborigine must give his or her name, address and a 'rough idea' of age to the protector. Wood recommended a large fine for any European found guilty of kidnapping Aborigines.[2] He was thinking along the lines of the Queensland *Native Labourers' Protection Act* of 1884 which attempted to redress similar abuses, although the Queensland parliament was chiefly concerned with the actions of ships' masters in abducting Aborigines to work in the pearlshell and trepang industries.

Parsons referred this report to Foelsche, who commented that it was difficult to legislate for the better treatment of the Aborigines. The authorities, who had proclaimed that whites and blacks were equal under the law, lost sight of the fact that it took many years for Aborigines, who had been governed by their own tribal laws, to become civilized. Laws specifically framed for them until they were 'reclaimed from savagery' would, he argued, be more effective than laws which 'control and regulate the most advanced stage of civilization'. The need for separate legislation for the Aborigines had 'occupied [his] mind for a good many years', but knowing that class law was against English principle he had refrained from suggesting it to the government.[3] Foelsche had touched on one of the key problems in the history of Aboriginal–European relations in Australia. If British law was to be applied equally to all races, one race could not be protected from the abuses arising from the advantages enjoyed by another. This legal question remained unresolved until the Queensland parliament in 1897 enacted the Aborigines protection legislation and so took the historic step of separating the Aborigines from other races for their own good.

In case the government felt disposed to consider separate legislation for the Aborigines, Foelsche further suggested that all offences by Aborigines, except murder and those cases which came within the jurisdiction of the Minor Offences Act, be heard and determined by a local court of full jurisdiction, and that in all cases the courts should have the power to impose corporal punishment. All Aborigines not in regular employment should be debarred from any town between 7 p.m. and 5 a.m.; no Aborigine in any town should be allowed on any premises at night unless regularly engaged as a servant; no Aborigines should be taken away on any boat or ship without the sanction of the protector; the protector should have jurisdiction over all Aborigines arriving in the Territory; any persons bringing Aborigines into the Territory should report their arrival and be responsible for their support and return to the colony from which they came; and, to discourage prostitution, any person illegally cohabiting with or having intercourse with an Aboriginal woman should be punished by a fine or imprisonment. In their proposals, Wood and Foelsche had anticipated the main provisions of the Queensland legislation without its principle measure, enforced segregation of the races.

Parsons referred Wood's and Foelsche's reports to the minister in Adelaide, R. C. Baker, saying this subject was of great importance and remedial measures were urgently required. He said the need for an Aboriginal Act to deal with offences committed by Aborigines was obvious, notwithstanding all that might be said about the genius of the English constitution. For the good government of the Territory, Acts were required for both the Aborigines and the Chinese, 'as neither of these races are fitted by nature or habits for ordinary English legal procedure'.[4] This was the first proposal for separate law to cover the special needs of Territory Aborigines not able to accommodate themselves to English law. It was ignored by Baker, who simply ordered that Parsons's recommendation and the attached reports be filed.

Parsons had suggested in January 1885 that large reserves should be set aside for the Aborigines so they could continue to live in their traditional way, free from contact with Europeans, but apparently he did not, at that time, feel so strongly about reserves as he did about the need for a separate law. In May 1886 Cockburn told Parsons he wished reserves to be established for the different tribes in the Northern Territory. He asked Parsons which tribes should be provided with reserves and the most suitable locations. Parsons's advice is not known, but nothing came of this. Instead, the first specific proposal came from C. T. Hemphill, of Douglas and Hemphill, owners of Helen Springs station near Powell Creek, just south of Newcastle Waters. In November 1887 he urged J. C. F. Johnson, minister in the Playford government, to set aside a reserve near the Powell Creek overland telegraph station 'for humanitarian reasons' — and, he added, 'to enable the station owners to more readily keep natives off the waters needed for the cattle'. Hemphill said not many such reserves were required at present but, as the country became more settled, it would only be fair that the Aborigines should have the use of certain tracts of country. Obviously Hemphill's motives were not altruistic. He displayed the common pessimistic attitude towards the Aborigines' future when he added that such reserves would revert to the government as the Aborigines disappeared before civilization 'as disappear they evidently must'.[5] Johnson thought that there was merit in the proposal and he instructed that inquiries be made with a view to having a tract reserved. Again, nothing came of this proposal.

No reserves were created in the Northern Territory until 1892 — when action was taken in response to a recommendation in Swan and Taplin's report of September 1890 and to the urging of F. J. Gillen even before he was appointed sub-protector in the Centre in October 1891. On 25 September Gillen advised the minister that three reserves should be proclaimed as quickly as possible near Tennant Creek, Barrow Creek and Charlotte Waters. Five days later W. G. Stretton, now magistrate at Borroloola, recommended to J. G. Knight, who became government resident after Parsons retired in 1890, that another be created between the McArthur and Robinson Rivers. The Commissioner of Crown Lands, F. C. Ward, thought this area, 540 square miles, was too large and would deprive Amos Brothers and Broad, owners of McArthur River run, of half their coastal frontage. Knight thought half the area would be sufficient. Putting Aborigines onto reserves not only kept them away from the water required for the runholders' cattle; it now had financial advantages as well. In the worsening economic situation of the 1890s, government funds were becoming scarce and it was hoped large reserves would enable the Aborigines to support themselves. Knight remarked: 'It is too much to suppose that the government can afford to supply rations to all the blackfellows in the N. Territory'.[6]

Other reserves were suggested to the government and on 28 March 1892 it approved the creation of nine. These were 20 square miles for the Larakia near Adelaide River, 366 square miles for the Woolna at South Chambers Bay, 388 for the Waggites at West Anson Bay, 154 square miles for the Woolwonga near the Mary River, 100 square miles for the Mallae near Daly River, 366 square miles for the Manassie near South Alligator River, 150 square miles near Tennant Creek, 100 square miles near Barrow Creek and 200 square miles near Charlotte Waters— a total of 1844 square miles out of the Territory's 523 620 square miles. No tribal names were associated with the last three. The owner of Crown Point station, however, objected to the excising of part of his run to provide the reserve at Charlotte Waters. By the end of the year he was able to point out that the Aborigines did not use the reserve and so it was cancelled. Stretton's proposal for a reserve in the McArthur River district was not accepted. Another was considered for the Victoria River district and Foelsche's son-in-law, H. W. H. Stevens, manager of Goldsborough Mort's station there, proposed a large reserve between the Victoria and Daly Rivers. This he said was 'indifferent' grazing land but was well watered and had always been a favourite spot for the Aborigines; it would provide sufficient country for all the Aborigines in the locality. Ward thought this area, taking in 160 miles of coastline, was unnecessarily large. Knight believed no great harm would be done by creating a reserve as large as this, 'as whenever the time arrives for disposing of the land to the public the proclamation of the reserves may be cancelled or modified according to the circumstances'.[7] While Knight had proposed that large reserves be created so Aborigines could be self-supporting, he envisaged no permanent right to such security. The demands of the Europeans should come first.

In his report for the end of 1889, Parsons again surveyed the condition of the Aborigines.[8] In the neighbourhood of Palmerston and in the settled country north of Katherine they had been peaceful and the Larakia appeared to be maintaining their numbers, but the tribes which had originally occupied the goldfields were dwindling. The blacks were beginning to understand the conditions under which the white man held

J. L. Parsons, Government Resident at Palmerston 1884–1890, was the first official to understand the plight of the Territory Aborigines

C. E. Herbert, Government Resident 1905–1910, reported on the deteriorating condition of the Aborigines

Hermannsburg mission on the Finke River, showing the 'wurlies' built for adult Aborigines in the early 1890s

William Willshire, head of the Native Police patrol in Central Australia until his arrest for murder in 1891

C. J. Dashwood, Government Resident 1892–1904, who unsuccessfully presented Aboriginal protection legislation in 1899

Native Police Camp, Gordon Creek. Victoria River Downs.

A drawing by Willshire, officer-in-charge at the camp 1892–1895

their country, of which they considered they had been robbed. An old Aborigine had told a station manager some time previously: 'I say, boss, whitefellow stay here too long with him bullocky. Now time whitefellow take him bullocky and clear out. This fellow country him blackfellow country'. Parsons said that after careful inquiry he believed this was the general attitude of the Aborigines towards the Europeans. 'Entrance into their country was an act of invasion. It is a declaration of war, and they will halt at no opportunity of attacking the white invaders'. He had visited Melville Island and was convinced it was useless to attempt to win the friendship of the Tiwi people with tucker or gifts. As soon as his party had arrived an old man had come to their camp, ordered them away, and warned that if they slept there the blacks would come from all points of the compass and spear them. Parsons's party had attempted to propitiate this man, his wives and a 'scout' who was with him by going to them with food, handkerchiefs and other gifts, which they took only from the end of a pole and then threw away. That night the Tiwi attacked Parsons's camp and next day speared Phil Saunders, his party's guide and leader of one of the civilian parties which had hunted the Daly River murderers. Shots were fired in self-defence, although not directly at Tiwi. On the last day of the visit, just as they were leaving, five spears were flung at the Europeans. None were hit.

The incident did not make Parsons hostile to the Aborigines. Instead, it confirmed his views of the moral and political problem which faced South Australians:

The primary fact which philanthropists must accept is that the aborigines regard the land as theirs, and that the intrusion of the white man is a declaration of war, and the result is simply 'the survival of the fittest'. There is a straight issue presented for the philanthropist, the statesman, and the capitalist to consider. Does the land inalienably belong to the aborigines, because they have from time immemorial occupied it and exercised tribal rights over it? If so, the pastoralist must clear out, and the philanthropist and the missionary must come in. If the land is, however, too wide for the nomadic population, how shall the 'real property' interests of the aborigines be preserved?

He had given serious attention to this question and had had long conferences with Foelsche and E. O. Robinson (the Cobourg Peninsula buffalo hunter) who, Parsons said, knew more about the Aborigines of the north coast than any other man in the Territory. During his time as government resident he had pressed upon successive governments the absolute duty of the state to consider the condition and provide for the future protection of the wild tribes living on the Territory's coast, but recorded in his report for 1889 that 'Up to date all my suggestions...have passed without attention from either Parliament, press or pulpit'. The first duty of the state was to create reserves within which the Aborigines would have absolute rights and sole control. This would mean that some pastoral tenants would be excluded from water, 'but the "bullocky" and the blackfellow cannot live and drink at the same places'. If reserves were not created, the result of white intrusion would be inevitable. Tasmania had 'civilized the native race off the island', and in South Australia, Victoria and New South Wales the blacks had almost died out: 'Rum, the bullet and syphilis have mowed them down'. Leave the native question alone and the natives would be obliterated, he said. Parsons again asked the government to 'take some decisive action' and state a policy for the Aborigines of the Northern Territory.[9]

Once more Parsons's pleas fell on deaf ears. South Australian governments were often pressed by persons with vested interests in the Territory to repress the Aborigines, especially in the Centre, whereas no groups exerted effective pressure on behalf of the Aborigines, even the missionaries. The Aborigines' Friends' Association was so quiescent that, after Corporal Montagu's report on the Daly River murders, it was accused in letters to the *South Australian Register* of being culpably negligent of the Aborigines' interests. Stung, it protested to the minister, Cockburn, about the treatment of the Aborigines by Montagu's party but not about the general treatment of the Aborigines in the Territory. The association took no serious interest in the Territory until December 1888, when it asked for an inquiry into the treatment of five Aboriginal prisoners in Palmerston gaol. Jemmy Miller had been sentenced in May 1881 to life imprisonment, Mandab to twelve years and Jacky for just over nine and a half years, all with hard labour, for the murder of Holmes, the publican at Collett's Creek. The association said that friends of the dead man had later remarked that the blacks should not have been charged. These friends had said that Jemmy's wife had been kept a prisoner in the house and that Jemmy and his associates had been attempting to rescue her when Holmes was slain in a scuffle. Wandy Wandy had been sentenced in August 1880 to ten years' imprisonment for the manslaughter of Wingfield on Croker Island, to which had been added hard labour for escaping from prison. The association now said Wandy Wandy had only struck the slain man after death 'in accordance with the well-known tribal custom'. Another man, who had struck the fatal blow, had not been arrested. The association protested against the 'cruel' treatment of a man named Nim, who was kept at work in the gaol yard during illness until he collapsed. Leg-irons were kept on him during his illness and removed only after his death. The association asked that an inquiry be held into these three cases. It also asked the government to assist a tribe near Tennant Creek, which was reported to be almost starving.[9]

Charles Todd had instructed his staff to supply rations to Aborigines near the telegraph stations but generally in return for work. Strangely, the first plea for welfare assistance for the Central Australian Aborigines came from Mounted Constable William Willshire, whose other activities there, as we have seen, were far from humanitarian. In August 1887 Willshire wrote to Sub-Inspector B. C. Besley at Port Augusta, who was also a sub-protector of Aborigines, that many sick, blind and crippled Aborigines at Alice Springs were constantly applying to him for food. He asked Besley to provide him with a small quantity of food for their relief, as 'It is hard to see these poor creatures suffering for want of food and my means are too limited to give them much'. Willshire asked for 600 pounds of flour, 150 pounds of sugar, 150 pounds of rice, 25 pounds of tea and tobacco, 20 pounds of split peas, plus 25 blankets, 6 tomahawks and 24 shirts. All of this was approved by the minister, J. C. F. Johnson. At the time a serious drought was developing in the Centre. The following November, Grant and Stokes, proprietors of Idracowra station on the Finke River, due south of Alice Springs, asked Johnson to appoint their station as a ration depot for Aborigines. They said that for some time they had supplied rations to twenty to thirty people usually camped near the waters on the station. Besley recommended that a small quantity of stores be sent to Idracowra and also to Erldunda and Tempe Downs where, he said, 'sick and infirm natives are numerous'. The police commissioner, George Hamilton, advised: 'The extension of depots in the Interior of South Australia would, I believe, have a good effect in tending to establish a better understanding between the natives and European settlers by a judicious distribution of articles of clothes and food etc.' The Commissioner of Crown Lands approved. The government was not so charitable in the Top End. In June 1888 George Warland of Elsey station told Parsons he had killed cattle to save the blacks in that district from semi-starvation: 'In the tribe here are many aged blacks and several young children who are unable to go far in the quest for food but are forced to hang around the main waters which in such a season as the present yield but little for them to eat'. Warland asked the government to authorize the station manager to kill beasts as food for the Aborigines and to deduct the cost from the rent on the run. The protector in the Top End, Dr Percy Wood, thought that, because managers obtained work and valuable information from the young adults, they should provide food without 'debiting it to the government'. Parsons and Johnson agreed.[10]

Mr Justice Pater, judge of the Northern Territory, had recently died, and the death of J. G. Knight in office in January 1892 presented the government of South Australia, still struggling against economic difficulties, with the opportunity to save more expenditure on its unprofitable province. It combined the two offices and selected Charles James Dashwood as successor to both.[11] Dashwood tried harder than Parsons to protect the Aborigines, his efforts culminating in the draft Aborigines' Bill of 1899 which failed to become law because of the lobbying against it by pastoralists with interests in the Territory. Born near Kangarilla, south of Adelaide, in 1842, he was educated at St Peter's College, Adelaide, and studied civil engineering in Ghent, Belgium, for a year. He returned to South Australia in 1865 and worked on the land and then as an articled clerk before being admitted to the Bar in 1873.

Dashwood won the seat of Noarlunga in 1887 and was 'a fluent and forceful debater but reluctant to accept party discipline and rather impulsive'. He had not had a remarkable career in the law, appearing in court in only seven significant cases from 1878 to 1889. In parliament he was considered to be a liberal progressive, standing to the right of his lifelong friend, C. C. Kingston, a radical liberal. The first serious matter relating to Aborigines with which Dashwood had to deal after arriving in Palmerston was police action following the murder of George Clark and Charles De Loitte on Creswell Downs, near Anthony Lagoon, in January 1892. A report of the murders in the *Brisbane Courier* of 23 March caused William Forrest, a powerful squatter and member of the Queensland parliament, to write about the matter to the South Australian Treasurer, W. B. Rounsevell, minister controlling the Northern Territory in the Playford government.[12] Early in March the Queensland Police Commissioner telegraphed his counterpart in Adelaide that police from Anthony Lagoon had pursued and shot dead several Aborigines and a 'strong party of settlers [was] still in pursuit'. Dashwood was asked for an explanation. Mounted Constable Ernest Smith reported that on 27 February he had led a party of eight white men to an Aboriginal camp. As they approached, he said, they were attacked with boomerangs and in the fight six Aborigines fell. Dashwood sent Smith's report to Adelaide in May and the government considered whether Smith's group was a revenge party or a party lawfully attempting to arrest murderers. The evidence against Smith was not strong enough, especially as he got three Europeans on neighbouring stations to countersign his second report in which he claimed the killings occurred in self-defence. The Attorney-General decided to let the matter lapse.

On arrival Dashwood quickly established himself as a 'hanging judge'. Early in 1892 rumours reached Palmerston that a Macassan prau had been wrecked on the Arnhem Land coast and that the crew had been killed by Aborigines. After John Lewis had surrendered the lease on the Cobourg Peninsula run, his last manager, E. O. Robinson, had set up a buffalo-hunting camp on Bowen Strait where he also acted as sub-collector of customs, collecting duties and licence fees from the Macassan trepang fishermen who still visited this coast. In October Robinson reported that the massacre had taken place at Cape Brogden, about forty miles east of his camp, and that Wandy Wandy was the ringleader. Wandy Wandy had served his sentence for the manslaughter of T. H. Wingfield in December 1879 and had lived for some time with the Jesuits at Rapid Creek before returning home. Foelsche proceeded with a party including the sub-collector of customs at Port Darwin, Alfred Searcy, by steamer to Port Essington. He hoped to pick up information from the local people, but Lewis's old station was deserted. They did, however, encounter Flash Poll at Bowen Strait and she guided Searcy and two policemen as they searched on Croker Island for an important witness, whom they found. At Cape Brogden they found parts of the wrecked prau and another guide, Mangerippy, led them inland where they found six skeletons. The police captured eight men, including Wandy Wandy, at Malay Bay. The prau was not a regular visitor to the coast. It was a small one from the Aru Islands and had been blown off course, but the captain seemed to have known he was on the Arnhem Land coast because he asked the Aborigines for guidance to Robinson's camp. The Aborigines began to escort the crew to Bowen Strait, carrying their boxes, but after only a short distance they ran away with the boxes. The Macassans and Aborigines then conferred at a camp, but the visitors were suddenly attacked and killed and their vessel partly burnt in case some 'white fellow might see it'. Mangerippy himself confessed to having been present during these events and to spearing the men after death.[13]

Wandy Wandy and the five others were taken to Palmerston where, along with two other Aborigines charged with other murders, they appeared before Dashwood and a jury in November 1892. The jury took only five minutes to find all eight guilty, and Dashwood sentenced each one to death. Next day he sentenced an Aborigine, Wurrama, to death for the murder of a Chinese on the Daly River, and on the last day of the three days of sittings, he sentenced a halfcaste, Charlie Flanagan, to death for the murder of Sam Croker at Auvergne station on the Victoria River in September 1892. Early in July 1893 the death sentences on four of the Bowen Straits murderers and on Flanagan and Wurrama were confirmed. There was opposition in Adelaide to these sentences and the Playford government promised to consider a reprieve for the four Bowen Strait murderers sentenced to death.[14] But there was no reprieve for Flanagan who was hanged on 15 July, the first person to be executed at Palmerston gaol. On that day Dashwood telegraphed Playford recommending that, of the Bowen Strait prisoners, only Wandy Wandy should die, because he had had sufficient experience of European ways to understand the consequences of his actions. He suggested hanging Wandy Wandy at the scene of his crime in the hope that this would help to preserve law and order on the coast. The government obtained the reprieve of three more Aborigines and approved Dashwood's plans for Wandy Wandy. He was taken to Malay Bay and hanged in the presence of about thirty members of his tribe. The scaffold was left standing as a warning to others.

In August 1894 Dashwood sentenced two Aborigines, Myanko and Mululurun, to death for the murder of an unknown Chinese on the Roper River. He acknowledged it was unsatisfactory that the court was trying 'two creatures who stand there utterly ignorant of what is going on'. He recommended Myanko's reprieve, because he was the younger of the two, and Mululurun was executed at Crescent Lagoon on the Roper before about fifty Aborigines in January 1895. Dashwood was clearly inconsistent in his thinking: he had recommended that all of the Bowen Strait murderers except Wandy Wandy be reprieved, because they did not understand the white man's law, but he executed Mululurun even though he conceded the man was 'utterly ignorant' of his offence under English law. The people near Elsey station today tell of the spearing of a Chinaman for his swag and food on the Strangways River near Crescent Lagoon by Mululurun, a rainmaker who was one of the owners of the lagoon. Their forebears were brought to the spot to witness the hanging, were told not to grieve and were given tobacco, blankets and some food.[15]

By means of hanging, Dashwood was combining his two roles — as a judge required to apply the law and as an administrator required to solve a social problem of violence. He used the most extreme punishment as a means of frightening Aborigines into refraining from violence. Dashwood sentenced only one more Aborigine to death — in April 1901, when Jimmy was hanged at Shaw's Creek on Bradshaw's Run in the Victoria River district for the murder of a white man named Larson on a boat on the river in 1900. Joseph Bradshaw mustered a large number of Aborigines to witness the execution. Dashwood's objective now was the same as before — to have a 'salutary effect upon the natives'. He justified his action on the grounds that, since the execution of Wandy Wandy in Bowen Strait and Mululurun at Crescent Lagoon, there had been no trouble in those districts. By hanging Aborigines at the scene of their crimes Dashwood may have discouraged Aboriginal violence and persuaded Europeans not to take the law into their own hands, thus ending the dominance of Aboriginal policy by frontier expedience as practised by Price and Foelsche; but he was simply using a different form of pacification. The vengeance party had been replaced by the gallows. For the Aborigines the result was the same — subjugation.

On arrival in Palmerston, Dashwood had sat only in the Circuit Court, where he heard major cases, but early in 1894 he was authorized to sit in the lower or magistrates' courts, where most of the cases involving offences against Aborigines were heard. His experience there changed his attitude towards the Aborigines. He heard evidence of raids by police on Chinese brothels and gambling houses, where often 'black gins were found in various stages of opium addiction'. These cases were brought before the courts under the gaming or liquor-licensing legislation. As Foelsche had pointed out in 1885, no legislation provided for the punishment of persons for the abuse of Aborigines as such. The only South Australian laws which dealt specifically with Aborigines were the 1840 Act dealing with destitute Aboriginal children, the 1849 Act on admission of Aboriginal evidence in court, some provisions of the Criminal Law Consolidation Act 1876 and the Licensed Victuallers Act 1880. On the other hand, under Governor Hindmarsh's proclamation of 1836, Aborigines were deemed to be equal under the law. This meant that the protectors of Aborigines had no legal authority to deal with persons who persuaded or coerced Aborigines into actions against their own interests. Protectors's actions were largely confined to issuing food and blankets, providing some medical aid and reporting conditions. Dashwood's experience in hearing lower-court cases persuaded him of the inadequacy of the law. It also helped him to understand better the Aborigines' side of some cases. For instance, in March 1896 he dismissed a charge against a Victoria River Aborigine of assaulting two white men, when he learned they had chastised him after supplying him with liquor. In July that year he dismissed another Aborigine accused of murdering a Chinese on the Daly River because the police had obtained his confession under duress and had little other evidence. In December of the same year, Dashwood discharged three Aborigines charged with murdering a white man on Wave Hill station on the grounds that the police had gained the prisoners' statements improperly — they had not cautioned them in advance. These actions alarmed the local press, but Dashwood was indifferent to its censure.

The Europeans were not always antagonistic to the Aborigines and sometimes showed unusual sympathy. In March 1898 Dashwood sentenced two men, Naboloora and Copperung, to death for the murder of white buffalo-hunters, Moore and Mackenzie, on King River, about sixty miles east of Malay Bay. The jury had recommended mercy because the Aborigines had been provoked. On Premier Kingston's recommendation to the governor, they were released immediately. In December 1895 Bradshaw wrote to Kingston asking that Rodney Claud Spencer be set free. Spencer had been convicted in 1890 of the murder of an Aborigine, Manialucum, one of several assisting him in buffalo-hunting at Bowen Strait. Judge Pater had commuted the sentence to life imprisonment after a recommendation for mercy from the jury. Evidence had been given at the trial that, on Spencer's orders, two Aborigines held Manialucum down while he was shot. One Adelaide newspaper was outraged at the suggestion that Spencer be released. It said Spencer had lived five years longer than he would have if the reasonable claims of justice had been satisfied. It congratulated the Kingston government on refusing the request, saying that to 'lavish philanthropy upon such a miscreant is simply to burlesque the gracious virtue of mercy'.[16] Spencer was released from gaol in Adelaide five years later, returned to the north coast and began trepanging. In 1904 he established a camp at Arnhem Bay but, while his Aboriginal assistants were working away from him, he was attacked by some of the local tribe and killed. As a later writer put it: 'This was one case in which the Territory police were not especially interested in rounding up the murderers'.[17]

Dashwood had already begun to take an interest in the general condition of the Aborigines, particularly their health. In August 1895 he had sailed along the western coast looking for a site for a leper colony for Aborigines and others. He chose the Peron Islands at the mouth of the Daly River, but Bradshaw the pastoralist and Father McKillop, superior of the Jesuit mission on the Daly, objected to this choice, saying they did not wish to have lepers near their operations. The total inadequacy of the law in dealing with abuses against Aborigines was emphasized when a Chinese man was charged with carnal knowledge of a child under twelve years. The man was found guilty but appealed, and Dashwood's decision was disallowed in the South Australian Supreme Court on the grounds that the child's age could not be proved, Aborigines' births not being registered.[18] A similar case, involving a white man and an Aboriginal girl aged between thirteen and sixteen years added to Dashwood's concern. From 1895 he and the protector reported increased incidents of the abuse of children, prostitution, venereal diseases and opium-smoking among the Aborigines and the growing number of halfcaste children. The linking of the Chinese and other non-Europeans with these problems occurred at a time when anti-Asian feelings were rising in Australia and miscegenation had become a public issue. The radical-liberal government of Kingston, Dashwood's friend, was in office in South Australia at this time and was more sensitive to pressing social problems than its predecessors. Like Queensland early in the 1890s, South Australia was now beginning to realize that it had a serious Aboriginal problem in the Territory, but did not know how to deal with it. On 10 November 1897 the Queensland Aborigines protection legislation was introduced into parliament and quickly passed by both houses with general agreement that it would solve that colony's Aboriginal problem. In the next month, F. W. Holder, treasurer in the Kingston government and minister controlling the Northern Territory, asked Dashwood for a report on race relations in the Territory. This report was to lead to the first serious attempt in the history of South Australia to legislate to protect the Aborigines.

Chapter 12

Dashwood's Bill

Dashwood set about obtaining the most comprehensive information on the condition of the Northern Territory Aborigines yet gathered. On 30 December 1897 he wrote to officers in charge of police stations asking them to report on such conditions and on relations with Europeans and Chinese, and to suggest ways of improving conditions. He followed this with another request on 26 January and received reports from the protector, who was then Dr F. Goldsmith, Foelsche and several police officers. Dashwood did not reply to F. W. Holder until 12 July, explaining that he had waited until able to obtain a copy of the Queensland Act and to study it.[1] The information provided extended far beyond relations in the Palmerston and goldfields districts, where most Chinese lived, and for the first time indicates some of the effects of the pastoral invasion upon some tribes in the Top End. It must be remembered that many Aborigines, particularly in Arnhem Land, much of the western coastal belt and most of the arid stretches between the Top End and the Centre, were not greatly affected by white intrusion — their lands not being suitable for grazing. Even so, there was some intrusion by other whites, such as the buffalo-hunters of the north coast and the goldminers at Tennant Creek and Arltunga. Also, the information collected by Dashwood omits reference to the Centre, which was effectively outside his administration and jurisdiction.

Dashwood said in his covering letter to Holder that the reports he had received confirmed his own experience on the bench. Undoubtedly the practice on some stations outside the settled districts was to take Aborigines against their will to employ them as stockriders and otherwise, 'the gins, with or without consent, being appropriated by those employed on the station'. When practicable these people were taken from tribes whose country was situated a considerable distance from the station. They were afraid to attempt to return to their own tribes, because this would involve travelling across country inhabited by hostile tribes: 'In such cases their position could only be compared to that of slaves'. In the settled districts, he said, prostitution was extensively carried out by Aboriginal women, which 'was not to be wondered at considering the disproportion of the sexes in the European and Asiatic races'. In some cases they lived with Europeans and Asians and in others they prostituted themselves promiscuously with the consent of and connivance of their husbands for money, food, tobacco, opium and other considerations. In the settled districts, many children were 'demoralized' at a very early age, particularly by the Chinese, and with the consent of their parents.

He believed venereal disease was prevalent among the Aborigines in 'up country' districts. Many died yearly because of influenza, malaria and pulmonary complaints. Their numbers in the settled districts, he said, were rapidly decreasing. The advent of the whites to the Territory would, in the course of time, result in the extinction of the black race, as had been the case in other colonies. The praiseworthy efforts of the Jesuit missionaries on the Daly River had not so far been successful. He did not believe the supply of intoxicating liquor and opium to Aborigines was increasing. This had been happening for many years but only lately had public attention been drawn to it. The law introduced in South Australia recently to deal with the opium problem had not yet had a fair trial. He did not favour establishing ration depots at police stations in the north, where native food was plentiful, although it might be expedient to do so in the southern districts where it was not. If food were distributed to the old and infirm in camps, he said, the 'hangers on and loafers' would benefit. Such a food-distribution programme would result in a significant increase in government expenditure on the Aborigines, which apparently he did not favour, perhaps having in mind the government's financial difficulties. Australia was now deep in a great economic depression, as serious as that of 1929–39, which started with the financial crash of 1893 and was extended by drought until 1906. It was not the time for any social reformer to be advocating increased government expenditure.

Goldsmith had been in the Territory only two years and in his report to Dashwood said his knowledge was based mainly on hearsay. He had asked for information from the police. The curse of Aboriginal life, he said, was the introduction of intoxicating liquor and opium for which the Aborigines had developed a great taste. To gratify this taste they would spend any money they earned and the women would prostitute themselves. Because of police activity the supply of liquor was kept fairly well within bounds, but opium-smoking flourished. It was difficult for the police to bring strong enough cases before the courts. Of the thirty-eight prisoners then in the Palmerston gaol, sixteen had been convicted for supplying opium or intoxicating liquor to the blacks. Of these sixteen, fourteen were Chinese. Goldsmith wanted any Asian sentenced for any offence against the Aborigines to be deported. This, he said, would 'rid us of a most undesirable class of people who are confirmed opium smokers and consequently incapable of useful employment and who simply live upon the scanty earnings of the blacks'. Imprisonment had no terrors for the Asiatics, he said. In fact, the majority of them rather liked it.[2]

In his report Foelsche said the condition of the Aborigines in the settled districts had considerably altered since he had written his report of August 1882 before the Jesuits had come to the Territory. At that time the Aboriginal men and women in and about Palmerston had been 'in a fair way of becoming good and useful workers'. At present, with a few exceptions, they were quite the reverse and 'ladies find it difficult to get lubras to assist in household work' and the men as a rule 'pass their time away in idleness, and very few will accept work when offered them'. This was not so much the case 'up country' and on the goldfields, where both men and women to some extent worked for their living 'although there is no perceptible difference in their general condition'. The principal causes of the contamination of Aborigines in contact with European and other races were their acquired fondness and craving for intoxicating liquor and opium and the prostitution of the women, encouraged by their husbands. Even some girls, not more than ten or eleven years of age, were involved. The severe punishment provided by the law for supplying Aborigines with liquor and opium had not deterred this trade. Coloured races were the chief transgressors but many Europeans deemed it no offence to give them a glass of grog occasionally, he said. Only when they became drunk did the matter come to the notice of the police, but many offenders escaped punishment. Many of the 'boys' who worked on the pastoral stations had been, and perhaps still were, obtained by 'running them down' and forcibly taking them to stations some distance from their tribes. Young girls were still obtained by this practice which, he believed, had been introduced from western Queensland. Eighteen years ago a Queensland squatter had arrived on the goldfields with a mob of fat cattle, his only assistants being three or four so-called black boys, who were really young women dressed in men's clothes and obtained by 'running them down'. On some stations nearly each male employee had his 'lubra', mostly obtained in this way against the will of their relatives. As a rule they accompanied these men while out on the run. There was strong reasons to believe, he said, that the Aborigines so obtained were treated brutally, leading to retaliation which in turn led to attacks on sometimes innocent persons. 'More than half of the offences of violence committed by natives are attributable to obtaining gins forcibly or otherwise'.[3]

William Sowden, the Adelaide journalist who accompanied Parsons to the Territory in 1882, commented on this 'Queensland' custom:

We met one of them who had a little black, dressed in boy's clothing, travelling with him as servant. It transpired that this little fellow was really a girl, and what her life may be I know nothing of. In the particular case I refer to I suppose it may be comfortable enough, for I believe the master is a good-hearted man, but in most cases these feminine boys are the victims of their masters' debasing passions . . . Some of these thoughtless bushmen have, in the stealing of their black servants, had 'brushes' with the male relatives of the latter and shot them down. The natives make reprisals, and sometimes kill guilty and at other times innocent men. The whites resident in the district then have a 'revenge' party, and shoot down a score blacks or so, and call it English justice . . . These blacks live and die like sheep, only that their lot is even more degraded. *And the whites degrade it.* [4]

In an oft-quoted passage, Alfred Searcy described in 1907 the value of having Aboriginal women as stockmen:

There can be no doubt that many of the murders were caused by the white men taking away the black women from their tribes. Nearly all the drovers, cattlemen, and station hands had their 'black boys' (gins). No objection was raised by the black men to interference with their women so long as they were not abducted. It is the taking away of the women that has been the cause of so many white men having been rubbed out by the niggers. These women are invaluable to the white cattlemen, for, besides the companionship, they become splendid horsewomen, and good with cattle. They are useful to find water, settle the camp, boil the billy, and track and bring in the horses in the mornings. In fact, it is impossible to enumerate the advantages of having a good gin 'outback'. [5]

Searcy was an apologist for the cattlemen and his bumptious good-humour does not disguise the true position of these women and their relatives, as indicated by Sowden, Foelsche and another policeman, R. C. Thorpe.

Continuing his report to Dashwood, Foelsche said prostitution was undoubtedly responsible for the spread of venereal disease among the Aborigines and this, together with other causes, had led to a decrease in their numbers in the more settled districts. The number of halfcaste children had been increasing. In his opinion, 'nothing but severe measures' would change this situation. The methods adopted would have to be different to those used in the south, where the 'whole circumstances' were different. Some reserves had been declared in 1892 but nothing more had been heard of them and he believed the reserve system was impracticable. Instead, the system of distributing rations to the old, decrepid and sick, as applied in the Centre, might be adopted in the north. No supplies should be given to those able to work for their living or procure food for themselves. In most parts of the north, especially along the coast, there was abundant fish and game. The gathering of tribes near townships, where they remained most of the year, should be discouraged. With only short intervals, the Woolna, Alligator and Minaedge tribes stayed at Palmerston throughout the year and lived off the prostitution of their women. Plenty of food was available in their own tribal areas and they should be compelled to stay there except for short friendly visits to the Larakia once a year, as had been their custom. 'This would greatly lessen prostitution, drinking, and opium-smoking, and improve their health', Foelsche wrote. Missions stations receiving concessions from the government should be compelled to accept halfcaste children and civilize them. These children, he believed, would make excellent servants. He did not anticipate any difficulty in getting mothers to give up their halfcaste children, 'for I believe any of them may be had for a bag of flour'. Few halfcaste children lived beyond twelve to fifteen years, he said, most being taken into the bush by old members of the tribe and killed. He proposed that births and deaths of Aborigines be recorded as far as practicable — especially the births of halfcastes, as this information would be valuable in proving the age of females in cases of carnal knowledge, such as had been before the courts recently. Foelsche recognized that conditions in the Territory were quite different to those in South Australia. Special laws would have to be passed for the Territory, but he felt sure that 'many of our legislators will not be able to so shape their ideas on this subject as to meet its requirements'.[6] The inability to see that legislation requirements for South Australia and the Territory differed was one of the chief reasons for the failure of parliament to accept Dashwood's draft Bill next year.

The most compassionate statement on behalf of the Northern Territory Aborigines in the South Australia period came from Mounted Constable R. C. Thorpe, a South Australian policeman stationed, by arrangement with the Queensland authorities, at Camooweal, just east of the border. His job was to patrol the Herbert River (Georgina River) on the eastern edge of the Territory and along the drovers' trails from Queensland to Anthony Lagoon and McArthur River. In his reply to Dashwood's request for information, addressed to Foelsche, Thorpe said half the young Aboriginal women on the stations in that district would say they had been 'run down by station blackguards on horseback, and taken to the stations for licentious purposes, and there kept more like slaves that anything else'.[7] He had heard it said these women had been locked up for weeks while their 'heartless persecutors' had been mustering cattle. Some men had taken their women with them and tied them up securely at night to prevent them escaping. These allegations, he said, were very difficult to prove against any individuals. He urged that temporary protectors be appointed in each police district with power to engage Aborigines to 'fit and proper' persons. His descriptions are graphic:

The so-called traveller with four or five horses, styling himself a *bona fide* stockman, I would debar from being allowed to have a blackboy or gin at all, for these are the very worst individuals; they are invariably illiterate and cruel, and live under the impression that after the blackboy has walked miles for his horses the proper and orthodox thing for him to do is to bring him down with a stirrup-iron, whether the poor boy deserves it or not. These men are generally good horsemen, and carry firearms; the boys and gins know this, and through fear are compelled to suffer this perpetual hell. The next thing we hear is that the boy has cruelly murdered his tormentor...I have often passed these so-called stockmen (they are pure bush larrikins, and are the flashiest of the flash), on a bitterly cold morning, travelling over the plains on a cold winter's morning. They themselves were comfortably clothed and muffled, whereas their blackboys were a mere bundle of dirty, torn rags, a shivering pinched-up mortal in a black skin. 'Why don't you clothe your boy?' I have often asked. 'Oh, he's only a b----- nigger', is the reply.

Thorpe said the practice of distributing blankets each Queen's birthday was often abused by the squatters, who were the first to benefit by it. He had seen such blankets on stockmen's beds. Instead of giving blankets, the government should force squatters engaging Aboriginal labour to sign before a protector an agreement promising to feed and clothe the employee 'in a proper manner' and pay them five or ten shillings a week. Such wages should not be paid to a man or woman but placed in the hands of some reliable person, who would purchase food, clothes and blankets for the aged, infirm and sick Aborigines. This, he said, would 'go a long way to ameliorate the sufferings of the poor old creatures'. Thorpe said that, by taking the young people from the tribes, the squatters had deprived the old people of their children's assistance in hunting over 'these endless plains' and during drought these old people, when alone, had to traverse many miles before finding anything. 'I have frequently met poor old gins', he wrote, 'sitting down under a currant bush, fairly knocked up. She [*sic*] has, of necessity, to carry a big coolamon of water all the time, and after walking very many miles may only succeed in finding a few small lizards and an iguana occasionally'. Thorpe said every father of a halfcaste child should be compelled to register its birth and contribute towards its support through a protector. He continued:

Some mean fellows think it a very clever and manly thing to saddle a young lubra with a half-caste child, then leave her to battle as best she can for its keep. Very probably, before being saddled with this half-caste child, the gin was earning her own living; but the moment she had a child no one would be bothered with her; and she dare not go amongst most of the bush tribes or they would kill her and her half-caste child. What is this poor gin to do but to sit about and become diseased. One time the gins used to kill these half-caste children, but they have learnt to fear the consequences of such unlawful acts.

Thorpe urged strong punishment for bushmen who, knowing they suffered venereal disease, cohabited with the Aboriginal women. 'I have seen', he wrote, 'poor young gins, mere children between 11 and 14 years of age, suffering from syphilis in all its stages. The old blacks assured me that white men had run them down and ruined them'. The Aborigines commanded the Europeans' sympathy and assistance, he said: 'It is the one word *fear* all through. No matter what it is these poor creatures have to submit to it is simply through *fear*'.

In his reply to Holder, Dashwood recommended the introduction of consolidating legislation which, in addition to the existing powers, would provide for employment of Aborigines under written agreement of Aborigines and halfcastes with the approval of the protector for a fixed period. He urged that no persons should employ an Aborigine or half-caste or allow one to be on his premises except as provided under the Act. The legislation should also prohibit the removal of an Aborigine or halfcaste from his country or beyond the Territory without the consent of the protector. Every blanket issued to Aborigines and half-castes should remain the property of the government, and persons found in possession of them should be penalized. Fines for supplying intoxicating liquor to an Aborigine or halfcaste should range from £10 to £50 with the option of imprisonment. Persons supplying opium, in addition to being fined or imprisoned, should be whipped. Native camps should be prohibited within two miles of a township, except for those Aborigines employed under provisions of the act. When a person was charged with an offence against a child under a certain age and the child appeared to be under that age the child would be so deemed unless the contrary were proved. Dashwood also proposed several regulations under the Act. They would define the duties of the protectors and other officials, preserve the mode of distributing money voted by parliament for the benefit of Aborigines, provide for the transfer of any halfcaste child being an orphan or deserted by its parents to an orphanage, and prescribe the conditions under which an Aborigine or halfcaste might be apprenticed or placed in service with suitable persons.[8]

Dashwood had been influenced by the Queensland legislation, especially by the resort to written agreements between Aborigines and their employers, the exclusion of Aborigines and halfcastes from townships and European premises, the prohibition on movement from their country or province without permission, and the stronger sanctions against supplying intoxicating liquor and opium. As its name implies, the Queensland *Aboriginals Protection and Restriction of the Supply of Opium Act* paid much more attention to the opium problem; it contained greater powers for police to search travellers, conveyances and premises for opium and it excluded whites from Aboriginal camps and reservations. It gave the minister the power to prescribe an Aborigine or halfcaste as being a person defined under the Act, which gave him and the protectors great authority to remove that person to a reserve. The Queensland Act was much more concerned with morality; any Aborigine, especially a woman or child, who was considered to be in moral danger by living with a non-Aboriginal man or being supplied with liquor or opium, could be removed by force — for that woman or child's supposed good. It clearly divided Aborigines and halfcastes into two types — those who were useful to the Europeans by working for them were excluded from its provisions, while those not so working were subject to removal to a reserve at any time. Dashwood had not suggested the creation of more reserves and those which had been created appeared to have been ignored both by the Aborigines and the government, as Foelsche had implied. Dashwood did not recommend compulsory separation of Aborigines and non-Aborigines for the good of the indigenous people. This was a fairly mild version of the Queensland legislation and in many respects more humane in that Dashwood was not proposing that Aborigines be removed from their own lands by force or that Aboriginal families be torn apart for moralistic reasons.

When Kingston read Dashwood's report and its attachments, he commented: 'This chapter of errors is a blot on our colonization'. He suggested that Dashwood draft a bill 'to deal with these evils'. Dashwood did so with enthusiasm, preparing a Bill for 'An Act for the Protection and Care of the Aboriginal and Half-caste Inhabitants of the Province of South Australia, and for other purposes'. Although opium-taking had been noted as a problem by Territory officials for about a decade, the emphasis in Dashwood's Bill was much more upon miscegenation. It is difficult to see why, as very few halfcaste children had been indicated by reports over that time. In his report to Dashwood, Foelsche had merely stated that during the decade 'half-caste children have been on the increase', without giving numbers. In 1900 Goldsmith said there were 'over 60 half-caste children of various ages' between Port Darwin and Katherine, while in 1909 the then protector, W. G. Stretton, estimated about 150 half-castes throughout the whole Territory.[9] By comparison the estimated Aboriginal population of the Territory in 1911 was 22 000. The attention to halfcastes in the Bill and its title indicates the seriousness with which the mixing of the races was regarded in South Australia and elsewhere in Australia at that time.

Although Dashwood's report excluded conditions in Central Australia, the government did have information in the annual reports of F. J. Gillen, who had been appointed sub-protector for much of that region in 1892. The health of Aborigines in the Centre had been good, Gillen had said in his report for 1896, although in previous years influenza and its complications had caused deaths at several of the ration depots. The deathrate during the year had been more than the birthrate. The Aborigines' conduct had been satisfactory, he said, only one case of cattle-killing having occurred and the offender having been sent to gaol. Because of the absence of rain, Aborigines had been forced in upon the waters on Tempe Downs station where they had killed a few cattle, but because of constant police patrols no serious depredations were expected. Rations supplied at Illamurta police station were 'much appreciated' by them, Gillen said, and others at Barrow Creek and Tennant Creek were well cared for. He praised the work of the missionaries at Hermannsburg and recommended that the government subsidy be raised from £200 to £300 a year. Pointing out that the children there were not trained in the use of Aboriginal weapons, he said they would find it very difficult to obtain food if the station were to close because of lack of funds. He believed Hermannsburg would be self-supporting in a few years. In his report for 1897, Gillen said that there had been more Aboriginal deaths due to influenza but that for the first time since he had begun reporting the number of births exceeded the number of deaths. The whole district had been suffering a severe drought and the Aborigines were finding it difficult to procure food, especially around the settlements, where stock were 'slowly but surely' driving off the native fauna. As native foods became scarcer the demand for rations would increase and in a few years it would be necessary to 'largely augment' the annual supplies to the depots. Addressing the general condition of the Aborigines, Gillen said Aborigines could not seek food in country unoccupied by the whites because each tribe had its own tract of land to which it was bound by the 'strongest ties of sentiment and tradition'. If Aborigines sought to settle elsewhere, they would be regarded as aliens and killed or driven off. He went on:

It is this feeling in the native mind which makes it so difficult to devise a comprehensive scheme by which large numbers could be benefitted. Mission stations for this reason have only been able to extend their ministrations to local groups within a radius of a few miles of the station, while the large majority of the tribes have been untouched.[10]

Apart from food supplementation, Gillen did not address himself to any of the pressing social issues covered by Dashwood. Because of his long residence in the Centre and membership of the Horn scientific expedition of 1894, he had come to be regarded as the region's resident expert on the Aborigines. He so impressed Baldwin Spencer that they were preparing a joint anthropological report on the work they carried out during that expedition. Like Foelsche, Gillen's interest in the Aborigines was completely detached. He had no empathy with them and, as was revealed in his evidence during the select committee examination of Dashwood's draft Bill, his sympathies lay with the squatters. While Foelsche was conscious of some of the abuses suffered by the Aborigines and some of the problems requiring solutions Gillen, apart from the growing shortage of food, seemed to prefer to believe that other problems did not exist.

The Kingston government was still in power, and Holder was still minister controlling the Northern Territory, when Dashwood's draft

Bill was introduced in the House of Assembly in July 1899. It was substantially the same as first proposed by Dashwood, the chief change being the setting of a penalty for carnal knowledge — up to two years imprisonment without the option of a fine. The Bill passed through the Assembly with little trouble and was introduced in the Council on 11 July. There it received the support of J. H. Gordon, who had shown himself to be partial during the public argument involving the Hermannsburg missionaries and the Central Australian settlers. Gordon described the Bill as almost a copy of the Queensland Act, adding that 'it was not the work of an Exeter Hall man'. By this he may have had in mind Dashwood's reputation as a 'hanging judge'. As we have seen, it was not almost a copy of the Queensland Act, several distinctive features of that legislation having been omitted. The government let the Bill lie on the table of the Council for a month to allow members to consider it. Most were not impressed. Among them was John Lewis, now a powerful squatter with interests in several stations, who was elected as one of the six members for the North-Eastern District in June 1898 and remained a member of the Council until his death in 1923.

When debate resumed in mid-August, members expressed sympathy with the objectives of the Bill but doubted that its provisions were practical or even necessary. M. P. F. Basedow successfully moved that the Bill be referred to a select committee of the Council, of which he was appointed chairman. Lewis was made a member. A journalist, educationist and later a social reformer but not a squatter, Basedow had been a Legislative Assembly member for Barossa during 1876–90 and during 1894–1900 he represented the North-Eastern District in the Legislative Council. The committee sat from 16 August to 14 November, taking evidence from twenty-one persons. Oral evidence was given by Dashwood, Parsons, Gillen and the two Legislative Assembly members for the Northern Territory, Walter Griffiths and Vaibon Louis Solomon; written evidence was taken from Finke River missionaries, G. J. Rechner and C. Strehlow, the Territory pastoralist, Joseph Bradshaw, and the policemen, Foelsche and Thorpe. Dashwood, in Adelaide at the time on other government business, was the first witness. He alleged that Aboriginal women were sexually exploited by white men and that whites 'shot the blacks down like crows'. This latter comment especially offended some members of both Houses, and when challenged to substantiate it Dashwood had difficulty in finding evidence from his own period, except the 1892 activities of Constable Smith and his volunteers after the killing of Clarke and De Loitte on Creswell Downs. J. L. Parsons reminded the committee that, while government resident, he had pressed upon successive governments the duty of the state to provide for the wild tribes living on the Territory's coast by creating reserves. 'The country belongs to these people and they are entitled to have a fair portion of it', he said. Parsons showed some naivety when he said that if the blacks could be induced to go upon Bathurst Island, for instance, and 'form a commonwealth of their own, it would be a most delightful solution of the difficulty'. Under questioning he agreed that Aborigines were reluctant to leave their own lands and that members of different tribes placed on an island would fight. The committee was not impressed with his pleas for more reserves.[11]

When called, Gillen disagreed with Dashwood's sexual exploitation claim, saying Dashwood had no personal knowledge of the blacks in the wild state. He also said proposals to require work permits and employment agreements would lead to slavery of the blacks. Modern critics also have said this of the Queensland legislation, stating that previously Aborigines could leave bad employers whereas under an agreement they could not do so until the term had expired. Such criticism ignores the position of Aborigines like those mentioned by Thorpe, Foelsche and Dashwood, who, without agreements, were enslaved on remote stations. Gillen repeated his praise for the Hermannsburg missionaries, although he believed they had not succeeded in making Christians of any of the blacks. In fact, he did not think it possible to make a Christian of a South Australian Aborigine. He showed his pessimistic attitude towards the Aborigines when he said: 'The missionaries are making the natives' path of extinction easier, and every man in Australia who is doing that for the blackfellow helps him'. He showed some appreciation of Aboriginal society, however: 'I think the missionary, in trying to make Christians of the blacks, destroyed all that was good in their organization, and gave them nothing in return'. But the Australian Aborigines, he believed, were the lowest in the scale of the barbarian races as well as the lowest in human intelligence. While he favoured extending the provisions of the Bill by giving the protector power to prosecute employers who ill-treated Aborigines and those who gave them opium, he opposed the clause which would have prohibited the harbouring of Aborigines in Europeans' houses, boats and premises, because it would be 'a hardship on the blacks if any settler was obliged to send them away'. Gillen did not appear concerned about the concubinage of Aboriginal women, although he said the settlers often used the young females as servants in their houses. He even stated that settlers in Central Australia did not 'harbour' Aborigines in their houses. When asked whether he would be prepared to give a licence to everyone who employed blacks in Central Australia, he replied: 'With one or two exceptions, yes'. John Lewis in 1910 said that Gillen had studied the native question more than any man in Australia. His old friend, Paul Foelsche, and Archibald Meston, architect of the Queensland legislation, may have been offended by that remark.

It was true that Dashwood's information had related only to the Top End and the eastern districts, whereas, apart from the claims made by the Hermannsburg missionaries in 1889–90, reports on the Centre during the previous decade had not mentioned any such 'immorality'. In January 1900, however, the new sub-protector at Alice Springs, T. A. Bradshaw, in his report for the previous year, commented on the committee's findings:

I feel compelled to take exception to the statement which has been made that the keeping of gins for immoral purposes is a rare occurrence even in bush centres...It is the rule and not the exception for lubras to be used for the purpose specified, as the number of half-caste children in the country will indicate. In the native camp near this station there are eleven half-castes as against nine black children, under (say), five years of age, and in the camp at the township—one and a half miles distant—the percentage of half-caste children is very much higher, a black child being a rarity.

The committee, unaware that Gillen was not telling the truth, was impressed with his evidence, Basedow remarking that it was 'among the most valuable evidence we have on record so far'. The pastoralists had lobbied heavily against the Bill and Gillen's evidence, supporting the status quo, was probably what many members of the upper house wanted to hear. Much of the evidence presented to the select committee contained objections to the proposed legislation because it was 'impracticable'. The committee's report, tabled in the Legislative Council in mid-November, said the Bill in its present form would be 'inoperative for any beneficial purpose, and, in some respects, might be injurious to the aboriginals'. It recommended that the Bill be withdrawn and a new one introduced to permit certificates to be issued to reputable persons to employ Aborigines and halfcastes, and to prevent the illicit intercourse of such persons or their employees with female Aboriginal and halfcaste employees. The new Bill should also prohibit the removal of Aborigines from their own districts unless stringent provisions were made for their return, and should provide increased powers to protectors enabling them, among other things, to prosecute offenders against the law. It should effectively prohibit the sale of intoxicating liquor and opium to Aborigines and halfcastes and prevent Chinese and other sellers of such goods from harbouring such persons. It would also prevent bartering of goods supplied by the government to them, facilitate proof of age in cases involving females under age, make it the duty of the government to take care of helpless orphans, encourage bona fide mission stations, and permit the exemption of certain Aborigines and halfcastes from the provisions of the Act. The Kingston government could do nothing to implement these recommendations, because parliament was prorogued and elections held on 28 November. The new government of V. L. Solomon lasted only one week until the Holder government replaced it.

Dashwood's Bill was doomed to failure from the start. He had accepted an invitation to draft legislation without receiving clear direction from the government as to what it wanted. Lacking strong support when introduced in parliament, it became his Bill rather than the government's. Dashwood's handling of his own evidence was maladroit and he seems to have confirmed his reputation for impetuosity by making charges he could not substantiate. The long period over which the inquiry was held, three months, allowed the pastoral interests to marshal strong opposition to its provisions, especially those relating to terms of employment and harbouring of Aborigines. When it came to a disagreement between one expert, Gillen, and another, Dashwood, the man of practical experience was favoured over the lawyer driven by moral indignation. Dashwood had intended that his legislation apply in South Australia and the Territory, but he had ignored Foelsche's warning that conditions in the two provinces were different and would require separate legislation. It was pointed out during the inquiry that the provisions of the Bill were not appropriate for dealing with Aborigines in the settled districts of South Australia. The Aboriginal population in South Australia had declined from about 15 000 when the whites arrived to less than 5000 in 1901, when there were 365 000 whites. In the same period, the Aboriginal population in the Territory had declined from perhaps 50 000 to just over 27 000 in 1901, compared with a white population of only 1055. There were 2690 Chinese in the Territory at that time but, because they held no political and little economic power, they have little bearing on this comparison. In the south, the Aboriginal minority was almost entirely absorbed into European society, either as inmates of mission reserves or as low-caste workers on pastoral stations; in the Territory, however, the numbers and proportion so absorbed were still very small, there being only one mission catering for about 100 Aborigines in 1899 and the pastoral intrusion being far from universal. A large part of the Territory's Aborigines in 1901 was still uncontrolled by the Europeans and many of those who provided labour on the cattle stations were free to leave if they wished. Despite the incidence of 'riding down' of Aborigines and of slavery practised by some pastoralists and drovers, probably more than half the Aborigines were still 'wild' in the European sense. They were still outside the European economic system, law and administration. Dashwood's Bill was designed to protect Aborigines who were still largely tribalized, whereas most of those in South Australia were detribalized. The chief reason for the pastoralists' objections was the interference in their relations with Aboriginal labour, especially at a time of economic crisis. Any interference which forced up the price of Aboriginal labour would have made their situation more perilous. Dashwood blamed the 'opposition of the pastoralists and others' for the failure of his Bill to pass through the Legislative Council, but it was also a victim of bad timing. The South Australian parliament was preoccupied with the coming colonial election, with the coming of federation and with the growing financial burden of the Northern Territory. For some time South Australians had realized that they had made a mistake in acquiring the Territory and were beginning to hope the forthcoming Commonwealth would take it, and its Aborigines, off their hands.

Despite his failure, Dashwood did not abandon his crusade. He remained in Palmerston until going on leave to Adelaide in 1904. During this last period he frequently reminded the government of the need for appropriate legislation for dealing with the Aborigines. Often he reported abductions of Aborigines by Europeans, pointing out the inadequacy of the law in dealing with such cases. He was conscious of the inequities suffered by Aborigines in the existing European justice system. In October 1900 a Palmerston jury recommended mercy for an elderly Aborigine charged with killing another Aborigine, because the murder was a consequence of tribal custom. Dashwood showed that he accepted the influence of tribal law on Aboriginal offenders when he accepted the jury's recommendation. Aborigines' right of access to waterholes and hunting grounds was a condition of leases issued to pastoralists in the Northern Territory, but conveniently ignored by leaseholders who drove them away. Dashwood angered the cattlemen by defending these rights. Charles Edward Herbert, a solicitor who had been practising in Palmerston since 1896, acted as government resident until Dashwood resigned to take up an appointment as Crown Solicitor in April 1905, then was appointed to the post. 'Northern Territory Charlie', as he was called, may have failed as a reformer on behalf of the Aborigines but he pointed the way South Australia was to go in the near future.

Chapter 13

The Last Decade

Successive South Australian governments tried to create in the Northern Territory an agricultural economy based on tropical crops such as sugar, cotton and rice, but all failed. The early discovery of gold had suggested to some enthusiasts that the northern province may hold great mineral wealth, but gold production declined after 1894 as the Chinese, the more successful miners since the original rush of 1872–78, were forced out by restrictive legislation. The *Northern Territory Land Act* of 1886 had precluded Chinese from new goldfields in the first two years after their proclamation, and immigration to the Territory was forbidden in 1888 as anti-Chinese feelings increased throughout Australia. A new *Northern Territory Gold Mining Act* in 1895 excluded Chinese from holding new mining leases but did not succeed in attracting Europeans instead. Chinese numbers in the Territory dropped from 6122 in 1888 to 1387 in 1910, while the number working in mining fell from 2055 in 1894 to 602 in 1910. Other minerals, such as copper, tin and precious stones, failed to provide bonanzas. This left the Territory's fortunes almost entirely in the hands of the pastoralists, but the 1890s had been catastrophic for them. Between 1889 and 1898 the area held under pastoral lease dropped by 30 per cent but the area declared stocked fell by 80 per cent, although cattle numbers increased very slowly over the decade.[1] Failures were most common in the Centre, the Palmerston and east Arnhem Land districts.

On the northern tablelands the thirty months to January 1894 were almost continuously dry, while 1897 and 1899 were hardly any better. The Victoria River district was hit badly in 1891–92 and the Centre suffered drought in 1889–93, and another longer drought began there at the end of the century. The 6000-square-mile Florida station in Arnhem Land was relinquished by John Macartney in 1893. Frew River station, south-east of Tennant Creek, was abandoned in 1894 and the Tempe Downs Cattle Company forsook its lease, south-west of Alice Springs, by the end of the century. John Costello abandoned

Valley of Springs on the Limmen Bight River between 1893 and 1895 and sold other stations in the area, losing a quarter of a million pounds on his Territory ventures. Even in relatively good times, Dr W. J. Browne, the most venturesome of the South Australian capitalists, for whom Alfred Giles had established Springvale station near Katherine in 1879, found the cost of labour, fencing and supplies was too great. He sold two of his Territory properties in 1888. During the 1890s, as drought and redwater fever reduced stock numbers, incomes dropped and many cattlemen were financially trapped. There were no buyers for their stock and property and it was extremely expensive to move stock out of the Territory. Because of the climate, isolation, poor food, threat of illness and attack by Aborigines, European labour had to be attracted to the Territory with offers of wages, which in 1895 were reported to be higher than elsewhere in Australia. For this reason, the pastoralists depended increasingly upon Aboriginal labour which was cheap and reliable. Without native labour the pastoral industry would have totally collapsed in the 1890s and, with it, the Northern Territory economy. As it was, this was the only Territory industry to show an upturn at the turn of the century and its output gradually rose during the remainder of the South Australian period.

The contribution of Aboriginal resistance to the difficulties of the Northern Territory pastoral industry has been exaggerated. Certainly, Aborigines attacked the early explorers such as Stuart and the overlanders with their herds coming up from the south in the 1870s but without effect on the southern ingress of Europeans and their animals. Resistance to others on the Queensland tracks from 1878 was much stronger and caused such experienced and determined drovers as D'Arcy Uhr to complain that the blacks 'were getting worse each trip he made'. Drovers and stockmen were killed as part of this resistance and stock was slaughtered, maimed and 'perished', particularly in the Limmen Bight region, but still the cattlemen came. In the Centre, Aborigines did not resist the invasion at first but once stations had been established they preyed on the herds, especially those of Glen Helen and Tempe Downs. Stock losses on some stations ran to hundreds a year and Willeroo station in the Victoria River district was abandoned in 1895 because of the Aborigines' killing and molesting of cattle, but Aboriginal depredations were rarely the sole cause of stations being abandoned. Gillen and Baldwin Spencer traversed Australia from Adelaide to Borroloola on an anthropological expedition in 1901. At Alice Springs Gillen noted in his diary that his old friend, Coulthard, 'had been nearly ruined by the drought and niggers'. Of five hundred head of cattle he had only seventy left, and the 'niggers' had killed and eaten fifty-two of his best horses. He claimed Coulthard's run abounded in game, the blacks were well treated and there was no excuse for their depredations. 'I feel that if they treated me this way I should feel bound to take the law into my own hands', he wrote. He quoted an Aborigine at Barrow Creek, who had arrived from the Barkly Tableland, as saying no blacks were left in that country. They had all been 'shot or driven off on account of their murderous attacks on settlers and their continual depredations among the cattle'. At McArthur River station results were very unsatisfactory after eighteen years. It had started with 14 000 head, mostly breeding cows, but the manager doubted he could muster that number now, 'owing to the persistent depredations of the natives who are killing continually'.[2]

The attacks on stock of the Eastern and African Cold Storage Company in eastern Arnhem Land in the first decade of this century have been given as evidence of sustained and effective Aboriginal resistance to the pastoral invasion. A British company with grandiose plans, it bought Macartney's old Florida station in 1903 and also Elsey, Hodgson Downs and Wollogorang stations, and was said to have had capital of £450 000. One of its directors was Sir John Cockburn, former South Australian premier and one-time minister controlling the Northern Territory. It has been claimed that within two years Aborigines had killed a thousand cattle, attacked a homestead, killed several gardeners and crazed the herds by incessant stampeding and scare-tactics. This, it is inferred, led to the failure of the company, which went bankrupt in 1909.[3] The resistance in eastern Arnhem Land appears to have been as strong and persistent as on Tempe Downs in Central Australia, but there is little evidence to prove that Aborigines were responsible for the company's failure. Rather, it seems, failure was due chiefly to bad management decisions. The eastern and central Arnhem Land country was unsuitable for cattle, as Macartney had found, because of ticks, distance from markets and the poor soil on which the stock could not thrive. They had to be moved frequently to fresh pastures. Because of its unsuitability for cattle, large Aboriginal reserves could be created in Arnhem Land early in this century, and the whole region was made one reserve in 1931. Oral history sources suggest that, to deal with the Aborigines, the company employed two gangs of blacks led by a white man or halfcaste to shoot down the local blacks on sight, and that one such leader, George Conway, 'asserted that the party he led in 1905 or 1906 killed dozens of wild blacks'.[4] Conway may have said that, but such actions are not supported by other evidence. The Eastern and African, sometimes referred to as the Arafura Company, did not complain to the government resident in Palmerston or the government in Adelaide of any attacks by Aborigines or losses of stock. In view of the success which single white constables assisted by native troopers were having at that time in repressing cattle-killing in the Centre, it seems that the company, because of its political connections through Cockburn and economic value to the Territory, would have called on the government to deal with this problem rather than risk public censure by taking the matter into its own hands. The company's term falls within a period of increasing government sensitivity to criticism of ill-treatment of the Aborigines, especially in the Territory. In the absence of better evidence than oral history, the claims made for large-scale black resistance and white retaliation in Arnhem Land are unconvincing. The only indisputable evidence of a pastoral station in the northern Territory being forced to close because of Aboriginal actions relates to Willeroo. There may have been killing as described, but it is the scale which matters most and oral sources are not reliable on that point.

Undoubtedly some Aboriginal aggression was genuine resistance. The Tiwi people were successful in keeping out permanent invaders until 1900, when the buffalo-hunter, Joe Cooper, and his Cobourg Peninsula assistants went back after being forced out in 1897. The Warramanga strongly tried to prevent foreigners passing through their land from 1860 to the late 1870s. The actions of the Western Aranda at Glen Helen and the Kukatja or Southern Aranda or both at Tempe Downs for ten years or more from 1884 appear to have begun as attempts to drive the whites out of their land. Afterwards, the chief reason appears to have been the need for a new source of food as cattle replaced wild game. Finally, as drought reduced herds and police patrolling became more effective, the Central Australian Aborigines were forced to rely more upon European employment and rations in order to survive. This acceptance of white presence and hegemony came at a time when the pastoralists were becoming more dependent upon black labour. Rather than destroying the Northern Territory pastoral industry, the Aborigines saved it. In the northern Queensland pastoral industry in 1886, 55 per cent of labour was black.[5] Similar conditions applied in the Northern Territory but the higher cost of European labour there and the disastrous financial situation of the 1890s would have been added incentives for employing blacks. By 1892 the majority of station employees were blacks. These were their working conditions:

The natives did work which white men were unwilling to tackle; they were excellent stockmen and toiled not only cheerfully but for a remuneration which in many cases made all the difference between working at a profit instead of a loss. In a very few cases partly-civilized natives received payment in money, but usually, at least in 1912, the remuneration consisted of two or three suits of clothing yearly, two or three pairs of boots, one or two blankets, one or two mosquito nets, an ample supply of meat and flour, tea, sugar, tobacco and pipes. Estimates of keeping an aboriginal in regular employment on a station varied from one pound to two pounds a month. It should be stressed, though, that lessees not only fed the natives actually employed, but also large numbers of dependants and hangers-on . . . [6]

A handful of whites assisted by Aborigines could manage a pastoral run carrying up to 100 000 cattle. For instance, at Banka Banka, north of Tennant Creek, in 1901, two white men and a number of Aborigines ran the station. But this is an oversimplification. Aborigines were good stockmen and because of their local knowledge were much more successful in keeping cattle on unfenced runs. The supply of white labour was never certain, while the pool of black labour never ran dry. On the other hand, Aborigines did not easily adapt to skilled trades such as fencing, carpentry and well-sinking, for which the owners had to pay white men high wages, although such work would have been periodic and in bad times neglected altogether. Also, individual Aborigines were generally unreliable, working slowly and inefficiently, requiring constant supervision and often absenting themselves when they felt like it. On northern Queensland runs, it was generally believed one European was worth two Aboriginal workers, but four Aborigines could be engaged for the price of one European. Although the number of people involved was small, because of the special conditions affecting the Territory's pastoral industry and its fundamental economic position, Aborigines and Europeans there were more dependent upon each other for survival than elsewhere in Australia at the beginning of the last decade of South Australian administration.

In the north, the conditions of the Aborigines were now deteriorating rapidly and seriously, as Dashwood took every opportunity to point out to the government during his last five years. Reporting on 1900, he urged the introduction of legislation. Relations between the white and black races continued to be 'most unsatisfactory', he said. No matter how injurious to the welfare of the Aborigines these relations might be, 'the authorities have no power to interfere unless offences against the criminal law are committed'. He pointed out that the select committee had recognized the 'absolute necessity for legislative interference'. He had read the report of the protector for north Queensland, Dr W. E. Roth, which, he said, showed that the Queensland Act was of 'great benefit to the Aborigines, and does not operate in any way to the detriment of the bona fide employer of black labour'. Dashwood was not to know that some north Queensland pastoralists had strongly protested against Roth's interpretation of the employment provisions of the legislation nor that the methods used in administering it were only just beginning to lead to disastrous consequences for the Aborigines it was meant to protect. In the Territory, the protector, Dr Goldsmith, reported that in May 1900 three hundred Aborigines attended the annual distribution of blankets in Palmerston; the presence of few children indicated, he thought, that the local Aborigines were gradually becoming extinct. Between Port Darwin and Katherine were more than sixty halfcaste children of various ages. He strongly urged that provision be made for their removal from their surroundings and educated 'to a certain extent', so that ultimately they might become useful members of society, 'and not — as too often happens when allowed to run wild in the blacks' camp — become a source of danger to the community'.[7]

Goldsmith was also concerned about the spread of leprosy. It was said to have spread from the Alligator Rivers to neighbouring tribes and, if so, he feared that it endangered the white population. It was reported that, whereas the Alligator Rivers tribe had numbered about 190 seven or eight years previously, only about sixty now survived, a large proportion of the deaths having been due to leprosy. Goldsmith admitted that this was a most difficult matter to treat. The Territory administration was certainly becoming alarmed but the government was as yet unconcerned by Aboriginal health. As diseases spread in both the north and south, however, this would become an important influence upon the government. In 1902 the acting protector, Dr T. E. F. Seabrook, remarked that long imprisonment was a frequent cause of phthisis among Aboriginal prisoners. The daily routine and environment of prison life, and the Aborigine's 'continual brooding and hankering to be with his tribe, his native soil and environments... affect his physical system deleteriously much more than they do the white man'. Goldsmith returned to his halfcaste theme, saying that the increasing number would make it necessary to provide for their welfare. They should be removed from the native camps to an institution where they could be taught trades and household work. The next protector, Dr Kensington Fulton, was alarmed that the 'curse of smoking and eating opium was spreading through these innocent people, causing them to lose what little morale still remains in them'. Opium-addiction reduced them to a deplorable condition and he asked that the introduction and sale of it in the Territory be prevented. The police had made strenuous efforts to suppress the trade and, when caught, offenders were severely punished. There were many cases of Aboriginal drunkenness but, although the police had been vigilant, this 'evil' still existed, he said.[8]

The South Australian government tightened the anti-opium legislation in 1905 and this 'removed one of the worst dangers threatening the Aborigines', according to Dashwood's successor, Charles Herbert.[9] Habitual smokers among the Chinese had been 'suffering from want of the drug' and had none to spare for the Aborigines. During the year rations had been sent to Daly Waters and Powell's Creek in answer to reports of distress among Aborigines there. None were distressed near Palmerston, however. With few exceptions the services of Aborigines were now hard to obtain, Herbert said. Europeans tended to recruit them from foreign areas, because they believed such staff worked better away from home. Often the willing recruit was transformed into an enforced servant, this being 'one of the evils which legislation is necessary to remedy'. Like Dashwood, Herbert urged that legislation based on the Queensland model be introduced.

In 1906 Herbert again called for legislation. Its application would be expensive but this could be lessened and better controlled if the law were applied by proclamation to the settled districts and extended later as required. And early in 1908 he pointed out that the Territory was now the only part of Australia with a considerable Aboriginal population but 'no legislation worthy of consideration'. In recent years it had often been necessary to take some action to protect Aborigines without authority. More often, no action could be taken, because 'it could not be persisted in'. Year after year the decrease in the number of Aborigines in the settled districts was observable, he said, particularly the number of young full-blood children:

In addition to disease (unfortunately rife among these people) which is one cause of the decrease, this result is further contributed to by the fact of so many lubras permanently leaving their camps and living openly with men of nationalities other than their own. The women, as a rule, are chosen because they are young and of a superior physique to others of their tribe. Their absence, therefore, naturally tends to hasten the race extinction, which is slowly but certainly approaching.

It is utterly impossible in the present state of the law to interfere in these cases unless the lubra is under the age of consent. Invariably no evidence of age is available.

In his report for 1908 Herbert said the condition of the Aborigines remained unchanged, except that those frequenting white settlements had become more disinclined to work and prone to indulge in the 'evils to which for many years they have been exposed without check or guidance'. He realized that it was not possible to frame legislation which would meet with general approval. The fact that views on the Aboriginal question were widely divergent was not an answer to the demand for protective legislation. For the first time a European official acknowledged the contribution which Aborigines had made to the European development of the Territory:

For economic reasons, too, ordinary prudence calls for the preservation of a people who have done much to aid, and comparatively little to obstruct, pioneering in this country, and who under a reasonable law will be of material assistance in furthering schemes for future settlement.

Unauthorized removal of Aborigines from the Territory was still a problem. Preventative action was taken locally when possible, and recently Herbert had asked the minister to seek the help of authorities in another state in returning a young halfcaste woman 'impudently enticed out of the Territory from a good home'. No law existed to meet such a case, he said. If the self-constituted guardian of the girl opposed her return, the only recourse was to operation of the Aboriginal legislation in that state. Such dependence upon the laws of other states was undesirable, he added. Because of the pressure of other work, the government medical officer had been relieved of his other duties and W. G. Stretton, who had been a magistrate and sub-protector at Borroloola, was appointed protector in 1908, a post he held until 1911. At the same time officers in charge of police stations were made sub-protectors. Writing in 1907, Alfred Searcy had regarded Stretton as a 'great authority on the aboriginals, especially those of the Gulf of Carpentaria'. In fact Stretton had, in 1893, sent to the director of the South Australian Museum a paper on the customs, rites and superstitions of the tribes of that region.

In January 1909 Stretton proposed restricting entry of Aborigines to white settlements. He had visited all native camps within the Palmerston town boundary and told them to keep their camps clean. There had been a great improvement in the camps after a few days but, nonetheless, he was impressed with the idea of establishing a permanent camping ground outside the boundary. This would not destroy their peaceful relationship with the whites, and the Aborigines would, he believed, be better out of the township. Only those employed by whites should be allowed in. Those employed on stations away from the settled districts appeared much healthier than those around towns. Stretton had opened a register of halfcastes, in which were noted 48 males and 51 females aged from one to twenty-five years. He believed their total number in the Territory to be 150, but they were not shown in any Aboriginal population figures — which he considered overestimated. During his time in Borroloola he had encountered, among the tribes 'best known to civilisation', none with more than 80 members. This was the position in other localities, where some numbers were much lower. For instance, the full strength of a group on the South Alligator River at Kaparlgo was only 22. Stretton estimated that Aboriginal populations in occupied areas in 1909 were: coast Aborigines from Victoria River to Robinson River (20 000 square miles), 5600; 'up river' tribes and intervening country (30 000 square miles), 4600; inland tribes from Newcastle Waters to southern boundary (473 000 square miles), 3000; and Melville Island (2400 square miles), 400; total, 13 600. In 1905 Foelsche had told the Governor of South Australia, Sir George Le Hunte, then visiting the Territory, that the Aboriginal population was from 20 000 to 22 000. The basis for Foelsche's estimate was not given but, as it turned out, his estimate agrees with figures published in 1980.[10]

By the beginning of 1910, the long years of campaigning by Parsons, Dashwood and now Herbert were bearing fruit. In a report on his 1905 visit, Le Hunte had commented:

The aboriginal problem is difficult, and I do not think any attempt has yet been made to cope with it. Yet it certainly demands attention...What is required is a properly organised system of power and responsibility. There should be an official head, who should... be the Government Resident, under the Minister for the Territory; under him there should be an organised department, a specially selected Protector, who should be a Justice of the Peace and his chief executive, with powers and jurisdiction all over the Territory; he should be a travelling officer.[11]

In 1901 the then governor, Lord Tennyson, after a visit to Oodnadatta, had publically criticized the treatment of the Aborigines, condemning 'the white man's general neglect of them, and in some cases... the cruel ill-treatment of them'. Now the present governor was adversely referring to their treatment in the Territory. Le Hunte's report on the Territory was tabled in the federal parliament and the following year the Price Labor government reached the first tentative agreement with the Commonwealth on terms for handing over the Territory. South Australia's record in Aboriginal relations there might soon be examined by outsiders and be found wanting. In 1909 the government began to yield to pressure and asked the parliamentary draughtsman to prepare legislation. Reports by Stretton and Herbert were referred to him for guidance. When the first draft was sent to Herbert for comment, he was not satisfied. The government was still sensitive to the pastoralists' opposition to controls over employment. In his report on 1909 he 'earnestly advocated' the inclusion of provisions for control of the engagement and employment of Aborigines and for preventing men of other races cohabiting with female Aborigines. The absence of these provisions from the draft was a serious omission, he wrote:

A direct prohibition of cohabitation would perhaps prove to be unworkable as a check on immorality, but a provision regulating employment of the nature previously recommended by me, together with a provision against harbouring aborigines contrary to the Act and regulations would, I think, be effective.[12]

An example of the abuses of Aboriginal employees in remote districts is a case investigated by the police at Borroloola in 1910. The officer then in charge, Mounted Constable First Class R. Stott, had received a report in January that some weeks previously a halfcaste girl aged twelve or thirteen years in the employment of J. Bohning, a teamster, had been horsewhipped by Bohning's eldest son near McArthur station in the presence of his mother. The girl had been compelled to carry two buckets full of water, a task much beyond her strength. Stott instructed Mounted Constable Noblett to charge Mr and Mrs Bohning under the Children's Protection Act and, if necessary, take immediate possession of the child. Noblett went to the place but learned that the eldest son had been kicked in the stomach by a mare and had died. The Bohning family seemed to be deeply in grief. In the circumstances, the original informant, a man named Gilbert, did not wish to give evidence against any of the family concerning the horsewhipping. Stott reported that the police would therefore take no further action, but would watch future treatment of the girl.[13]

An example of the brutalizing influence of some whites upon their Aboriginal employees and associates comes from the same district.[14] In December 1908 William Hume and a halfcaste named Paddy Bull were arrested for the murder of an Aborigine named Alick. Hume and his partner, Thomas Williams, lived at Horse Creek. They made a living mustering cattle on the western boundary of Tanumbirini Downs station, south-west of Borroloola, under an agreement with the manager, Henry Coop, that they deliver all branded cattle to Coop and keep all cleanskins. A native of Kelso, Scotland, Hume was about sixty-five years of age at this time. According to the police, Hume and Williams led very immoral lives. Hume kept two Aboriginal women, Polly and Mary, for 'immoral purposes' and Williams kept a halfcaste girl for the same reason. Hume had a halfcaste son by Polly, and he and Williams employed the halfcaste Paddy and several fullbloods. About the beginning of September 1908 Hume and his son and Paddy left Horse Creek for Borroloola to obtain stores. It was alleged that on the morning after they left, Alick had raped or attempted to rape Mary, then had ridden to Tanumbirini Downs, where he left the horse and saddle, and went to the Aborigines camp near the homestead. Two days later Williams arrived and told Coop what had happened. On 24 September on the way back from Borroloola Hume called at the homestead. Hume vowed vengeance and several times threatened to shoot Alick, but the local people camped at Tanumbirini did not disclose his whereabouts. Eventually Hume heard where Alick was and asked Paddy to shoot him. Paddy agreed and one evening, taking Hume's rifle, went to the camp, told Alick he was clearing out because Hume 'growled' too much, and asked Alick to come with him. Alick took a lot of convincing, Paddy arguing with him for some hours. At last, when most of the camp were asleep, Paddy rose, saying he was going back to his camp, but without warning he shot Alick in the head. The people in the camp fled and next morning Paddy told Coop what had happened. Coop simply commented: 'Good job. You clear out. I don't want you'. Hume then burned Alick's remains.

Soon after this Coop arrived in Borroloola and remained until 10 November but did not report the murder. A month later rumours reached Stott, and he and Mounted Constable H. Higgs rode to Tanumbirini, picking up information on the way, and arrested Paddy. Coop denied he knew anything about the matter. He also said he had not considered the assault on Mary worth reporting when the police were there immediately after that event but before the murder. The police collected some human bones, arrested Hume as well, and returned to Borroloola with prisoners and witnesses on 22 December. Coop, who had a halfcaste woman living with him, denied Paddy had told him of the murder or that he had told an Aboriginal witness, Hector, not to say anything to the police about it. A man named Bunning, who was camped on Tanumbirini at the time and had talked to Hume after the murder, denied knowing anything about it. Bunning also kept a halfcaste woman, Lucy. According to Stott, Bunning had threatened to shoot Paddy because of jealousy over Lucy. 'Nearly every European in the District keeps Lubras for immoral purposes', Stott reported, 'and in most instances there is a considerable amount of jealousy. For this reason the sympathy for Hume is very pronounced'. Hume and Paddy appeared in Borroloola court on 29 December, but even there an attempt was made to influence Hume's son not to speak freely. Stott held all principal witnesses at the police station, saying that if any were allowed to leave they would be 'either tampered with or put out of the way'. Mary had given birth to a halfcaste girl six or seven weeks after the murder.

William Hume, Paddy Bull and witnesses were sent to Palmerston by steamer in February 1909, but the case against Hume failed. In court in April Paddy changed his story, denying Hume had incited him and saying he had shot Alick in self-defence during an argument. The Crown alleged that Paddy had been induced to change his story, but Hume was discharged nonetheless and Paddy was sentenced to death despite a strong recommendation of mercy from the jury. In July 1910 Hume was charged with supplying liquor to Aborigines at his camp near Borroloola. On 27 July 1910 Mary, who was then eighteen years of age, gave birth to a halfcaste boy, but died soon afterwards. Mounted Constable Higgs went to Hume's camp some days later and saw Mary's body lying under dirty calico in the sun. William Hume was lying helplessly drunk about twenty yards away, there were many empty whisky bottles and three or four Aboriginal women were sitting about Hume's dray, one of them nursing a halfcaste child. A native of the Wearyan River country, Mary had been with Hume since she was a piccaninni and this was the second child by him.

The birth of children of mixed race was a feature of life in the Gulf Country. In August 1910 Henry Coop reported the birth of a halfcaste male child to Minnie, an Aboriginal woman who slept in a room at Tanumbirini; Coop did not admit to being the father. In 1911 a child was born to another Minnie, who lived at McLeod's store in Borroloola. Born with a deformed foot, the child was killed by another Aboriginal woman at Minnie's request. Stott said there was insufficient evidence to bring charges. In 1908 a list of halfcastes in the district was kept at Borroloola police station. It contained twenty-seven names: three were of 'coloured' extraction, the rest white. The story of William Hume and Mary as well as the incidence of 'comboism', as it was called, which these records reveal, indicate in some measure one result of the overwhelming influence of European domination of Aboriginal lives in one district of the Territory at that time. Young Aboriginal women, particularly halfcastes, were from early years the possessions and prizes of the conquerers. They had no say in the matter.

Aboriginal health continued to be a serious problem. The government medical officer had stated in 1909 that of more than a hundred female Aborigines in the settled districts examined by him only one was found to be free from venereal disease. Herbert added that in the Northern Territory's non-Aboriginal community the adult male population exceeded the female by four to one. Stretton had received many complaints from young men of their women going away with white and coloured men and found they had done so willingly and in some cases with the consent, for the time being, of their husbands. Stretton said men of all nations had free use of the mature women, who were lured away from legitimate employment, and this must continue until legislative action was taken to protect the employer. The women were especially lured into the services of Japanese, Malays and Filipinos. Despite several newspaper accounts, it was not true to say that cases of criminal intercourse with young girls were common or numerous. Stretton now estimated the number of halfcastes in the Territory to be two hundred. Among them were unfortunate girls, 'too good for full blooded natives and not good enough for white men', who were driven to seek food and shelter in blacks' camps. These women were only too willing to live with white or coloured men and to 'submit to any degradation to obtain that end'. He appealed for protection and a home for these women. As for the long-predicted extinction of the Aborigines, Stretton said this was 'not yet within measurable distance', but civilization would untimately 'draw it to a close'. In the meantime, a race more difficult to manage, the persons of mixed blood, would have sprung up, 'and every endeavour should be made to ameliorate the condition' of these people. He believed few Aborigines in the Territory had not come into contact with white people. In 1909 South Australia had spent £1861 on the Northern Territory's Aborigines and, despite Stretton's estimate of 13 600, the official population was put at 16 000.

In March 1902, as the great drought set in, the telegraph master at Barrow Creek rode two to three hundred miles 'in all directions' around his station and reported that the country was destitute of fauna and water. Aborigines had been coming into Barrow Creek and dying of exhaustion. Others had died *en route*. The responsible minister, J. G. Jenkins, who was also Chief Secretary and Premier, immediately wired T. A. Bradshaw that he regretted the state of the Aborigines and had informed the police at Barrow Creek to provide relief for any Aborigines at once. By September 1906 the Adelaide press was carrying reports of starving Aborigines in Central Australia and early in 1907 the government was authorizing all rations necessary be sent to assist those west of Charlotte Waters, reported by the postmaster there to be 'in a bad way'.

On 20 April 1905 the *South Australian Register* carried a report alleging shocking treatment of Aborigines by missionaries at Finke River. A Captain Barclay, who had led a geological expedition in Central Australia, had claimed in an address in Melbourne that the missionaries at Hermannsburg had 'enriched themselves at the expense of the country, and possess thousands of cattle and horses' and had ill-treated the Aborigines. This was soon denied by the Reverend L. Kaibel of the Immanuel Synod in Adelaide. The minister's department advised that no report of such treatment had been provided by police but that the allegations were sure to get to London and that the South Australian agent-general should be advised. The minister said: 'Wait events'.[15] As it happened, the British government and the British press did not react, but the incident does show how sensitive the treatment of Aborigines had become in South Australia. Official police attitudes had changed since Hamilton's hardline policy following the Barrow Creek attack. When the police commissioner, L. G. Madley, learnt in 1905 that Mounted Constable Frederick Pflaum had inflicted corporal punishment on Aborigines suspected of killing cattle at Hermannsburg, he was incensed and dismissed him, saying: 'M/C Pflaum has not only disgraced himself, but has left a lasting stain on the Police Force as a whole. For years it has been a policy . . . to establish the kindliest and friendliest feelings between the Police and the Native Population'.[16]

The situation experienced by the Aborigines of Central Australia during the last decade of South Australian control remained grim, as indicated by the reports of Constable Charles Brookes, the trooper in charge of Illamurta police station.[17] In July 1906 he reported that the Aranda were still killing cattle on C. F. T. Strehlow's run, and in June 1907 he said the Aborigines were coming into Erldunda station because of the drought. They were in a 'deplorable condition', he said, and asked Bradshaw at Alice Springs to send half a ton of flour and ten pounds of tobacco to Henbury station and one ton of flour and twenty pounds of tobacco to Erldunda. Rations normally supplied to Illamurta were not sufficient to meet the demand from the blacks. In September that year Brookes reported that the health of the Aborigines was now good except for a few suffering colds, but that 'There is a small tribe of blacks about 120 miles S.W. of here, who are in a deplorable condition. Some of them came in here for rations then informed me that 2 old men & 6 lubras had perished for want of food. They also stated that water was scarce'. In December 1907 Brookes reported only one case of cattle killing in the past twelve months, and the owner of the beast had not wished to prosecute. He went on:

The frequent patrols & visiting the various camps has in a great measure stopped the cattle killing. The blacks in general have had a very rough time for the past three years during the drought and in some parts where there are small tribes kangaroos and wallabies are a thing of the past and how the blacks exist is a mystery. I saw some on the Palmer a few days ago whilst on patrol and they were simply walking skeletons.

This assessment by Brookes indicates the extent to which Aborigines in the Centre, deprived of natural game and denied introduced cattle, had become dependent upon European benevolence to survive. In these circumstances they had no course but to become 'quiet'.

So effective had pacification in the Centre become that, in each report over the next three years, Brookes was able to say that no cases of cattle-killing had been brought to his notice. Nor had he received any complaints from station managers. In December 1908 he said the issuing of rations to 'the outside blacks has a great deal to do with their good behaviour'. By 'outside' blacks, he meant 'wild' ones as distinct from those who had settled on stations. He had distributed food to all Aborigines who needed it, not just the old and infirm, as had been past policy. He had received a good supply of rations during the year for the Aborigines and they had come to Illamurta 'from all quarters'. As well, he reported in January 1910, station managers occasionally killed a beast for them. By July that year he had issued rations to more than 150 old and young people. He was also supplying tea, blue shirts and blankets but the supply was not enough to meet demands. In his last report on the South Australian period, dated 1 January 1911, Brookes said that Aboriginal conduct was still good, there was no cattle-killing and through the year he had distributed food to 300 people, young and old, from all parts.

There was still some violent resistance to European intrusion, especially in districts where the pastoralists had been established for some time but their numbers were small. In November 1905 F. M. Bradshaw, a Victoria River squatter and brother of Joseph Bradshaw who gave evidence to the 1899 select committee inquiry in Adelaide, set out by launch to Port Darwin. Bradshaw was accompanied by two friends and a Russian engineer, Ivan Egeriffe. This man had escaped when a Swede, Larsen, had been killed on a launch on the Daly River in 1900. On the way northwards Bradshaw called at Port Keats, where boring for coal had begun and where four Aborigines joined the launch. That night, forty miles north of Port Keats, the whites were attacked as they slept and their bodies thrown overboard. The launch and the bodies were later found. Two Aborigines, Combit and Donah, were convicted of murder but the jury recommended mercy, evidence having been given at their trial of repeated acts of cruelty by Egeriffe towards Combit. In June 1907 the sentences were commuted to life imprisonment. At the same time the camp at Port Keats was attacked, two of the boring party being struck but not seriously injured.[18] In contrast with previous major attacks on Europeans, no punitive action was taken against the tribe involved probably because frontier passions had cooled and the government now had better control of events in the Territory. Occasional spearings continued in the Victoria River district and elsewhere.These and similar incidents continued to receive press attention, but Aboriginal resistance to the European occupation of the Northern Territory was now passive, no further serious violence occurring until the Coniston and Lander River killings in Central Australia in 1928.

The last serious affair occurred in 1933 when a white policeman, investigating the murder of three Japanese pearl-fishermen, was speared to death at Caledon Bay in eastern Arnhem Land. Press reports that white parties had set out to relatiate alarmed southern whites and a missionary party was sent to the area to negotiate between the whites and the local people. An Aborigine, Tuckiar, was arrested and tried for the policeman's murder but his trial in Darwin was mishandled, the judge directing the jury to find him guilty even though the jury had suggested that there was insufficient evidence. Tuckiar was sentenced to death but the conviction was subsequently quashed by the High Court. This affair showed that it was no longer possible to hand out rough justice to Aborigines in the Territory without exciting the indignation of southerners, at least not in the open.[19]

In a study of the Victoria River district, Michaela Richards has pointed out that after the first cattlemen arrived in the early 1880s the local people had two options: they could sustain themselves by working on the stations, or continue their traditional way of life, compensating for the loss of natural game by spearing cattle. No doubt some pursued a combination of both styles. This choice of living with or away from European settlement was conducive to polarization and antagonism within Aboriginal society. By 1928, however, when serious drought was affecting the district, the pastoral industry was consolidated and the advantages of living traditionally had weakened, the choice began to disappear: 'A nomadic existence began to involve considerable hardship if it was, in fact, possible at all, and employment in the pastoral industry became a matter of survival'. As a result of these changed circumstances it was possible to detect a shift towards a harmonious and fairly uniform dissatisfaction with European settlement among many Aborigines in the district, leading to new co-operation between Aboriginal groups in the Victoria River district. This appears to be typical of the situation in all the settled districts in the first half of the twentieth century. European domination had given them a commonality of experience, out of which would arise a concensus of attitudes.

Chapter 14

Solving the Problem

After several years of dickering and despite the opposition of South Australian interests who wished to retain the Territory, the Labor government of Thomas Price in 1906 and 1907 worked out a tentative deal with the Commonwealth on the transfer of the Territory. The province's public debt had been gradually rising over the years and by 1910 it was just under four million pounds. South Australia could no longer afford to keep it but still hung out for the best possible deal. Price had wanted the Commonwealth to take over this debt, purchase the existing railway from Port Augusta to Oodnadatta and complete the railway to Port Darwin which, the South Australians hoped, would ensure they continued to receive any economic benefit from the Territory. Price died in May 1909 but, after more dickering, the Commonwealth finally accepted this deal and in September 1910 the Northern Territory Acceptance Bill passed both houses of the federal parliament. On 1 January 1911 control of the Territory passed to the Commonwealth.

On 27 July 1910, Thomas Crush, one of the two members for the Territory, had obtained leave to introduce in the House of Assembly a Bill to 'make Provision for the better Protection and Control of the Aboriginal Inhabitants of the Northern Territory, and for other purposes'.[1] Debate lapsed before the end of that session but in the next session, immediately after the Commonwealth parliament passed the acceptance Bill, Price's successor, John Verran, introduced another aimed at the protection of the Aborigines in South Australia. A few days later, debate on Crush's Bill resumed, to the puzzlement of some members who saw no reason for proceeding with it when the Commonwealth was to take over the Territory in a few weeks. Its sponsors argued that South Australia should do something for the Territory before it parted with it. The Attorney-General, W. J. Denny, said the Assembly should pass as many Bills as it reasonably could in the short time still available 'and bring the legislation regarding the Northern Territory up to date. Then the Commonwealth could do what they desired. They would thus be doing good service to the Commonwealth'. It seems that, now they were getting rid of the Territory after forty years of failure, South Australians were anxious to leave it in as good a condition as possible in the hope of avoiding national censure. Some members were also puzzled that such an important measure should have been introduced by a private member, but Denny declined to give a reason.

In his second-reading speech, Crush said that, owing to the absence of legislation in the past, the Aborigines were rapidly decreasing 'through disease, neglect and insanitary conditions'. Many among the tribes which had come into contact with civilization had deteriorated physically and morally. The police had no power to prevent them going where they liked and doing almost as they liked. The needs of the Aborigines in the Territory had been alleviated to some extent by the provision of food and blankets and other commodities, but this system, he said, had tended to make them lazy instead of self-supporting. They would work if they received good treatment and were able to make themselves useful, particularly among stock. He added:

Since country had been taken for pastoral purposes they had been deprived of former hunting grounds. The government had done nothing to recompense them in that respect. To improve their condition, the only thing to do was to establish reserves. There was plenty of country left that would be suitable and for the purpose, and provided that proper supervision was provided by practical men, they would solve the problem of the aborigines.

Crush was expressing the sentiments and ideals voiced when the Queensland legislation was introduced in 1897 — shame because of the ill-treatment of the Aborigines followed by the same draconian solution to the problem, pushing them off their tribal lands and onto reserves. The South Australians too had a naive belief that the Aborigines would be able to support themselves on these reserves by breeding horses, cattle, sheep, goats, pigs and cultivating the soil to provide vegetables at little expense. Crush said his Bill differed from the one introduced by the premier because of the different conditions in the Territory. His bill provided for the employment of Aborigines and the restricted use of firearms by them. The provisions relating to employment were similar to those in the Queensland legislation, as advocated by Dashwood and Herbert. Aborigines were to be permitted to carry firearms if licensed, or even if unlicensed when provided by an employer for their protection, because 'blacktrackers and aborigines who went into the bush needed firearms for their protection'. This provision had been adopted from the Western Australian legislation of 1905. The Bill provided for the creation of a chief protector, who would be responsible for the administration of the Act and have power to appoint superintendents and other protectors. Powers would be granted to resume Crown land and to grant certain areas for reserves. It provided for the employment of Aborigines under permits from the chief protector and for the employment of Aborigines on coastal vessels. Europeans found on Aboriginal reserves would be punished. 'That', Crush said, 'would tend to improve the morality of the blacks, and prevent the dangers of intermingling'. The other member for the Territory, John Brown, whose experience of Aborigines there dated from 1873, supported the Bill, saying that he had 'seen a great falling off' in their physical and moral condition. The regulations governing their employment must be revised. 'Decently treated', he said, 'the natives made good workmen, but they should be granted something like a fair and recognised wage'.

The Northern Territory Aborigines Bill when enacted made the chief protector the legal guardian of all Aboriginal and halfcaste children, 'notwithstanding that any such child has a parent or other relative living', until such children reached eighteen years of age. It gave the chief protector power to keep any Aborigine or halfcaste within the boundaries of a reserve or Aboriginal institution and forbade marriage between Aboriginal women and non-Aboriginal men without permission. It restricted the removal of Aborigines from one district to another within the Territory and from the Territory itself without permission and guarantees of return.

Despite continued grumbling by some Assembly members about the irrelevance of the Bill in the circumstances, debate on it continued sporadically over the next month. The government stressed that the 'main bill' introduced by Verran dealt mainly with Aborigines who had come into close contact with civilization, whereas the Territory measure dealt with those in their wild state. A former attorney-general in the Playford, Downer and Jenkins ministries, Robert Homburg, was not happy with the clause authorizing Aborigines to be removed to reserves, saying this was one of the drastic features of the Bill. It would be an extraordinary thing, he said, 'to practically incarcerate what was a nomadic race'. He asked members whether they would be prepared to experiment in this way when they had been assured such a measure would be unsuccessful. Crush replied that 'murders and depredations which were constantly being committed in the Territory would be checked by a system of reserves. Refractory characters would be sent to a reserve on one of the islands off the coast'. Other members claimed that to confine tribes, who were 'constantly at war', to reserves would defeat the objects of the Bill; they would be made slaves, but freedom was essential to the blacks. Crush and Brown dismissed these fears as being unfounded, saying the object of the Bill was to improve the condition of the blacks and only diseased ones would be forced to go to reserves. One member said some of the blacks were 'repulsive to the sight owing to disease' and he hoped the clause would remain. It did. There was quibbling on the proposed control of female Aborigines to prevent their marriage to undesirable people, and forcing of fathers to contribute to the maintenance of halfcaste children, but the principles of the Bill were preserved unchanged. The Assembly passed it on 9 November. In the Council the main critic was John Lewis, who was particularly critical of the proposed licensing system which was similar to the system proposed in the 1899 Bill. The Council agreed with Lewis's amendments which weakened the appropriate clause in favour of the pastoralists. The changes were accepted by the lower house and the Bill was signed into law on 7 December 1910.[2] With the transfer of the Territory, the Commonwealth adopted the South Australian law, which was embodied in the *Northern Territory Aborigines Ordinance* 1911.

The 'main' Bill, dealing with Aborigines in South Australia, had a more difficult journey. It lapsed in 1910, was reintroduced in 1911 but was not passed into law until December 1911. When it did appear it was apparent how successful the pastoralists had been in preserving their privileges. The Territory legislation required employers to be licensed by a protector for the district, but there was a right of appeal to the chief protector. Asians were specifically excluded from holding such licences, six-monthly returns of employees and wages had to be made to the local protector and if he did not comply the protector could recommend cancellation of licences to the chief protector. These clauses, and others relating to conditions of employment, did not appear in the 1911 legislation. The reason for the difference is not hard to find: the 'big men' of the Central Australian pastoral industry had been financially broken in the 1890s and had got out, leaving the field to the 'small men', former stockmen and miners, who had started with nothing but a few cattle they had bought with their meagre savings or duffed from the 'big men's' herds. They had no weight in the South Australian upper house; whereas, the 'big men' like John Lewis still had extensive interests in the northern districts of South Australia proper. They meant to preserve the old way of doing things in cases where their own interests were still concerned.

While South Australia had dithered, the principles of the Queensland legislation had been adopted by Western Australian in 1905. Now those principles covered 90 per cent of all Aborigines and 85 per cent of the Australian continent. From the concept of equality which Glenelg had attempted to impose in 1836 to the paternalistic concepts of 1911, the Aborigines had passed from being free men and women confronted with invaders of their lands to wards of a state in which they had no say. In some parts of Australia, the humanitarian intentions of the protective laws were ignored because of the inhuman detachment of white administrators. The power to remove Aborigines to reserves for their own good and to keep troublesome or diseased ones out of sight of whites now completed the process of dispossession, detribalization and control of Aborigines' lives, which had begun with the arrival of the first settlers in South Australia in 1836.

The opinion of Paul Foelsche on this legislation is not known, but his belief that separate legislation was required for the two provinces had been vindicated. He continued to maintain a detached, semi-academic interest in the Territory Aborigines throughout his life, although his comments on them suggest that, to him, they were simply the more interesting of the local fauna. He never showed any deep understanding of Aboriginal culture nor genuine sympathy for them in the problems which resulted from European invasion. He continued to take hundreds of photographs of Aborigines and local views and is justly famed as the leading Territory photographer of that time, more because of the quantity than the quality of his work. Nonetheless, his photography and his few articles on the local tribes and flora earned him some recognition. He corresponded with Ferdinand von Mueller in Melbourne, who named a tree, *Eucalyptus Foelscheana*, in his honour. A small river in the Gulf of Carpentaria, near McArthur River, carries his name, and so do a street in Darwin, a mountain and a headland. He received a gold medal from Kaiser Wilhelm for his contributions to natural science and was honoured by King Edward VII with the Imperial Service Medal. As late as 1920 copies of Foelsche's Aboriginal studies were being sent to overseas universities and many of his original prints survive in Australian archives. It seems that he visited Shanghai, possibly accompanying Lewis, who called at Port Darwin in February 1909 on a ship going to Japan. It had been twenty-five years since they had last met. Foelsche retired from the police force in January 1904 after taking one year's leave. He had maintained his connection with Freemasonry during the long years in the Territory and was one of the founders of the Port Darwin lodge, which was named after him. Apparently he was not entirely happy with the coming of the Commonwealth, telling Lewis in July 1913 that when the new federal government came to power it was 'plainly visible the old officers that were taken over by the Commonwealth were not wanted but got rid of as soon as possible. New offices were created and officers appointed at enormous high salaries and travelling allowances, when there was nothing to do for them...' As good a gossip as ever, Foelsche said Maurice Holtze, who had been government secretary for years, had lost his position so that a relative of the administrator, S. J. Mitchell, could be put in his place. Holtze had worried over this until it brought on other complaints which caused his death. Foelsche remarked in this last letter to Lewis that he was 'still laid up with my bad foot and am writing this with my leg resting on a chair'. In fact, he was confined to a chair over the last two years of his life, suffering much pain. Paul Foelsche, the founder of the Northern Territory Police Force, so-called expert on the Aborigines and the man at the centre of Aboriginal–European relations for more than thirty years, died in Darwin on 31 January 1914.[3]

The *Northern Territory Aboriginals Ordinance*, which incorporated the main provisions of the South Australian legislation of December 1910, came into effect on 7 June 1911. As far as the Aborigines were concerned it had no immediate effect, because of delays in implementing the legislation. Archibald Meston and Daisy Bates were among those who applied for the position of chief protector, but it went to Dr Herbert Basedow, anthropologist, geologist, explorer, medical practitioner and youngest son of M. P. F. Basedow, who had chaired the 1899 inquiry into Dashwood's Bill. Basedow seemed eminently qualified for the position and took it up in May 1911 with enthusiasm and energy, 'but he was over-idealistic and became rapidly disillusioned and dissatisfied' and resigned on 30 August, claiming the legislation was unworkable. He had also clashed with Mitchell. Work stopped until Walter Baldwin Spencer was appointed special commissioner and chief protector. Baldwin Spencer arrived in Darwin (as the capital was now called) in January 1912, visited the Daly River, Pine Creek and the Alligator Rivers region. In September he and Mitchell drove to Newcastle Waters, Anthony Lagoon, Borroloola, back to Katherine, westwards to the Flora River and northwards to Pine Creek. In November he visited Bathurst and Melville Islands. He did not visit Central Australia but, because of his previous visits, claimed to be fairly well acquainted with conditions there. D. J. Mulvaney has commented that Baldwin Spencer's anthropology derived from Darwinian evolutionary theory as applied to social and religious institutions; 'His fieldwork and his analysis of data, however, were filtered through the preconceptions and value systems of both Evolution and Empire'. Mulvaney has added that Baldwin Spencer conceived of Aborigines as surviving fossil remnants from the remote past, whose social and belief systems reflected this pristine condition.[4] With these reservations in mind, we can approach the report which Baldwin Spencer submitted to the Commonwealth government in May 1913 as the most valuable contemporary report on the end of the South Australian period.[5]

Baldwin Spencer showed some respect for Aboriginal culture by saying in his report that the Aboriginal moral code was very different to the European and that it would be a serious mistake to interfere with it 'until we can give them something better and something which they can understand'. In many cases, he said, the tribes, as in the neighbour-hood of Darwin, were 'not only demoralized but decimated'; the old rules could not be enforced but, except in these cases, the Aborigines should be encouraged to adhere to them. Later in his report, however, he proposed amendments to the Aboriginals Ordinance aimed at destroying their culture. As an example of the stereotyped thinking to which this early anthropologist was disposed, he remarked in his report that generally speaking the uncivilized Aborigine was honest whereas the 'so-called uncivilised aboriginal who has given up his old habits and become often a mere loafer, in many cases, is not'. He did not ask why the change from 'uncivilised' to 'civilised' had made such a drastic change in the Aborigine's moral behaviour.

Baldwin Spencer adds to our knowledge of the part played by Aborigines in the pastoral industry. On some stations, he said, they were still harassing and killing cattle and this was a matter very difficult to deal with in a way fair to both whites and blacks. In many areas there was little such trouble 'and it is only right to say that the personality of the white man counts for a certain amount'. Practically all the stations depended upon Aboriginal labour and 'could not get on without it, any more than the police constables could'. He gave this picture of life on a cattle station:

> They do work that it would be difficult to get white men to do and do it not only cheerfully but for a remuneration that, in many cases, makes all the difference at the present time between working the station at a profit or a loss. Out on the run the first thing that one hears, often long before daybreak, is the call to the boys to get up and go out in search of the horses. They are up without a murmur or anything to eat and off they go into the bush with bridles in their hands, often shivering, through grass and scrub heavy with dew, until, after anything up to a two or three miles trudge, they find a horse, mount him bare-back, track all the others up and bring them into camp. Then, in intervals of packing, they eat their breakfast and all day long ride behind, seeing that the pack-horses with their loads are kept on the track. When mustering they are hard at work from early morn to late evening, just as their masters are.

Baldwin Spencer praised the usefulness and selflessness of the Aborigines. On one occasion in Darwin 'twelve stalwart aboriginals' had assisted in the unloading of steamers and on another, when white men refused to work, ten of them loaded sixty-three tons of coal into trucks outside Darwin and then went to the ship and unloaded half of it, working on into the night until they could work no longer, 'laughing and cheerful the whole time'. When he and Mitchell ran out of petrol while travelling by motor car to Borroloola, an Aborigine whom they had taken with them walked forty-six miles to the nearest cattle station then, on a borrowed horse, rode another fifty miles to their nearest supply of petrol. Two years beforehand, an Aborigine, Aya-I-Ga, also known as Neighbour or Nipper, arrested for supposed cattle-killing, was being brought with others in chains to Darwin by a mounted constable. As they were fording a swollen stream, the policeman's horse slipped and fell, kicking him unconscious. Aya-I-Ga, seeing what had happened, wound his chains around the constable's neck and dragged him onto land, where he recovered. For this action he was awarded the Albert Medal.

On the condition and treatment of Aborigines in the Territory, Baldwin Spencer believed that in all parts where they were in contact with outsiders, 'especially with Asiatics, they are dying out with great rapidity'. Those living in towns had long become degenerate and had lost all their old customs and beliefs, he said. Many were employed by whites but, since the passing of the *Aboriginals Act* 1910, no permits to employ them had been granted to Asians. The most serious 'evil' the Aborigines Department had to deal with was the supplying of Aborigines with opium and spirits and the wholesale prostitution of native women, which were common practices among the 'great body of Asiatics'. As a result of contact with the Chinese, he claimed, the 'lubra ceases to bear children, abortion being undoubtedly practised in many cases, and becomes a physical wreck'. Then he remarked, apparently with Eurocentric blindness, that in regard to intercourse between the whites and Aborigines, 'there is no such physical degradation of the lubras'. The department's general policy was to prevent Asians coming into contact with Aborigines. A compound for Aborigines was being formed at Darwin and when this was operating it would be easier to implement this policy. The problem of what to do with Aborigines living in areas where closer settlement of Europeans was intended, as on the Daly and Roper Rivers, was serious and awaited immediate solution, he said. The alternatives were to allow the Aborigines in these areas to wander about as outcasts or to establish a reserve for them under proper control. He did not propose doing anything about those living in large pastoral areas, because the stations were largely dependent upon the work done by black 'boys', the number on each station varying from two or three to thirty or forty. The practice of drovers and teamsters travelling with an Aboriginal woman must be stopped, although the law did not deal directly with this matter and must be amended so this 'deplorable practice can be carefully controlled without inflicting hardship on either aboriginals or whites'. Practically nothing was known about Aborigines living on wild, 'unoccupied' land, but many of the wild tribes who lived on the coast came into contact, much to their detriment, with pearl and trepang fishermen. The area involved was so great that complete and effective control was at that time impossible.

The Aborigines Department in 1912 consisted of a chief protector, Baldwin Spencer, a chief inspector, who was also a protector, two other protectors and a clerk. In addition, the officers in charge of the fourteen police stations throughout the Territory were protectors. Baldwin Spencer now recommended that some reliable and reputable settlers and officials, who should include women, be appointed honorary protectors. The legislation, he pointed out, 'affords every protection to the aboriginal' but it offered no remedy to the white employer if an Aborigine misbehaved himself by, for example, walking away from his post and leaving his employer helpless. While he did not advocate a system of indenture, he believed it necessary to make the Aborigine feel a sense of responsibility. 'This can only be done by giving the Chief Protector the power of summary punishment', and would mean locking up the offender for no more than twenty-four hours. The spread of venereal disease among Aborigines and 'white men of low morality' was so serious that there was no course other than to follow the example of Western Australia and establish 'lock-hospitals for men and women to which, if necessary, they can be forcibly removed and where they can be detained until cured'. These should be established on islands. Baldwin Spencer was concerned at the unfair position occupied by Aboriginal prisoners compared with white men, arising from the former's ignorance of European law. He recommended that no Aborigine be permitted to plead guilty, except with the consent of an official protector, and that none be convicted on evidence other than that which would convict a white man accused of the same offence. Crimes committed by 'wild' Aborigines against Aborigines should be dealt with under tribal law. Those Aborigines who offended against European law should not be sent to gaol, because the average one did not think it a degradation or hardship to go to Fanny Bay gaol. Instead, Aboriginal prisoners, except murderers, should go to a special reformatory.

Halfcastes continued to be seen as a social problem. Baldwin Spencer hoped that as the Territory became more populated, the proportionate number would become less. There were now between 100 and 150 in the northern and the same number in the southern part. 'One thing is certain and that is that the white population as a whole will never mix with half-castes', he said. Because they were the children of Aboriginal mothers of a very low intellectual grade and the fathers belonged to the coarser and more unrefined members of the higher races, he said, they were not likely to be, in most cases, of much greater intellectual calibre than the more intelligent Aborigines. No halfcaste should be allowed to remain in a Aboriginal camp but should be withdrawn and placed on stations. As far as possible this was now being done. As was advocated in Queensland at that time, Baldwin Spencer advocated that, except in individual and exceptional cases, the best and kindest thing for the halfcastes was to place them on reserves with fullbloods, train them in the same schools and encourage them to marry among themselves. This was another way of limiting the 'contamination' of the European race. Under the 1910 legislation the payment of wages to Aboriginal workers was not made compulsory. Baldwin Spencer believed a definite wage should be paid in the settled districts and part of the wage handed to a protector for investment in the worker's name. During the early days of reserves, when 'wild' Aborigines were resident, the remuneration for labour should be food, clothing and tobacco, but as they became civilized a system of payment might be adopted. On the large pastoral areas it was not expedient to enforce payment, he said. As well as the workers, who had no knowledge of or use for money, the stations supported the families and a large number of 'hangers-on'. If money were substituted for goods, the result would be hardship for large numbers now indirectly maintained by the station's workers. These dependants would then become a tax upon the government. Baldwin Spencer recommended that the Commonwealth be given responsibility for all Aborigines, that a new Act be drafted and new regulations drawn up. No action was taken. The States were jealous of their powers and the Commonwealth did not acquire the right to legislate for Aborigines until 1967.

Baldwin Spencer believed government policy should preserve and 'uplift' the Aborigines within the context of European pastoral and agricultural expansion. A primary objective of the Commonwealth government at that time was to settle whites permanently on land in the Territory, but at the same time it was saying that something should definitely be done about Aboriginal administration. It was under pressure from scientific and religious bodies for a more precise statement of policy but the government had no more policy than that expressed in the South Australian legislation of 1910; by 1914 Commonwealth interest in the Territory was flagging. Administrative economies were made and several senior civil service posts were abolished including that of the chief protector, whose responsibilities were given to the government secretary. The Aboriginals Ordinance of 1918 was introduced in an attempt to reduce intercourse between Aboriginal and part-Aboriginal women, and men of other races. It also broadened the definition of an Aborigine to include all female part-Aborigines except those legally married to men substantially European and living with their husbands. All other Aboriginal women were required to have ministerial approval to marry. In 1919 control of the Aborigines passed into the hands of the police where it remained until 1927, when a chief protector, a doctor with a medical staff who made some effort to improve Aboriginal health, was appointed. The Aborigines, however, did not see any dramatic changes in the way they were regarded by the administration. The emphasis on control was maintained by the Aboriginals Ordinances of 1933 and 1936 and the halfcaste problem remained the central concern of the administration. The Welfare Ordinance of 1953 made all Aborigines in the Territory wards of the state.

It is beyond the intention of this history to examine Aboriginal–European relations in the Northern Territory during the Commonwealth period. The racial and social problems which South Australians perceived as having resulted from acquisition of the Territory were not solved in the period before 1911. In fact, the Commonwealth, despite some early enthusiasm for solving the problem from the point of view of white Australians, also failed specifically because of neglect of its responsibilities during the period between the two world wars. The hardship system devised in 1953 came closest to the original nineteenth century concept of protection of a disadvantaged people. But the supposed Australian article of faith, a 'fair go' for all, did not extend to the Aborigines. Even though they outnumbered the whites in the Territory until 1955, they were never asked what they wanted.

Conclusion: *The Northern Territory Experience*

The only attempt by an Australian colony to establish another colony on the continent failed. Continued European presence in the Northern Territory was sustained by large government expenditure for which South Australia received little in return. Because of unreal expectations, mismanagement and economic disasters, white settlement of the Territory was always limited by the few resources attractive to Europeans and the meagre financial support which the continually changing governments in Adelaide voted it over more than forty years. Climate, poor soil, distance from markets and high costs, limited mineral resources and other factors discouraged settlement. When South Australia finally got rid of its 'white elephant' on 1 January 1911, the number of Europeans in a land of more than half a million square miles was only about 1200 and the total non-Aboriginal population was only 2800. The Aboriginal population during the period of South Australian administration decreased from perhaps 50 000 to about 22 000. These simple population facts help to illustrate some of the ways in which Aboriginal–European relationships in the Northern Territory were both similar and different to those in other parts of Australia during the same period.

The obvious similarity is that European intrusion contributed to Aboriginal population decrease. In the first parts of Australia settled by Europeans — the present New South Wales, Tasmania, the south-west corner of Western Australia, the central districts of South Australia and all of Victoria — numbers declined rapidly. The indigenous people were overwhelmed by force of numbers and in some cases by force of arms in Tasmania and Victoria. Populations were severely reduced in New South Wales and South Australia but in Queensland, which is well watered, the situation was different: Aborigines there numbered about 120 000 before the arrival of the whites and, although they were ultimately overwhelmed by land and gold-hungry foreigners, their numbers in 1911 were still substantial at 22 000, the same number as in the Territory at that time. Nonetheless, Aborigines in Queensland were a subject race, practically and legally, by 1897. By contrast, although the South Australian Act of 1910, which was incorporated in the *Northern Territory Ordinance* of 1911, also treated Aborigines as a subject people, special circumstances allowed most to avoid subjugation.

One such circumstance, of course, was the relatively tiny number of whites compared to the large black population; another was the huge area, which made it extremely difficult to implement any policy of subjugation such as that successfully followed in Queensland after 1859. While there were some vast tracts of grasslands in the northern part of the Territory and some marginal tracts in the southern, most of the province was inhospitable to foreigners. Also, even in the well-watered north, some areas were too rugged for grazing and did not appear to have mineral wealth. For the tribes in the many traditional lands not desired by the whites, there was little disturbance to Aboriginal culture, little competition for natural resources, little contact with Europeans and Asians and little decline in population, at least arising directly from contact. While Australian tribes were generally restricted to precisely defined homelands, they did have rights to visit parts of other tribal lands which allowed them some freedom of movement for religious, ceremonial and, in special cases such as drought, for food-gathering purposes. Also, while the whites might have occupied a part of a tribal area, the remainder of the area might have been undesirable, especially rugged country. For these and other reasons, many Aborigines, probably the majority in the Northern Territory during the South Australian period, were able to get away from the Europeans if they wished. In all other parts of Australia this was difficult, in most cases impossible, except perhaps in the northern and eastern districts of Western Australia and the remote corners of South Australia. This low density of whites and relative freedom from white intrusion was a major reason for the survival and subsequent political strength of the Aboriginal people in the Territory.

The decline of the Aboriginal population since the arrival of the Europeans and others has become a topic of popular interest in recent years, some persons claiming that much of the indigenous population was deliberately wiped out in a campaign of genocide. This is not true. There were many killings especially in Gippsland, New England and most parts of Queensland before 1880, but the numbers who died in those conflicts were, with rare exceptions, tiny, because of the technology available to the whites, especially in the period before the breech-loading rifle was introduced in the mid-1860s. While the number of individuals and groups of Aborigines murdered no doubt totalled several thousand throughout Australia in 150 years, the population decline from an estimated 314 000 in 1788 to an estimated low-point of 68 000 in 1933 was due not so much to malicious action on the part of the Europeans but rather to the unintentional consequences of invasion. Introduced disease, deprivation of natural resources and reduction in reproduction appear to have been the chief causes. If the evidence available from western Queensland is a reliable indicator, venereal diseases were endemic in the Australian pastoral industry in the latter part of the nineteenth century. The decline in Aboriginal population in the Territory was due chiefly to the same inherent and inadvertent consequences of invasion and contact as applied elsewhere in Australia.

Similarly, claims that Aboriginal people as a whole resisted European invasion are too general and exaggerated in some cases to be credible. The Tasmanians resisted strongly at first but were soon controlled; the South Australian people, apart from a few along the Murray River near the New South Wales border and on Eyre Peninsula, were relatively docile. The people of the New England district of New South Wales resisted sporadically but ineffectually. Those of the rugged central districts of Queensland as well as of the Selwyn Ranges and Cape York Peninsula fought strongly and at times effectively, threatening to turn back the flood of Europeans and their stock. Others, after a brief contest of wills, readily capitulated. In the Territory, resistance was almost entirely confined to the overlanders' tracks through the Gulf Country, along the Roper and, later, into the Victoria River district on the way to the Kimberley goldfields, as well as areas south and west of Alice Springs. Other incidents appear, on the evidence, to have resulted from personal feuds over women, infringement of obligations and desire for European goods. The evidence, scanty in many cases, suggests that brigandage was a major factor in most attacks on Europeans. The motive for the attack on Charles Johnstone and his companions on the Roper River in 1875 may have been desire for the goods on their waggon; it may have been desire for revenge for the provocations of the Queensland 'hard cases' overlanding cattle and working on the telegraph line for several years before then; but there is no evidence that the motive was to drive out the white intruders. The evidence given in 1885 by three of the accused in the Daly River murders case does not suggest resistance. By contrast, some indigenous people welcomed the Europeans: the tribes of the Cobourg Peninsula and Croker Island, the Larakia at Port Darwin and the several tribes in contact with the Jesuit missions on the Daly River appear to have seen some benefit in the European presence. Relations between Europeans and the Central Aranda at Alice Springs and the Kaititja of Barrow Creek were, apart from the 1874 incident, generally amicable. Aboriginal claims to have resisted European invasion of their lands rest more firmly on their success in maintaining spiritual and cultural links with the past than on any evidence of physical violence.

The process of European invasion in the Territory was different to that in the other colonies. In south-eastern Australia the whites fanned outwards from Sydney into the Port Phillip District, the western plains of New South Wales and the Darling Downs of Queensland. Other ingressions were made into Queensland, notably at Rockhampton, Bowen, Townsville and Normanton, but generally the frontier moved in a line across the colony. In the Territory, occupation occurred almost from within. The building of the overland telegraph line along Stuart's track meant that overlanders followed it and pastoralists selected runs east and west of it. To a lesser extent the cattlemen could fan out from the east-west tracks from Queensland. There was no moving frontier in the sense of a line with the invaders on one side and the defenders on the other. Some Territory people were quickly dominated by strangers who appeared among them, and others were left alone. Even in areas occupied without a fight, there was a better chance of survival than in Queensland or South Australia. Because the European economy applied to the Territory was largely and increasingly pastoral after the first decade of the South Australian period, and because of special factors applying to that industry, Aborigines were more likely to be preserved as workers than forced off their lands.

Certainly, there were gross abuses of Aboriginal labour and victimization of individuals, especially women, on the stations, but most were employed in their homelands and so could maintain their cultural associations. There was some abduction of labour from one land to a station in another tribe's land but, given the size of the industry and the number of whites, resulting disruption to Aboriginal society was small compared with what happened in Tasmania by 1836. In Victoria, New South Wales and South Australia by the 1880s, the only home for most Aborigines was a mission station to which they were sent by the whites. In the Territory there were no such forced migrations during the South Australian period and in some districts, such as Arnhem Land, there was no serious and long-term disruption of traditional life.

The few missions established in the Territory had little permanent effect. Gillen's opinion that the young people at Hermannsburg were so out of touch with traditional hunting methods that they would not be able to survive if the mission were closed down is implausible. There were no more than two hundred Aborigines at Hermannsburg at any time in the South Australian period out of a total of several thousand Aranda. Gillen ignored the determined preservation of customs by Aborigines even when almost totally dependent upon Europeans. He was not aware of the 'intelligent parasitism' which professional anthropologists, such as A. P. Elkin and W. E. H. Stanner, were to observe. Hermannsburg, like most nineteenth century missions, failed to convert Aborigines to Christianity, but in some cases the missions did facilitate an honourable accommodation between two very dissimilar races, societies and economies which was largely successful in sustaining Aborigines, and therefore their culture, in the face of European depredations.

There is considerable evidence of the corrupting influence of contact with whites in the reports of Foelsche, Price, Parsons, Dashwood and others. They indicate declining numbers in specific areas and increased disease, prostitution, alcoholism and opium-addiction. Promiscuity changed from a courtesy extended to visitors to a means of sustaining life for some tribes in districts heavily populated by foreigners, particularly on the goldfields. But the extent of disease, malnutrition and opium-addiction in the Territory during, for instance, the 1890s appears to have been much less than in western Queensland in the same period. In south-western Queensland at that time, Aborigines would not work on many stations unless supplied with opium, but in the Territory opium-addiction appears to have been confined to the goldfields and Port Darwin areas and kept out of the pastoral districts.

Because of the size of the Territory, the small non-Aboriginal population and the limited resources put into it by the South Australian government, its administration was always small. Policemen probably played a more important part in the public service of the Territory than in any other colony. Life for a Territory policeman was possibly harder than elsewhere, perhaps except in the remote districts of Western Australia. When racial conflict broke out, the Territory police, like police elsewhere, had to intervene and report. They were at the centre of Aboriginal–European relations and appear to have been given greater discretion in suppressing Aboriginal violence than in eastern Australia, because of the great distances from Palmerston and Adelaide. In the reactions to the first serious incidents, policemen like Gason, Montagu and Stretton appear to have been given a free hand. Yet, apart from the excessive responses of 1874–78, restraint was stronger in the Territory than in Queensland, despite the difficulties in maintaining control, where no pretence at restraint was made until humanitarians led by the *Queenslander* began to have some effect in the 1880s. The police record in the Territory, compared with that of other provinces at the time, was good. Even William Willshire, who seemed to enjoy killing 'niggers', was the first to plead for aid for starving Aborigines in Central Australia. The cool detachment of men like Foelsche and Stretton permitted them to support the use of condign punishment as a method of dealing with rebellious subjects of the Queen. On the other hand, it allowed them to take a genuine interest in Aborigines, even though they, like the settlers, assumed the Aborigines would inevitably die out in the face of competition from a 'superior' race.

Northern Territory Aborigines, more than any others in Australia, demonstrated that their race was not dying out. Numbers and time were on their side. While humanitarian concern for their plight, and efforts to solve a social problem, as seen by the Europeans, developed there later than elsewhere, they were becoming public issues at a time when the Commonwealth was likely to take control of the Territory. Belated but genuine attempts were made to protect and preserve them, although the principles employed were racist and the methods were authoritarian. While Commonwealth policy towards Aborigines in the Territory floundered for forty years towards the wardship system, many still had a freedom unknown in the other parts of Australia. It is not surprising therefore that the first successful stirrings toward equality and land rights were made in the Territory by the Gurindji at Wattie Creek near Wave Hill in 1968 and by the Yirrkala mission people in 1971.

The whole Northern Territory experience can be seen as part of an historical process which began in London in the early 1830s. Humanitarians controlled Colonial Office policy at a time when settlement in South Australia was being planned, and the ideals on which the colony was founded in 1836 included the most protective yet expressed towards indigenous people in Australia. Even so, British policy in South Australia collapsed as rapidly as elsewhere in the face of frontier attitudes. The Colonial Office and, later, the colonial administrations could not reconcile humanitarianism with the inevitable inequalities of conquest. By 1863, when it began extending its rule over the Aborigines of the Northern Territory, South Australia had no Aboriginal policy other than meagre succour for the remnants of its original population. Its attempts at establishing good relations with the people of the new province were as futile as had been those of the Colonial Office and its representatives in Adelaide. The openly expressed attitudes of Edward Price and the secretly expressed views of Paul Foelsche in the 1870s show that when two races contest possession of land by violent means the attitudes of the frontier, not politicians more than a thousand miles away, decide official practice.

The humanitarianism of the last two decades of South Australian rule was never strong compared with that of Queensland, where the sight of drunken, diseased, emaciated and opium-addicted Aborigines was common by 1890. Public reaction to their plight became caught up in the growing fear of 'the yellow hordes of Asia', whose forerunners were blamed for the opium problem. Miscegenation was another factor in facilitating the passage through parliament of Queensland's answer to a growing social problem, the 1897 protection legislation. In South Australia, bedevilled with economic problems at home, the distasteful effects of Aboriginal–European contact in the Territory were so far away that they could largely be ignored. When Charles Dashwood tried in 1899 to get protection legislation through the South Australian parliament, his statements on the condition of the Aborigines in the Territory were scorned. It took the withdrawal of the big pastoralists from the Territory during the economic crisis of 1893–1906, the growing concern about miscegenation in South Australia itself, and the increasing interest of the Commonwealth in the Territory, finally to stimulate South Australians into doing something to protect Aborigines from the worst abuses of colonization.

The Northern Territory experience helps to show how easily well-intentioned official policy could fail when in conflict with the objectives of land-hungry Europeans. It also shows that, in contrast to what was happening to Aborigines in other parts of Australia during the period 1836–1910, the original people of the Territory had the greatest chance of survival, although it was not until the late 1960s that they began to assert their claims to at least part of their traditional lands.

Notes

Abbreviations

AA   Australian Archives
AIAS   Australian Institute of Aboriginal Studies
SAA   South Australian Archives
SAPP   South Australian Parliamentary Papers

Introduction

1 The Introduction, which deals with events outside the field and period of the history, is a summary of the work of other scholars, chiefly Kathleen Hassell, *The Relations between the Settlers and Aborigines in South Australia, 1836-1860*, and R. M. Gibbs, 'Relations between the Aboriginal Inhabitants and the First South Australian Colonists'.
2 Gibbs, 'Relations between the Aboriginal Inhabitants and the First South Australian Colonists', p. 62.
3 Quoted in Gibbs, p. 65.
4 Copy of Hindmarsh's proclamation, State Library of South Australia.
5 Hassell, p. 23.
6 Gibbs, p. 68.
7 Gibbs, p. 71.
8 Gibbs, p. 65.
9 Earl Grey to Fitzroy, 5 November 1850, encl. in Earl Grey to Young, No. 39, 21 May 1851, quoted in Gibbs, p. 75.
10 Smith, *Aboriginal Population of Australia*, p. 155.
11 Clyne, *Colonial Blue*, pp. 120-1.
12 Berndt and Berndt, *From Black to White in South Australia*, p. 70.
13 Mattingley and Hampton, *Survival in Our Land*, pp. 37-8.
14 See 'Report of the Select Committee of the Legislative Council upon "The Aborigines"; Together with Minutes of Evidence and Appendix', *South Australian Parliamentary Papers*, 1860, Vol. 3, No. 165.
15 Rowley, *The Destruction of Aboriginal Society*, p. 203.
16 Gale, A Study in Assimilation, p. 100.
17 Berndt and Berndt, *From Black to White in South Australia*, pp. 70-1.
18 Rowley, *The Destruction of Aboriginal Society*, p. 216.

1 Early Overtures

1 Quoted in Hill, *The Territory*, p. 48.
2 Allen, 'Port Essington'.
3 Powell, 'Culture Contact', p. 91.

[4] Gregory and Gregory, *Journals of Australian Explorations*, p. 143.

[5] Ibid., pp. 152-3.

[6] Ibid., p. 158.

[7] Quoted in Birman, *Gregory of Rainworth*, p. 147.

[8] Thonemann, *Tell the White Man*, Sydney, p. 22.

[9] All quotations concerning Stuart's expeditions are from Mudie, *The Heroic Journey of John McDouall Stuart*, pp. 108, 113, 115-6, 118-20, 121, 199-200.

2 Escape Cliffs

[1] For details of early European settlement of the Territory *see*: Donovan, *A Land Full of Possibilities*, pp. 29-33; and Powell, *Far Country*, pp. 70-4.

[2] Stokes, *Discoveries in Australia*, Vol. 1, pp. 413-15.

[3] Instruction 18, quoted by F. Rymill, under 'Charge 4' in 'Report of the Commission appointed by the Governor in Chief to inquire into the Management of the Northern Territory Expedition; together with Minutes of Evidence and Appendix', *SAPP*, 1866, No. 17.

[4] Rowley, *The Destruction of Aboriginal Society*, p. 211.

[5] Quoted by Gibbs, 'Relations between the Aboriginal Inhabitants and the First South Australian Colonists', pp. 74-5.

[6] For Finniss's account of the settlement at Escape Cliffs, see 'Report of the Northern Territory Commission', p. xxii.

[7] Ibid., McMinn's evidence, pp. 37-8; Rymill's summing up, no page numbers.

[8] From Finniss's reply to Rymill, ibid., pp. xxii-iii.

[9] Schrire, *The Alligator Rivers*, p. 19.

[10] Lockwood, *The Front Door*, p. 26.

[11] Quoted in Powell, *Far Country*, p. 83.

3 Colonization Begins

[1] Donovan, *A Land Full of Possibilities*, p. 77.

[2] Description of events at Millner's camp is drawn from the journal of J. Stokes Millner, Acting Government Resident, included with his report from Palmerston, 1 July 1870, to Commissioner of Crown Lands, 70/80, attached to Government Resident's report, 1 July 1870, 70/81, to Commissioner of Crown Lands: both in AIAS MS 1042. Also the diary of Geo. G. MacLachlan, senior surveyor, attached to the same Government Resident's report.

[3] Donovan, *A Land Full of Possibilities*, pp. 83-9.

[4] Burns on Douglas in *Australian Dictionary of Biography*, Vol. 4, Melbourne, 1972, p. 92.

[5] Douglas, Palmerston, 1 July 1870, to Commissioner of Crown Lands, 70/81, in AIAS MS 1042.

[6] Douglas, Palmerston, 13 April 1871, to Commissioner of Crown Lands, 67/71, and attachment to 22 October 1870, 130/70; and civil service list and salaries in attachment to Douglas to Commissioner of Crown Lands, 1 July 1870, 81/70: all in AIAS MS 1042.

[7] See his diary entries of 25, 29 June, 6, 8, 18, 29 August and 29 September.

[8] Diary, 28 November and 9 August.

[9] Douglas, Palmerston, 13 April 1871, to Commissioner of Crown Lands, 67/71, AIAS MS 1042.

[10] Ibid.; and report by Millner to Douglas on the Binmook incident attached to Douglas, Palmerston, 2 June 1871, to Commissioner of Crown Lands, 28/71, AIAS MS 1042.

[11] Douglas, Palmerston, no date, to Commissioner of Crown Lands, 32/71, AA, Canberra, CRS 1640.

[12] Millner to Douglas, encl. with Douglas, Palmerston, 2 June 1871, to Commissioner of Crown Lands, AIAS MS 1042.

[13] Diary, 29 September 1870.

[14] Douglas, Palmerston, 13 April 1871, to Commissioner of Crown Lands, 67/71, AIAS MS 1042.

15 Daly, *Digging, Squatting and Pioneering Life in the Northern Territory*, pp. 75-6.
16 Ibid., p. 186.
17 Powell, *Far Country*, pp. 92-3.
18 Burns on Douglas in *Australian Dictionary of Biography*, Vol. 4, Melbourne, 1972, p. 92.
19 *South Australian Register*, 2 February 1914.
20 Lockwood, *The Front Door*, p. 58.
21 Douglas, 10 July 1872, 67/71, and Millner's report on population attached; Scott, Palmerston, 22 April 1876, to Minister of Education, 212/76; Price, Palmerston, 14 September 1876, to Minister of Education, 453/76 and 8 March 1878, 178/78 and 1 August 1878, 458/78; G. B. McMinn, acting Government Resident, to Minister of Education, 30 December 1880, 63/81: all in AIAS MS 1042; Price, telegram to Minister, 24 October 1881, 542/81, SAA GRG790.
22 For population details *see* Smith, *Aboriginal Population of Australia*, pp. 208-9; and Donovan, *A Land Full of Possibilities*, pp. 107-8, and Table 5, p. 173.

4 The Overlanders

1 Ashwin, Recollections of Ralph Milner's [*sic*] Expedition . . . , pp. 11-21.
2 Diary, entries for 17 November 1871 and 14 January 1872.
3 Lewis, *Fought and Won*, p. 83.
4 Scott, Palmerston, 13 October 1874, to Minister of Justice and Education, 1012/74, AIAS MS 1042.
5 Lewis, *Fought and Won*, pp. 129-51.
6 Ibid., p. 151.
7 Hill, *The Territory*, p. 126.
8 Giles, The First Pastoral Settlement of the Northern Territory, pp. 3-4, 33, 39-43.
9 The incidents set out in this paragraph are recorded in Merlan, 'Making People Quiet', pp. 76-7.
10 Giles, 'The Adelaide and Port Darwin Telegraph Line'.
11 Todd, 'Report on the Post Office, Telegraph and Observatory Departments'.

5 Frontier Practice

1 Gillen, *Gillen's Diary*, pp. 107-8.
2 The attack at Barrow Creek is documented in Research Note 174, South Australian Archives.
3 Ibid.
4 Ibid.
5 Hartwig, The Progress of White Settlement in the Alice Springs District and its Effects upon the Aboriginal Inhabitants, 1860–1894, p. 275.
6 Basedow, *Knights of the Boomerang*, p. 93.
7 Hartwig, p. 270.
8 Clyne, *Colonial Blue*, p. 183.
9 Daer's report, as written by W. J. Randall, Daly Waters, 13 July 1875, duplicate enclosed with J. A. G. Little papers.
10 Foelsche, Palmerston, to Lewis, addendum dated 15 July 1875 to letter dated 14 July 1875, in Lewis papers.
11 A. Dewhurst Gore, Roper Bar, 10 December 1899, to S. C. Stirling, Protector of Aborigines, Adelaide, 50/1900 SAA GRG790; and J.A.G. Little, Roper River, 29 August 1875, duplicate with Little papers.
12 Little to Todd, with Little papers. Correspondence on murder of Johnstone, 589/75; Scott to Minister, telegram, 27 December 1875, 639/75; both in SAA GRG790.
13 Scott, Palmerston, 15 November 1875, to Minister forwarding copy of diary of Walker's Blue Mud Bay Gold Prospecting Party, AA, Canberra, CRS A1640, 75/623.
14 Downer, *Patrol Indefinite*, p. 38.
15 Foelsche to Lewis, part of a letter, place and date unknown, SAA PRG247/2.

16 Price to Minister, telegrams 21, 22 January 1878, 83/78, 84/78; Price to Minister, letter, 26 January 1878, 87/78; Price to sub-protector of Aborigines, telegram, 8 February 1878, 50/78; Price to Minister, 28 February 1878, 118/78: all in SAA GRG790.
17 Price, Palmerston, to Minister, 28 February 1878, 118/78, SAA GRG790.
18 Price, Palmerston, 8 March 1878, to Minister, AA, Canberra, 179/78 CRS A1640.

6   A Policeman's Lot

1 Foelsche, Palmerston, 12 September 1876, to Lewis, SAA PRG247; and biographical note on Lewis family in SAA PRG247 series list.
2 Foelsche, Palmerston, 2 September 1876 and 15 May 1877, SAA PRG247/2; and clipping from unnamed newspaper, 21 December 1893, on death of Price, in Minister's press cutting book, vol. 4, SAA GRG9/4.
3 Foelsche, Palmerston, 15 May 1877, to Lewis; addendum of 19 May 1877; Foelsche to Lewis, 6 October 1877; Charlotte Foelsche to Lewis: all in SAA PRG274/2.
4 Foelsche, Palmerston, 19 December 1877, 18 May and 24 July 1878, to Lewis, SAA PRG247/2.
5 Foelsche, on board *Flying Cloud*, *en route* to Port Essington, 24 July 1878, to Lewis, SAA PRG247/2.
6 Foelsche, Port Essington, 24 July 1878, and Port Essington, 25 July 1878, to Lewis, SAA PRG247/2.
7 Price, Palmerston, 17 May 1877, to Minister of Justice and Education, AA, Canberra, A1640, 77/295.
8 Foelsche, Palmerston, 5 March and 30 July 1879 to Lewis, SAA PRG247/2.
9 Foelsche, The Shackle (Yam Creek), 19 December 1879, and Palmerston, 31 January 1880, to Lewis, SAA PRG247/2.
10 Interview with Robinson in *The Sun*, 23 December 1910.
11 Little, 1 March 1878, to Lewis: Foelsche, Palmerston, 31 January 1880, to Lewis: both in SAA PRG247/2. Price to Minister, Palmerston, 1 January 1880, 1/80, SAA GRG790.
12 Foelsche, Palmerston, 5 June 1880, to Lewis, SAA PRG 247/2.
13 Foelsche, Port Essington, 10 June 1880, addendum to letter of 5 June, and Palmerston, 7 September 1880, all to Lewis, SAA PRG247/2.
14 Price, Palmerston, 19 February 1878, to Minister of Justice and Education, and Minister's notation, 78/144; also Price's telegram to Minister, 12 August 1880, and Minister's notation, 434/80: all in SAA GRG790.
15 Price, Palmerston, 12 March 1880, telegram to Minister, 114/80; and letters, 16 March and 2 November 1880, 639/80: all in SAA GRG790.
16 Foelsche, Palmerston, 28 September 1881, to Lewis, SAA PRG247/2.
17 Foelsche, Palmerston, 7 September 1880, 28 September 1881 and 23 August 1882, to Lewis, SAA PRG247/2.
18 Foelsche, The Shackle, 5 August 1883; Palmerston, 15 August 1884; telegram, 2 December 1884; letter from Palmerston, 28 January 1885: all to Lewis, SAA PRG247/2.
19 Lockwood, *The Front Door*, p. 174, quoting the *Northern Territory Times*, June 1881.
20 Quoted in Downer, *Patrol Indefinite*, pp. 36-7, no source given.
21 Foelsche, The Shackle, 5 August 1883, to Lewis, SAA PRG247/2; Foelsche, 'Notes on the Aborigines of North Australia'; and Curr, *The Australian Race*, pp. 250-7, 270-3.

7   Pastoral Invasion

1 Buchanan, *Packhorse and Saddle*, pp. 44-55; Government Resident, telegram to Minister, 10 January 1879, 61/79, SAA GRG790.
2 Buchanan, *Packhorse and Saddle*, pp. 55-8, 63-4.
3 Giles, The First Pastoral Settlement of the Northern Territory, pp. 67-8, 136, 138.
4 Duncan, *The Northern Territory Pastoral Industry*, pp. 33, 37; G. R. McMinn, acting Government Resident, Palmerston, 30 December 1889, to Minister, AIAS, MS 1042.
5 Price, Palmerston, telegram to Minister, 30 June 1881, 326/81; Foelsche, Palmerston, 2 July 1881, to acting Commissioner of Police, attached to above: both in SAA GRG790.

6 Price, Palmerston, no date, 355/81, SAA GRG790.
7 Price, Palmerston, 17 July 1882, two telegrams to Minister, AIAS MS 1042; Price, 11 September 1882, telegram to Minister, 571/82, SAA GRG790. Government Resident, J. L. Parsons, Palmerston, to Minister, 12 November 1885, 1211/85; Parsons to Minister, enclosing inquest depositions on Charley, 49/86 and report by J. A. Palmer, 74/86: both in SAA GRG790.
8 *See* Costello, *Life of John Costello*.
9 Ibid., pp. 162-8, 170-2.
10 Cuthbertson, 21 January 1886, report on visit to Borroloola, 86/225, AA, Canberra, CRS A1640.
11 D'Arcy Uhr, member of deputation to R. C. Baker, Minister controlling the Northern Territory, *South Australian Register*, 10 September 1884. Parsons, Palmerston, 11 November 1884, to Minister, 1008/84 and 12 July 1888, to Minister, 665/88: both in SAA GRG790.
12 Donegan, Borroloola, 18 and 24 October 1886, 22 May and 29 August 1888: all to Foelsche and all in Borroloola Police Station Letter Book, Vol. 1, 1886–94, AA, Darwin, CRS F275.
13 Donegan, Borroloola, 22 May, 14 August, 5 and 6 September 1888, to Foelsche, Borroloola letter book, see note 12 above.
14 Power, Borroloola, 20 July and 7 December 1889, to Foelsche; Foelsche, Palmerston, 13 October 1889, to Power: all in Borroloola letter book, see note 12 above.
15 Mounted Constable First Class J. J. East, Prospect Police Station, 14 November 1888, to Minister, 1074/88, SAA GRG790.
16 Price, Palmerston, 10 December 1881, to Minister, 74/82, SAA GRG790.
17 Buchanan, *Packhorse and Saddle*, p. 100.

8 The Daly River Murders

1 Corporal George Montagu, Yam Creek, 17 October 1884, to Foelsche, *SAPP*, 1885, Vol. IV, No. 170.
2 Parsons, Palmerston, 1 October 1884, to Minister; also telegrams, 13 and 22 September 1884: all in SAA GRG790 861/84 and 869/84. Foelsche to Parsons, 8 October 1884, SAA GRG790 990/84.
3 Little, Southport, 2 October 1884, to Government Resident, attachment to Parsons, Palmerston, 1 October 1884, SAA GRG790 861/84.
4 Parsons, Palmerston, 1 October 1884, to Minister, SAA GRG790 861/84.
5 Montagu, Yam Creek, 17 October 1884, to Foelsche, *SAPP*, 1885, Vol. IV, No. 170.
6 Ibid., and Montagu, Yam Creek, 28 October 1884, to Foelsche, SAA GRG790 1060/84.
7 Parsons, Palmerston, 1 October and 5 November 1884, to Minister, 861/84 and 1109/84: both in SAA GRG790.
8 Parsons, Palmerston, telegrams, 10 and 13 September 1884, to Minister, 836/84 and 851/84; Parsons, Palmerston, 22 September 1884, to Minister, 869/84: all in SAA GRG790.
9 Various items in 'Correspondence re Suspension, Etc., of Dr. Morice in the Northern Territory', ordered by the House of Assembly to be printed, 3 November 1886, in *SAPP*, Vol. III, No. 137.
10 Unnamed newspaper, no date but soon after 10 October 1885, in Minister's Northern Territory press cuttings book, SAA GRG9/1, p. 16.
11 Parsons, Palmerston, to Minister, 22 October 1884, 966/84; 22 December 1884, 1158/84; 10 June 1885, 681/84; 10 December 1885, 1309/85: all in SAA GRG790.
12 See note 11.

9 Native Police

1 *South Australian Register*, 10 September 1884.
2 Giles, Springvale, 9 January 1885, to Parsons; Foelsche, Palmerston, 20 May 1878, to Government Resident, SAA GRG790 329/78. For a history of the formation and early years of the Queensland Native Police Force, see Skinner, *Police of the Pastoral*

Frontier; for estimates of numbers of Queensland Aborigines killed, see Reynolds, 'The Other Side of the Frontier', and Loos, *Invasion and Resistance*.

3 A particularly valuable source for this chapter has been Hartwig, The Progress of White Settlement in the Alice Springs District. Baker, Adelaide, to Chief Secretary, memo, 2 December 1884, 1092/84; Parsons, Palmerston, 14 October 1884, telegram to Minister, 926/84; Parsons to Minister, 29 October 1884, 980/84; Parsons, 24 December 1884, telegram to Minister; Seymour, Brisbane, to Parsons, 4 December 1884; Parsons, Palmerston, 23 January 1885, to Minister, 133/85: all in SAA GRG790.

4 Parsons to Baker, letter, 30 January 1885, enclosing guidelines, 174/85, all correspondence in SAA GRG790.

5 Parsons, Katherine, telegram to Cockburn, 20 May 1886, 438/85; Foelsche, Palmerston, to Parsons, 6 December 1886, 13/87; Parsons to Minister, 637/87: all in SAA GRG790.

6 Eylmann, *Die Eingeborenen der Kolonie Sudaustralien*, Ch. 25.

7 Willshire, *The Land of the Dawning*, pp. 20-1 and 14-16. Besley's instruction on dispersals comes from Richard Kimber of Alice Springs.

8 Schmiechen, The Hermannsburg Mission Society in Australia, p. 85.

9 Willshire, *The Aborigines of Central Australia*, pp. 7-8.

10 *South Australian Register*, 31 August 1888.

11 Willshire, Finke River, to Inspector Besley, Port Augusta, 8 January 1890, 40/90, and attached press cutting, no name, 20 February 1890; also Lewis to Rounsevell, 19 January 1893, Police Commissioner to Besley, 15 February 1893, Besley to Police Commisioner, 20 and 22 February 1893, 61/93: all in SAA GRG790.

12 Eylmann, *Die Eingeborenen der Kolonie*, Ch. 25.

13 Clyne, *Colonial Blue*, pp. 188-9.

14 Unnamed newspaper report, 'Inquiry into the Shooting of Donkey and Roger', quoted in Willshire, *A Thrilling Tale of Real Life in the Wilds of Australia*, pp. 53-4.

15 Unnamed newspaper report, letters from 'A Colonist of 44', and 'Tom C. Fowler', all quoted in ibid., pp. 56-7, 60-2.

16 Goldsborough, Mort & Co. Ltd, Melbourne, 4 January 1892, to Treasurer as minister controlling the Northern Territory; and C. J. Dashwood, Government Resident, Palmerston, to Minister, 15 December 1892, both 26/92, SAA GRG790.

17 Willshire, *Land of the Dawning*, pp. 42-3, 50, 66, 74-5.

18 Read, A View of the Past, pp. 120-30.

19 Willshire to Foelsche, 26 January 1895; Treasurer to Chief Secretary, memo, 8 May 1895: both 121/95, SAA GRG790.

20 Treasurer to Chief Secretary, 16 September 1898, 143/98, SAA GRG790.

10 The Missionaries

1 Schmiechen, The Hermannsburg Mission Society, pp. 67-9, 72-3, 74, 83; Hartwig, The Progress of White Settlement in the Alice Springs District, pp. 449-500.

2 Schmiechen, The Hermannsburg Mission Society, pp. 526-7.

3 The Adelaide *Observer*, 27 September 1890, reported upon the subsequent reaction and investigation.

4 Detail of the Hermannsburg Mission is drawn from Hartwig, The Progress of White Settlement in the Alice Springs District.

5 Foelsche, Palmerston, 15 August 1882, to Government Resident, attached to Price to Minister, 579/82, AIAS, MS 1042.

6 Anthony Strele, Norwood, 31 March 1883, to Minister, 85/402, AA, Canberra, CRS A1640. Detail of the Jesuit missions is drawn from O'Kelly, The Jesuit Mission Stations in the Northern Territory, 1882-1899.

7 D. McKillop, Uniya, 12 March 1892, reporting on 1891, and Joseph Conrath, Uniya, 1 August 1893, reporting on 1892, attached to Government Resident's reports for 1891 and 1892, in *SAPP*, 1892, 1893.

8 Conrath, Uniya, 12 April 1894; McKillop, Daly River, 3 March 1896; J. F. O'Brien, Daly River, 12 January 1897; Conrath, Daly River, 13 January 1899: all attached to government resident's reports for 1893, 1895, 1896 and 1898, in *SAPP*, 1894, 1896, 1897, 1899.

9 W. E. H. Stanner, 'Daly River Tribes', quoted in O'Kelly, The Jesuit Mission Stations in the Northern Territory, 1882-1899, p. 102.
10 Charles E. Herbert, annual report on the Northern Territory for 1906, Appendix on Aborigines, *SAPP*, 1907, Vol. 3, No. 45.
11 McKillop, Daly River, 3 March 1896, attached to Government Resident's report for 1896, in *SAPP*, 1896.

11 The Humanitarians

1 Mounted Constable First Class W. H. Summers, Southport, 27 September 1884 and 31 January 1885, to Foelsche, SAA GRG10/1374/A7687; and Foelsche, Palmerston, 23 February 1885, to Parsons, attached to above.
2 Wood, Palmerston, 6 August 1885, to Parsons, AA, Canberra, CRS A1640, 85/995.
3 Foelsche, Palmerston, to Parsons, 18 August 1885, AA. Canberra, CRS A1640, 85/995.
4 Parsons, Palmerston, 19 August 1885, to Minister, AA. Canberra, CRS A1640 85/995.
5 Cockburn to Parsons, 21 May 1886, 442/86; and Hemphill, Helen Springs, 15 November 1887, to Johnson, 905/87: both in SAA GRG790.
6 Gillen, Alice Springs, 25 September 1891, telegram to Johnson, 645/91; Stretton, Borroloola, 30 September 1891, to Knight, 829/91; and R. Sandford, Blood's Creek, to Minister, 20 March 1893, 144/93: all in SAA GRG790.
7 Stevens to Knight, 28 November 1891, 826/91, and attached comments by Ward and Knight and list of proposed reserves, SAA GRG790.
8 Government Resident's report on the Northern Territory for end of 1889, *SAPP*, 1890, Vol. 2, No. 28.
9 F. W. Cox, chairman, A.F.A., to *South Australian Register*, 20 November 1885; and Cox, 22 December 1888, to Minister: both in 35/1889. SAA GRG790.
10 Willshire to Besley, 12 August 1887, 649/87; Grant and Stokes to Johnson, 25 November 1887, 936/87; and Warland to Parsons, 30 June 1888: all in SAA GRG790.
11 Detail of Dashwood's term of office is drawn largely from Elder, Northern Territory Charlie.
12 Graham Loughlin on Dashwood, *Australian Dictionary of Biography*, Vol. 8, pp. 214-15; letter from Forrest, Brisbane, 23 March 1892, to Rounsevell, 171/92 SAA GRG790.
13 Searcy, *In Australian Tropics*, pp. 211-17.
14 Unnamed newspaper, 29 October 1892, in Minister's press cuttings book, SAA GRG9/3.
15 Merlan, 'Making People Quiet', p. 80.
16 Unnamed newspaper, no date but late in December 1895, in Minister's press cuttings book, SAA GRG9/5, pp. 23-24.
17 Downer, *Patrol Indefinite*, p. 43.
18 *Queensland Parliamentary Debates*, 1897, Vol. 2, pp. 1010-911 *passim*.

12 Dashwood's Bill

1 Dashwood to Minister, 12 July 1898, 333/98, SAA GRG790.
2 Goldsmith, Palmerston, 12 March 1898, to Dashwood, attached to 333/98, SAA GRG790.
3 Foelsche, Palmerston, to Dashwood, 'Select Committee of the Legislative Council on the Aborigines Bill', *SAPP*, 1899, Vol. 2, Appendix, pp. 112-13.
4 Sowden, *The Northern Territory As It Really Is*, p. 42.
5 Searcy, *In Australian Tropics*, p. 173.
6 Foelsche to Dashwood, see note 3 above.
7 Thorpe's views are quoted from Thorpe, Camooweal, 5 March 1898, to Foelsche, 'Select Committee of the Legislative Council on the Aborigines Bill', *SAPP*, 1899, Vol. 2, pp. 113-14.
8 Dashwood to Minister, 12 July 1898, 333/98, SAA GRG790.
9 Kingston, 22 August 1898, to Holder, 333/98, SAA GRG790.
10 Gillen, Alice Springs, 12 February 1897, 137/97, and 31 January 1898, 150/98: both in SAA GRG790.

[11] 'Report of the Select Committee of the Legislative Council on the Aborigines Bill' 1899; and Bradshaw's report in unnamed newspaper, 9 March 1900, in Minister's press cuttings book, SAA GRG9/5.

13 The Last Decade

[1] Much of the detail on Aboriginal workers on cattle stations in this chapter comes from Duncan, *The Northern Territory Pastoral Industry*.

[2] Gillen, *Gillen's Diary*, pp. 8, 126, 312.

[3] York and Robinson, *The Black Resistance*, p. 102.

[4] Merlan, 'Making People Quiet', p. 81.

[5] May, *From Bush to Station*, p. 54.

[6] Duncan, *The Northern Territory Pastoral Industry*, p. 73.

[7] Dashwood, annual report on the Northern Territory for 1900, *SAPP*, 1901, Vol. 2, No. 45; and Goldsmith to Dashwood, attached to above.

[8] Seabrook to Dashwood, attached to Dashwood's report for 1902, *SAPP*, 1903, Vol. 3, No. 45; Goldsmith to Dashwood, attached to Dashwood's report for 1903, *SAPP*, 1904, Vol. 2, No. 45; and Fulton to Dashwood, attached to Dashwood's report for 1904, *SAPP*, Vol. 2, No. 45.

[9] Herbert, annual report on the Northern Territory for 1905, *SAPP*, 1906, Vol. 2, No. 45; report for 1906, *SAPP*, 1907, Vol. 3, No. 45; report for 1907, *SAPP*, 1908, Vol. 1, No. 44.

[10] Stretton's report to Herbert, included with Herbert's annual report for 1908, *SAPP*, 1909, Vol. 3, No. 45; Smith, *Aboriginal Population of Australia*, pp. 208-9.

[11] *Commonwealth Parliamentary Papers*, 1905, No. 37.

[12] Tennyson reported by unnamed newspaper on 27 August 1901, Minister's press-cutting book, p. 97, SAA GRG9/5; Herbert, annual report on the Northern Territory for 1909, *SAPP*, 1910, Vol. 3, No. 45.

[13] This and the following examples of Aboriginal abuse are derived from Stott, Borroloola, 28 January 1910, to Sub-Inspector N. Waters, Palmerston, Borroloola Police Station Letter Book, 1908-13, AA, Darwin, CRS F275, Vol. 2.

[14] Herbert's annual report for 1909, *SAPP*, 1910, Vol. 3, No. 45; Stretton to Dashwood, 19 September 1909, 566/09 and reply to request for information from Queensland, 407/1910: both in SAA GRG790.

[15] Newspaper cutting and comments by staff and Minister, 183/1905, SAA GRG790; and Clyne, *Colonial Blue*, p. 228.

[16] Brookes, Illamurta, 28 July 1906, 12 February, 1 June, 24 September and 13 December 1907, 14 December 1908, 25 July 1909, 1 January and 21 July 1910, 1 January 1911: all in Illamurta Police Station Letter Book, AA, Darwin, CRS F757.

[17] *South Australian Register*, 20 June 1907; Searcy, *In Australian Tropics*, pp. 190-1.

[18] Humphrey McQueen, *Social Sketches of Australia, 1888-1975*, Melbourne, 1978, pp. 146-7.

[19] Richards, 'Aborigines in the Victoria River Region: 1883-1928', pp. 33-4.

14 Solving the Problem

[1] For the progress of the Bill, see *South Australian Parliamentary Debates, House of Assembly*, 1910, pp. 672, 727-8, 956-8, 960; and Council, 1910, pp. 489, 562-3; Rowley, *The Destruction of Aboriginal Society*, p. 219.

[2] For detail of the legislation, see *An Act to make Provision for the better Protection and Control of the Aboriginal Inhabitants of the Northern Territory, and for other purposes*, No. 1024, 1910.

[3] Foelsche, Palmerston, November 1902, to Chief Secretary, 487/02, SAA GRG790; and Foelsche, Darwin, 5 January 1909 and 23 July 1913, to Lewis, SAA PRG247/2.

[4] Mulvaney, introduction to *The Aboriginal Photographs of Baldwin Spencer*, p. x.

[5] Spencer, 'Preliminary Report on the Aboriginals of the Northern Territory', esp. pp. 36, 39-52.

Bibliography

Archival Sources

Most of the official correspondence used in this history is located in the South Australian Archives, Adelaide, Government Resident Series, GRG790. Some correspondence relating to the South Australian period is located in the Commonwealth Archives, Darwin and Canberra, CRS A1640 and a few items relating to the end of the period in CRS A1 and A3. The Borroloola police station letter books, 1886–1913, CRS F275, and the Illamurta police station letter books, 1906–12, CRS F757, are held in the Australian Archives, Darwin, with copies in Canberra. A register of inwards correspondence to the office of the minister controlling the Northern Territory from 1870 to 1911 is held in the South Australian Archives, SAA GRG79i mfm, together with a register of correspondence received by the government resident in the Northern Territory, 1870–1911, SAA 1374. Press cuttings books, SAA GRG9/1–9, from the office of the minister controlling the Northern Territory, are also held by the South Australian Archives. In 1980 Ros Fraser prepared for the Australian Institute of Aboriginal Studies, Canberra, a guide to Commonwealth records to 1950 relating to Aborigines, which is helpful because it describes contents. That guide is available at the Australian Archives in Canberra.

Official Sources

Baldwin Spencer, W., 'Preliminary Report on the Aboriginals of the Northern Territory', *Commonwealth Parliamentary Papers*, 1913, No. 45.

'Correspondence re Suspension, Etc., of Dr. Morice in the Northern Territory', ordered by the South Australian House of Assembly to be printed, 3 November 1886, in *South Australian Parliamentary Papers*, 1886, Vol. III.

'Report of the Northern Territory Commission', *South Australian Parliamentary Papers*, 1866.

'Report of the Select Committee of the Legislative Council upon The Aborigines; Together with Minutes of Evidence and Appendix', *South Australian Parliamentary Papers*, 1860, Vol. 3, No. 165.

'Report of the Select Committee of the Legislative Council on the Aborigines Bill; Together with Minutes of Proceedings', *South Australian Parliamentary Papers*, 1899.

Todd, Charles, 'Report on the Post Office, Telegraph and Observatory Departments', 10 October 1884, *South Australian Parliamentary Papers*, 1885.

Manuscript Sources

Ashwin, Arthur C., Recollections of Ralph Milner's [*sic*] Expedition from Kopperamanna to the Northern Territory with Sheep and Horses in 1870–71 with an Account of his Subsequent Experiences in the Northern Territory', compiled in 1927, copied in 1930 from a manuscript copy made by L. A. Wells from Ashwin's original manuscript, photocopy in Australian Institute of Aboriginal Studies, Canberra.

Catchlove, Edward N. B., Diary, 24 June to 24 December 1870, SAA D5170 (L).

Elder, Peter, 'Northern Territory Charlie': Charles James Dashwood in Palmerston, 1892–1905, B.A. thesis, Australian National University, 1979.

Gale, Fay, A Study in Assimilation: Part-Aborigines in South Australia, Ph.D. thesis, University of Adelaide, 1960.

Giles, Alfred, The First Pastoral Settlement of the Northern Territory, handwritten reminiscences prepared after 1927, SAA 1082.

Hartwig, M. C., The Progress of White Settlement in the Alice Springs District and its Effects upon the Aboriginal Inhabitants, 1860–1894, Ph.D. thesis, University of Adelaide, 1965.

Krastins, Valda, The Tiwi: A Cultural Contact History of the Australian Aborigines on Bathurst and Melville Islands, 1705–1942, B.A. thesis, Australian National University, 1972.

Lewis, John, Papers, SAA PRG247.

Little, J. A. G., copy of Diary, 27 September to 20 November 1871 and 8 January to 21 April 1872, SAA PRG329.

Macknight, C. C., The Macassans: A Study of the Early Trepang Industry along the Northern Territory Coast, Ph.D. thesis, Australian National University, 1969.

Neal, Stephen, An Important Place: Borroloola 1881–1923, B.A. thesis, Australian National University, 1977.

O'Kelly, G. J., The Jesuit Mission Stations in the Northern Territory, 1882–1899, B.A. thesis, Monash University, 1967.

Read, Jay and Peter, A View of the Past, unpublished manuscript, MS 1318, Australian Institute of Aboriginal Studies, Canberra.

Richards, Michaela, 'An Australian Frontier ...': Aborigines and Settlers at the Daly River, 1912–1940, B.A. thesis, Australian National University, 1982.

Schmiechen, H. J., The Hermannsburg Mission Society in Australia, 1866–1895: Changing Missionary Attitudes and their Effects on the Aboriginal Inhabitants, B.A. thesis, University of Adelaide, 1971.

South Australian Archives, Genesis of the Police Force in the Northern Territory, Research Note 456.

——— Notes on Steps taken to capture the Natives concerned in the Attack on Barrow Creek Telegraph Station (Feb. 22, 1874) and the murder of Stapleton and Frank, Research Note 174.

Woodley, Peter, The Best Laid Plans: Government Policy Concerning Aborigines in the Top End of the Northern Territory, 1911–1927, Litt.B. thesis, Australian National University, 1982.

Contemporary Works

Curr, E. M. *The Australian Race*, Vol. 1, Melbourne and London, 1887.

Daly, Harriet W., *Digging, Squatting and Pioneering Life in the Northern Territory of South Australia*, London, 1887.

Eylmann, E., *Die Eingeborenen der Kolonie Sudaustralien*, Berlin, 1908.

Foelsche, Paul, 'Notes on the Aborigines of North Australia', *Transactions of the Royal Society of South Australia*, Vol. V, 1881–82.

Giles, Christopher, 'The Adelaide and Port Darwin Telegraph Line: Some Reminiscences of its Construction', *Journal of the South Australian Electrical Society*, Vol. 2, 1888.

Gillen, F. J., *Gillen's Diary: The Camp Jottings of F. J. Gillen on the Spencer and Gillen Expedition Across Australia*, Adelaide, 1968.

Gregory, A. C. and F. T. Gregory, *Journals of Australian Explorations*, Brisbane, 1884.

Gsell, F. X., *'The Bishop with 150 Wives': Fifty Years as a Missionary with an Epilogue by Andre Dupeyrat*, London, 1956.

Kelsey, D. E., *The Shackle: A Story of the Far North Australian Bush*, edited by Ira Nesdale, Adelaide, 1975.

Lewis, John, *Fought and Won*, Adelaide, 1922.

Searcy, Alfred, *In Australian Tropics*, London, 1907.

Sowden, William J., *The Northern Territory As It Really Is: A Narrative of the South Australian Parliamentary Party's Trip, and Full Descriptions of the Northern Territory; Its Settlements and Industries*, Adelaide, 1882, reprinted Darwin, 1984.

Stokes, J. Lort, *Discoveries in Australia; with an Account of the Coasts and Rivers Explored and Surveyed during the Voyage of the Beagle, in the Years [1837–43]*, London, 1846, facsimile edition, Adelaide, 1969.

Willshire, W. H., *The Aborigines of Central Australia: With Vocabulary of the Dialect of the Alice Springs Natives*, Port Augusta, 1888.

———— *A Thrilling Tale of Real Life in the Wilds of Australia*, Adelaide, 1895.

———— *The Land of the Dawning: Being Facts Gleaned from Cannibals in the Australian Stone Age*, Adelaide, 1896.

Later Works

Allen, Jim, 'Port Essington: A Successful Limpet Port?', *Historical Studies*, Vol. 15, 1972.

Basedow, Herbert, *Knights of the Boomerang: Episodes from a Life Spent among the Native Tribes of Australia*, Sydney, 1935.

Bauer, F. H., *Historical Geography of White Settlement in Part of Northern Australia: Part 2, The Katherine–Darwin Region*, CSIRO Land Research and Regional Survey, Divisional Report No. 64, Canberra, 1964.

Berndt, Ronald and Catherine, *From Black to White in South Australia*, Melbourne, 1951.

Birman, Wendy, *Gregory of Rainworth: A Man in his Time*, Perth, 1979.

Buchanan, Gordon, *Packhorse and Saddle: With the First Overlanders to the Kimberleys*, Sydney, 1933.

Butlin, N. G., *Our Original Aggression: Aboriginal Populations of Southeastern Australia 1788–1850*, Sydney, 1983.

Clyne, Robert, *Colonial Blue: A History of the South Australian Police Force, 1836–1916*, Adelaide, 1987.

Costello, Michael J., *Life of John Costello; Being the Adventures of a Pioneer, Pastoralist and Explorer in Queensland and the Northern Territory*, Sydney, 1930.

Donovan, P. F., *A Land Full of Possibilities: A History of South Australia's Northern Territory*, Brisbane, 1981.

Downer, S. F., *Patrol Indefinite*, Adelaide, 1963.

Duncan, Ross, *The Northern Territory Pastoral Industry, 1863–1910*, Melbourne, 1967.

Evans, Raymond, 'Don't You Remember Black Alice, Sam Holt?: Aboriginal Women in Queensland History', *Hecate*, Vol. VIII, 1982.

Feeken, H. J., Feeken, Gerda E. E. & Spate, O. H. K., *The Discovery and Exploration of Australia*, Melbourne, 1970.

Gibbs, R. M., 'Relations between the Aboriginal Inhabitants and the First South Australian Colonists', *Royal Geographical Society, S.A. Branch, Proceedings*, Vol. 61, 1959–60.

Hassell, Kathleen, *The Relations between the Settlers and Aborigines in South Australia, 1836–1860*, Adelaide, 1966, originally presented as an M.A. thesis, University of Adelaide, 1927.

Hill, Ernestine, *The Territory*, Sydney, 1951, reprinted 1963.

Jenkin, Graham, *The Conquest of the Ngarrindjeri*, Adelaide, 1979.

Lockwood, Douglas, *The Front Door: Darwin 1869–1969*, Adelaide, 1968.

Loos, N. A., 'Queensland's Kidnapping Act: The Native Labourers Protection Act of 1884', *Aboriginal History*, Vol. 4, 1980.

———— *Invasion and Resistance: Aboriginal–European Relations on the North Queensland Frontier, 1861–1897*, Canberra, 1982.

McGrath, Ann, *'Born in the Cattle': Aborigines in Cattle Country*, Sydney, 1987.

Macknight, C. C., *The Farthest Coast*, Melbourne, 1969.

———— 'Journal of a Voyage round Arnhem Land in1875', *Aboriginal History*, Vol. 5, 1981.

Markus, Andrew, *From the Barrel of a Gun: The Oppression of the Aborigines, 1860–1900*, Melbourne, 1974.

Mattingley, Christobel, and Hampton, Ken, *Survival In Our Land*, Adelaide, 1988.

May, Dawn, *From Bush to Station: Aboriginal Labour in the North Queensland Pastoral Industry, 1861–1897*, Townsville, 1983.

Merlan, Francesca, '"Making People Quiet" in the Pastoral North: Reminiscences of Elsey Station', *Aboriginal History*, Vol. 2, 1978.

Mudie, Ian, *The Heroic Journey of John McDouall Stuart*, Sydney, 1968.

Mulvaney, D. J., introduction to *The Aboriginal Photographs of Baldwin Spencer*, selected and annotated by Geoffrey Walker and edited by Ron Vanderwal, Melbourne, 1982.

Pike, Douglas, *Paradise of Dissent: South Australia 1829–1857*, second edition, Melbourne, 1967.

Powell, Alan, 'Culture Contact and Changes in Land Occupation on Cobourg Peninsula', *NARU Research Bulletin*, No. 8, 1982.

———— *Far Country: A Short History of the Northern Territory*, Melbourne, 1982.

Queensland, Police Department, *A History of the Native Mounted Police in Queensland*, typescript pamphlet, Brisbane, n.d.

Reynolds, Henry, 'The Other Side of the Frontier', *Historical Studies*, Vol. 17, No. 66, 1976.

———— *The Other Side of the Frontier: An Interpretation of the Aboriginal Response to the Invasion and Settlement of Australia*, Townsville, 1981.

Richards, Michaela, 'Aborigines in the Victoria River Region: 1883–1928', *Australian Institute of Aboriginal Studies Newsletter*, New Series No. 17, 1982.

Rowley, C. D., *The Destruction of Aboriginal Society: Aboriginal Policy and Practice*, Canberra, 1870.

Schrire, Carmel, *The Alligator Rivers: Prehistory and Ecology in Western Arnhem Land*, Canberra, 1982.

Sinclair, Keith, *History of New Zealand*, revised edition, London, 1969.

Skinner, L. E., *Police of the Pastoral Frontier: Native Police 1849–59*, Brisbane, 1975.

Smith, L. R., *Aboriginal Population of Australia*, Canberra, 1980.

Spillett, Peter G., *Forsaken Settlement: An Illustrated History of the Settlement of Victoria, Port Essington, North Australia, 1839–1849*, Melbourne, 1972.

Thonemann, H. E., *Tell the White Man*, Sydney, 1949.

Wilson, Helen J. and Estbergs, Elizabeth, *The Northern Territory Chronicle*, second edition, Darwin, 1984.

Wright, Judith, *The Cry for the Dead*, Melbourne, 1981.

York, Barry, and Robinson, Fergus, *The Black Resistance: An Introduction to the History of the Aborigines' Struggle against British Colonialism*, Melbourne, 1977.

Index

Aborigines: attitudes towards Europeans, 7, 21, 27, 55, 85-6, 139, 148-9; condition of, 129, 130-1, 145-6, 148-9, 151, 157-65, 175, 177, 182, 192-3, 201; drovers' 'boys', *see* Drovers' 'boys'; drug addiction, 156, 158-9, 164, 167-8, 176, 193, 199; education, 2, 7, 9-10, 12-13, 132, 136-8; evidence in court, 4-5, 71; halfcastes (persons of part-Aboriginal descent) 131, 161, 163-4, 168, 175-6, 178, 181-2, 195; health, 6-7, 10-11, 13, 18, 83, 141, 155, 156, 164, 193-4, 200; labour, 10, 163, 167-9, 172-5, 179-80, 192-5, 199; land rights, 7-8, 9, 13-14, 166, 200; prostitution, 6, 129, 156, 158-60, 168, 182, 193; protection, 3, 9, 12-13, 30-2, 36, 38, 76, 81, 128, 132, 161, 163, 167, 188-9, 193; prisoners, 12, 20, 33-4, 43, 46, 66, 75, 80, 90, 108, 114, 117, 122, 131, 145-6, 150, 153, 155, 176, 184, 194; reserves, 8-9, 12-14, 131, 147-8, 150, 160, 166-7, 193-4; resistance, 7, 22, 54, 56-7, 60, 70, 85, 89, 91, 93-4, 97-8, 121-2, 172-3; *see also* conflicts

Individual peoples: see Aranda, Bilignara, Dieri, Gurindji, Iwaidja, Kaititja, Kukatja, Larakia, Manassie, Marakai, Matuntara, Milmenrura, Minaedge, Mulluk, Mulluk, Mululurun, Nga liwuru, Ngarinman, Ngolokwonga, Nuboloora, Orunga, Pongaponga, Tiwi, Unalla, Unmatjera, Waggite, Wakaja, Warrama, Woolna, Woolwonga

Aborigines' Friends' Association, 11, 112, 150

Aborigines' Protection Society, 10, 31

Angas, G. F., 31

Anna's Reservoir station, 116-18

Aranda, 115, 118, 120, 129, 133, 174, 198

Argument Flat incident, 102-3, 105, 109, 144

Arltunga, 97, 130

Ashwin, A., 26, 49, 57, 58

Attack Creek incident, 26

Auvergne station, 125, 153

Bagot, E. M., 56, 97

Baines, A. P., 109, 112

Baines, T., 22

Baker, R. C., 93, 101, 105-7, 113, 147

Baludja, 23-4

Banka Banka station, 175

Barker, Captain C., 17, 56

Barker, J., 11

Barrow Creek attack, 62-6

Basedow, H., 65, 191

Basedow, M. P. F., 166, 168

Bates, D., 191

Bathurst Island mission, 140

Bennett, J. W. O., 35

Beresford, R. D., 107

Besley, B. C., 117, 123, 128, 150-1

Bilignara, 126

Binmook, 43, 45

Blyth, N., 70

Boko Jacky, 103, 145

Bond Springs station, 120

Borradaile, 54, 78

Bradshaw, F. M., 184

Bradshaw, J., 154-6, 166

Bradshaw, T. A., 168, 182-3

Bremer, Captain G., 17

Bridson, C., 69, 86, 102, 144

Broadmere station, 92

Bromley, Captain W., 3

Brook, W. H., 77

Brookes, C., 116, 183-4

Brown, J., 188

Browne, W. J., 88, 172